Insurer Accounting Management

Insurer Accounting Management

Edited by

Michael W. Elliott, CPCU, AIAF, MBA

1st Edition • 2nd Printing

The Institutes
720 Providence Road, Suite 100
Malvern, Pennsylvania 19355-3433

1st Edition • 2nd Printing • February 2016

Library of Congress Control Number: 2014950867

ISBN 978-0-89463-814-5

Foreword

The Institutes are the trusted leader in delivering proven knowledge solutions that drive powerful business results for the risk management and property-casualty insurance industry. For more than 100 years, The Institutes have been meeting the industry's changing professional development needs with customer-driven products and services.

In conjunction with industry experts and members of the academic community, our Knowledge Resources Department develops our course and program content, including Institutes study materials. Practical and technical knowledge gained from Institutes courses enhances qualifications, improves performance, and contributes to professional growth—all of which drive results.

The Institutes' proven knowledge helps individuals and organizations achieve powerful results with a variety of flexible, customer-focused options:

Recognized Credentials—The Institutes offer an unmatched range of widely recognized and industry-respected specialty credentials. The Institutes' Chartered Property Casualty Underwriter (CPCU®) professional designation is designed to provide a broad understanding of the property-casualty insurance industry. Depending on professional needs, CPCU students may select either a commercial insurance focus or a personal risk management and insurance focus and may choose from a variety of electives.

In addition, The Institutes offer certificate or designation programs in a variety of disciplines, including these:

- Claims
- Commercial underwriting
- Fidelity and surety bonding
- General insurance
- Insurance accounting and finance
- Insurance information technology
- Insurance production and agency management
- Insurance regulation and compliance
- Management
- Marine insurance
- Personal insurance
- Premium auditing
- Quality insurance services
- Reinsurance
- Risk management
- Surplus lines

Ethics—Ethical behavior is crucial to preserving not only the trust on which insurance transactions are based, but also the public's trust in our industry as a whole. All Institutes designations now have an ethics requirement, which is delivered online and free of charge. The ethics requirement content is designed specifically for insurance practitioners and uses insurance-based case studies to outline an ethical framework. More information is available in the Programs section of our website, www.TheInstitutes.org.

Flexible Online Learning—The Institutes have an unmatched variety of technical insurance content covering topics from accounting to underwriting, which we now deliver through hundreds of online courses. These cost-effective self-study courses are a convenient way to fill gaps in technical knowledge in a matter of hours without ever leaving the office.

Continuing Education—A majority of The Institutes' courses are filed for CE credit in most states. We also deliver quality, affordable, online CE courses quickly and conveniently through CEU. Visit www.CEU.com to learn more. CEU is powered by The Institutes.

College Credits—Most Institutes courses carry college credit recommendations from the American Council on Education. A variety of courses also qualify for credits toward certain associate, bachelor's, and master's degrees at several prestigious colleges and universities. More information is available in the Student Services section of our website, www.TheInstitutes.org.

Custom Applications—The Institutes collaborate with corporate customers to use our trusted course content and flexible delivery options in developing customized solutions that help them achieve their unique organizational goals.

Insightful Analysis—Our Insurance Research Council (IRC) division conducts public policy research on important contemporary issues in property-casualty insurance and risk management. Visit www.ircweb.org to learn more or purchase its most recent studies.

The Institutes look forward to serving the risk management and property-casualty insurance industry for another 100 years. We welcome comments from our students and course leaders; your feedback helps us continue to improve the quality of our study materials.

Peter L. Miller, CPCU
President and CEO
The Institutes

Preface

Insurer Accounting Management is the assigned textbook for the AIAF 114 course in The Institutes' Associate in Insurance Accounting and Finance (AIAF) designation program. This text provides learners with a broad understanding of insurance accounting, including United States generally accepted accounting principles (GAAP) and statutory accounting principles (SAP) required by the various U.S. states. While much of the content applies to both property-casualty and life insurers, the detailed explanations of premium accounting, loss accounting, reinsurance accounting, and tax accounting apply only to property-casualty insurers.

Assignment 1 explains accounting frameworks and concepts, including the fundamentals of insurer financial statements. International Financial Reporting Standards (IFRS) are introduced, along with their application to insurance contracts.

U.S. GAAP and statutory financial statements for property-casualty insurers and life insurers are covered in Assignments 2 and 3, respectively. Comparisons are made between GAAP for insurers and noninsurers and between GAAP and SAP.

Assignments 4 through 6 explain in detail various components of an insurer's financial statements. Property-casualty insurer premium accounting, including the concepts of written, earned, and unearned premium, are explained in Assignment 4. Property-casualty insurer loss accounting, including the transactions for paid and incurred losses, are covered in Assignment 5. The valuation of various types of insurer assets, including complex securities and deferred tax assets, is covered in Assignment 6.

Assignment 7 explains accounting and financial reporting considerations for various types of assumed and ceded reinsurance, including prospective and retrospective reinsurance. U.S. federal and state tax considerations, including the requirements for a company to be taxed as an insurer, are also covered in this assignment.

For more information about The Institutes' programs, please call our Customer Success Department at (800) 644-2101, email us at CustomerSuccess@TheInstitutes.org, or visit our website at www.TheInstitutes.org.

Michael W. Elliott

Contributors

The Institutes acknowledge with deep appreciation the contributions made to the content of this text by the following persons:

Michael M. Barth, PhD, CPCU, AU

Judith M. Vaughan, CPCU, AIC

Contents

Direct Your Learning ▶▶

1

Introduction to Insurance Accounting

Educational Objectives

After learning the content of this assignment, you should be able to:

▷ Explain the following qualitative accounting information criteria:

- Understandability
- Relevance
- Reliability
- Comparability and consistency
- Lack of bias
- Cost-benefit effectiveness

▷ Describe the frameworks and the intended users and focus of each of the following sets of accounting frameworks:

- Generally Accepted Accounting Principles (GAAP) accounting
- Regulatory/supervisory accounting
- Tax accounting
- Management accounting

▷ Explain the concept of a rule hierarchy and the sources of the following accounting frameworks:

- Generally Accepted Accounting Principles (GAAP)
- Regulatory/supervisory accounting
- Tax accounting

▷ Summarize the following accounting concepts:

- Fair value versus historical cost
- Recognition versus measurement
- Deferral-matching versus asset-liability

1

- Impairment

- Revenue recognition

- Reporting segment

- Liquidation versus going concern

- Change in accounting principle versus change in accounting estimate

- Principle-based versus rule-based

▸ Describe the purpose and primary components of these key schedules of an insurer's financial statements:

- Balance sheet

- Income statement

- Cash flow statement

- Notes and disclosures

▸ Describe International Financial Reporting Standards and their importance to insurers.

▸ Explain how the current FASB standards and the current and proposed IASB standards affect accounting for insurance contract liabilities.

▸ Explain the conditions under which an accounting framework may require deposit accounting for an insurance contract, and the operation of three general forms of deposit accounting rules.

Introduction to Insurance Accounting

QUALITATIVE ACCOUNTING INFORMATION CRITERIA

Accounting provides information for analysis. The degree to which the information that accounting provides is useful for decision making depends on its qualitative criteria.[1]

The purposes of accounting are to track and organize all the activities that affect an organization financially and to provide information useful for decision making. The five basic assertions of accounting are that the financial information is complete; valued correctly; exists; belongs to the company; and is properly classified, described, and disclosed.

Qualitative accounting information criteria that stem from these five basic assertions have been developed by various accounting standard setters.[2] Criteria vary slightly depending on the standard-setting body, but generally, the accounting information resulting from a set of accounting rules or requirements should meet these criteria:[3]

- Understandability
- Relevance
- Reliability
- Comparability and consistency
- Lack of bias
- Cost-benefit effectiveness

Understandability

Accounting information should be readily understandable to those who use it. Understandability can be evaluated in terms of both the intended users and the intended uses of the information. In general, to be understandable, information contained in financial reports (including financial disclosures) must be transparent, intelligible, and clearly disclosed.

Relevance

Accounting information should help its users make decisions. This typically means that the information must be timely, have predictive value, and provide useful feedback about previously made decisions.

Handwritten margin notes:

Five Basics
1) Financial Information is complete
2) Valued Correctly
3) exists
4) belongs to the company
5) properly classified described & disclosed

intended users
intended uses

* help make decision
→ timely
→ predictive value
→ useful feedback about previous decision

Reliability

To be considered reliable, accounting information should embody these criteria:[4]

- Representational faithfulness—The information represents what it claims to represent. For example, if the information is supposed to represent the expected total amount of ultimate claim payments, it should not be implicitly discounted (adjusted to reflect the time value of money) so that it is materially lower than the expected ultimate nominal payments. Similarly, if the reported value of a common stock holding purports to be the current market value, that value should be approximately what the stock could be sold for by the company holding it at the financial reporting date.

- Verifiability—Another person or entity should be able to recreate the reported value using the same information as the reporting entity.

- Completeness—The reported information should not omit any material fact or consideration.

- Neutrality—The information can be used for economic decision making without regard to how it may affect economic, political, or social behavior.

- Representational faithfulness
- Verifiability
→ Completeness
→ Neutrality

Comparability and Consistency

Accounting information must allow for comparisons between time periods and among entities (such as companies or industries) and therefore must be consistent. For example, comparisons of two companies could be potentially misleading if one company discounts all of its liabilities for future investment income, while the other does not discount any of its liabilities. Similarly, comparisons of the same company from one time period to another would be difficult if the company discounted its claim liabilities at one period-end but not at the subsequent period-end.

Lack of Bias

Biased information can be misleading. It is useful only if the users understand the bias; the bias is consistently applied across time periods, firms, or industries; and the users can adjust the reported results to reflect their own desired bias. When uncertainty is present, an accounting framework may require the reporting of unbiased values accompanied by sufficient disclosure of biased values (for example, prudent or conservative values) with the bias determined in a predictable, consistent fashion.

In the United States, Actuarial Standards of Practice (ASOP) 21 requires only that the actuary "be aware that a discounted reserve is an inadequate estimate of economic value unless appropriate risk margins are included." The Standards of Practice of the Canadian Institute of Actuaries (CIA) and federal insurance regulations in Canada require the reporting of policy liabilities that include both present value discounting and provisions for adverse deviation (that is, risk margin). The CIA Standards of Practice state that "a calculation should not include a provision if the related work requires an unbiased calculation. Otherwise, if a provision promotes expectations for financial security, then the calculation should include a provision [for adverse deviation]."[5]

Cost-Benefit Effectiveness

The development of accounting information consumes resources. Consequently, the cost of producing such information should be reasonable in relation to the expected benefit of the information. In many cases, this effectiveness is reflected through the application of materiality thresholds in accounting frameworks. For example, less strict or less complete application of the rules may be permitted for immaterial items if full compliance would result in unnecessary higher costs.

Considerations Within These Criteria

Associated with these qualitative criteria are the issues of the relationship between relevance and reliability, as well as between neutrality and reliability.

Comparing Relevance and Reliability

In many cases, a trade-off exists between relevance and reliability. For example, the value of an infrequently traded asset may be relevant if the owner clearly intends to sell that asset to meet a liability. The valuation of such an asset, however, may be difficult or impossible to determine. Different parties may place materially different values on that asset, making it impossible for an external party or auditor to verify the asset's value. The only reliable value for the asset may be its original cost, which might not be relevant to the user of the information. Therefore, the owner of the asset may have to choose between a relevant but unreliable value and a reliable but irrelevant value.

The relationship between relevance and reliability also affects the valuation of difficult-to-estimate insurance liabilities. While a value may be estimable by an actuary, the reliability of that estimate could be questioned. Can the user depend on that value, or could reliance on that value materially mislead the user? If a range of estimates could be produced, but only the low end of the range could be reliably determined, booking the low end of the range may produce a reliable estimate. However, the relevance of such a booked value could then be questioned. More disclosure, such as information that is not misleading or that does not lack material facts, may be required to make the information complete.

Comparing Lack of Bias and Reliability

A conflict can arise between lack of bias and reliability of information where uncertainty exists. Some accounting frameworks require conservatism or prudence in such circumstances. The rationale for requiring conservatism in the face of uncertainty is that an uncertain asset, or an asset of uncertain value, cannot be relied upon. This may lead to the delayed recognition of some assets until their value is more dependably known or until the ability to realize a gain from their sale is more certain (that is, the value of the asset is "reasonably certain"). With respect to uncertainty in liabilities, conservatism and prudence could lead an organization to report a high liability value, making it unlikely that a final settlement value would be greater than the reported value.

However, what constitutes conservatism depends on the context in which an estimate is made. For example, the buyer of an asset would apply conservatism by choosing a high estimate, while the seller would apply conservatism by choosing a low estimate. As another example, a high estimate of ultimate losses would be conservative when used to estimate claim liabilities, but optimistic when used to estimate agents' contingent commissions.

Also, different users have different risk tolerances. Therefore, any bias in accounting information could produce misleading information unless the end user can quantify or adjust for the bias. As a result, in the face of uncertainty, accounting frameworks may call for reporting of unbiased estimates accompanied by disclosure of the uncertainty rather than report biased estimates.

TYPES OF ACCOUNTING FRAMEWORKS

Different sets of accounting frameworks exist to meet the needs of different users.

The group into which a particular user of accounting information falls determines the accounting framework to be used to develop that information. In general, users of accounting information and the corresponding frameworks fall into these categories:[6]

- Investors, creditors, and owners (current and potential)—generally accepted accounting principles (GAAP)
- Regulators and supervisors[7]—Regulatory/supervisory accounting
- Tax authorities—Tax accounting

GAAP Accounting

Accounting frameworks designed for a broad range of users (including investors, creditors, and owners) are usually called general purpose accounting rules, or **generally accepted accounting principles (GAAP)**.

Generally accepted accounting principles (GAAP)

A common set of accounting standards and procedures used in the preparation of financial statements to ensure consistency of presentation and reported results.

The focus of GAAP accounting is typically on the value or performance of an organization as a going concern. That is, it assumes that the organization will continue to operate indefinitely. This is an important point, as many liabilities or assets would have a significantly different value for a going concern than they would for an entity in runoff (that is, an entity that is liquidating its assets). For example, the value of a tangible asset (such as large machinery or computer equipment) used by a going concern in its business may be the asset's replacement value, but the value for a company in runoff that no longer needs the asset may be the asset's liquidation market value. In the instance of a going concern, GAAP would focus on the asset's replacement value (or depreciated cost), as opposed to its liquidation value.

Regulatory/Supervisory Accounting

Regulators interested in solvency regulation may have more interest in runoff values than going-concern values. This may lead them to develop their own specialized accounting frameworks, such as the **statutory accounting principles (SAP)** produced by the National Association of Insurance Commissioners (NAIC) in the United States. Such rules may place more emphasis on realizable values for asset sale and liability settlement than general accounting rules do. Hence, they may require a different set of valuation assumptions (possibly including mandatory conservatism or bias), resulting in accounting values materially different from GAAP values.

Statutory accounting principles (SAP)

The accounting principles and practices that are prescribed or permitted by an insurer's domiciliary state and that insurers must follow.

Tax Accounting

Tax authorities may desire, demand, or be legally required to use their own specialized accounting frameworks in order to calculate the tax owed by an entity. Such accounting frameworks may be directed or influenced by social engineering, public policy, political, or verifiability concerns. As such, they may be materially different from either GAAP or statutory accounting frameworks.

In the U.S., the tax accounting rules for insurers are based on statutory accounting, with modification. In many parts of the world, GAAP, regulatory, and tax accounting rules are the same. One advantage to having one set of accounting rules is reduced cost and confusion in the creation of the information. One disadvantage is that because the needs of all the users are not the same, compromises must be made that are suboptimal to one or more sets of users. For example, accounting rules that are established based on public policy issues driven by tax or regulatory authorities may result in misleading information for investors.

Management Accounting

GAAP, regulatory, and tax accounting frameworks may still not meet the needs of an organization's management. As a result, many organizations create one or more additional sets of accounting frameworks on which to base their management decisions. These are generally based on either GAAP or regulatory accounting rules, with modifications.

For example, the incidence of large claims may require special treatment when evaluating individual business units in an organization. While a constant volume of large claims may be expected for the total results of an organization, their incidence may severely distort the evaluation of the individual business units that experience the large claims in the single year being analyzed. If a business unit were a separate organization, it might limit its exposure to such claims (for example, through reinsurance or coverage restrictions), but for the organization as a whole, retaining that exposure might make more sense. Therefore, management may wish to cap any claims at a certain level, when looking at its internal "management accounting basis" results for individual business units, or it may reflect a reinsurance pool among the business units in its internal accounting results. Such arrangements are often referred to as internal reinsurance.

The existing GAAP and/or regulatory accounting frameworks may not allow discounting of liabilities for future investment income, possibly due to reliability concerns. Management, however, may believe that such present value discounting of liabilities is necessary to properly evaluate the financial results of the business units. Within the operation, management may believe that any reliability concerns can be adequately controlled.

ACCOUNTING FRAMEWORKS AND RULE HIERARCHIES

Each accounting framework uses prescribed sets of rules.[8]

The rules on which accounting frameworks are based originate from accounting or securities standards boards, laws and regulations, professional associations, or internal management. Within any given accounting framework are typically several different sources of rules. Where the rules for a given framework potentially conflict, a predefined hierarchy must be followed. Rules from a source higher on the hierarchy overrule those from a source lower on the hierarchy.[9]

Generally Accepted Accounting Principles (GAAP)

For GAAP, the hierarchy is generally led by the organization in charge of securities regulation for the jurisdiction in question. (The International Organization of Securities Commissions, [IOSCO] Web site [www.iosco.org] lists such organizations.) The organization in the "top" position may defer the rule setting to a specified accounting standard setter, such as the International Accounting Standards Board (IASB), but it generally has the authority to add additional requirements or rules. It may also retain veto power over the designated accounting standard setter's proposed new rules. This describes the situation in the United States, where the Securities and Exchange Commission (SEC) retains veto power over new Financial Accounting Standards Board (FASB) standards.

SEC has veto power

Next in the hierarchy are the standards set by the specified accounting standard setter for the jurisdiction. The European Union (EU) has identified the International Financial Reporting Standards (IFRS) produced by the IASB as the accounting standards for companies with publicly traded securities, although any new IFRS statement must be explicitly endorsed by the EU before it becomes applicable. This endorsement is not automatic. For example, the EU did not adopt the hedge accounting rules in IASB's financial instrument standard (IAS 39) when it adopted the rest of the standard in 2004.

In the U.S., the SEC has designated FASB as the accounting standard setter under the SEC. These standards would be at the top of the hierarchy for companies that are not subject to publicly traded securities rules (for example, a privately owned firm).

Standards may be supplemented by industry-specific guidance. In the U.S., the American Institute of Certified Professional Accountants (AICPA), a separate organization of accounting professionals, used to provide some industry-specific guidance in the form of Statements of Position (SOPs). The FASB eliminated this role for the AICPA in 2002.

A rule hierarchy (such as within GAAP) also includes interpretations, such as those issued by the IASB's IFRS Interpretations Committee [10] and FASB's Emerging Issues Task Force. Interpretations are produced when timely guidance is needed, as they can be produced much faster than official accounting standards because of the shorter period required for due process. See the exhibit "Emerging Issues."

Emerging Issues

Accounting frameworks frequently contain a mechanism (such as an "emerging issues task force") for decisions on emerging issues where the existing guidance is unclear and the implications are material. An example of an emerging situation may be the proper treatment of a liability established by a new law. Mechanisms such as emerging issues groups can produce guidance faster than is required for official accounting standards.

While the exact hierarchy within a given accounting framework may vary, all accounting paradigms need some sort of hierarchy to determine which accounting rule(s) or interpretation(s) take precedence when conflicts exist.

[DA06546]

Regulatory/Supervisory Accounting

Regulatory accounting rules can consist of an independent set of standards, produced by or with the approval of the regulator, or can consist solely of additional specialized accounting schedules filed in addition to GAAP financial reports. In the U.S., regulators have developed a complete set of accounting rules, combining elements of both liquidation accounting and going-concern accounting.

Tax Accounting

Tax accounting rules can be based on GAAP accounting rules or statutory accounting rules or can be determined independently. This determination is generally based on the tax laws or regulations for the jurisdiction in question. Some countries rely on GAAP accounting reports to determine taxable income, while at least one country relies on statutory accounting reports with modifications.

SELECTED ACCOUNTING CONCEPTS

Knowledge of common accounting concepts helps the user understand the reasoning behind a given accounting rule and the differences between various types of accounting frameworks. It also helps the user understand the debate that occurs as accounting rules are being changed.

Common accounting concepts include these:

- Fair value versus historical cost
- Recognition versus measurement
- Deferral-matching versus asset-liability
- Impairment
- Revenue recognition
- Reporting segment
- Liquidation versus going concern
- Change in accounting principle versus change in accounting estimate
- Principle-based versus rule-based [11]

Fair Value Versus Historical Cost

Mark-to-model
The valuation of an asset based on financial models instead of market price.

Mark-to-market
The value of an asset or liability based on its current market price.

Fair value is the price that would be received to sell an asset or paid to transfer a liability in an orderly transaction between market participants at the measurement date.[12] Fair value is meant to represent market value given a sufficiently robust and efficient market. Where no such market exists, fair value is estimated conceptually. When the fair value estimate is based on a model rather than an actually observed market value, it is called **mark-to-model** rather than **mark-to-market**. Mark-to-market is sometimes referred to as "marked" to market, while mark-to-model is sometimes referred to as "marked" to model.

Historical cost is the price at which an asset or liability was originally obtained. Where historical cost is expected to be different from the final value when an item is no longer on the balance sheet, some amortization or depreciation of the value may be necessary. This can result in an amortized cost or depreciated cost value. These values are generally more reliably determinable, but less relevant, than fair value.

Recognition Versus Measurement

Accounting rules distinguish between when to recognize an asset or liability in financial reports and how to measure that asset or liability once it is recognized. The probability standard for recognition may vary from the probability standard for measurement. For example, the rule for when to record an asset may be to wait until the financial benefit from it is virtually certain, but the rule for measuring it at initial recognition may be to record its most likely value.

Multiple recognition triggers and measurement rules also may exist. For example, the rule for initial recognition may differ from the rule for the triggering of subsequent remeasurement. The rule for initial recognition of an asset may be based on "reasonable certainty" of economic value. The measurement basis may then be its fair value, which implicitly includes a present value discounting of future cash flows. This same initial measurement value may then be included without change in subsequent financial reports (that is, it would be "locked-in") until the remeasurement is triggered, ignoring the change in assumptions and facts since the original measurement. The rule for the triggering of subsequent remeasurement may be whether the undiscounted flows are likely to be less than the current value.

Deferral-Matching Versus Asset-Liability

The focus of **deferral-matching** is on the income statement more than the balance sheet. For example, under a deferral-matching approach, insurance premiums are not recognized when received but are instead recognized ("earned") over the policy term during the period the insurance protection is provided. Likewise, the related expenses and incurred losses are not recognized when paid or committed to but are instead recognized over the same period as the premium. This may lead to the deferral of some up-front expenses and the accrual of some losses that may take decades to pay. The deferral-matching approach requires the establishment of certain assets and liabilities to defer or accelerate recognition of revenue, expense, or loss in order to obtain the desired income statement effect.

For insurers, the two most common balance sheet accounts resulting from this approach are deferred acquisition cost (DAC) assets, used to defer certain

Deferral-matching

An accounting approach in which the focus is to coordinate the timing of income and expense recognition so that both occur when the triggering event that is the focus of the contract occurs.

up-front expenses so they are not recognized on the income statement during the current period, and unearned premium liabilities, used to defer the recognition of revenue. The unearned premium reserve can be considered an offset to the cash received or premium receivable, and the DAC asset an offset to the incurred expenses.

Under an asset-liability approach, the focus is on the value of assets or liabilities that exist as of the balance sheet date. An asset is booked if a right to a future stream of cash flows (or to an item that could be converted to future cash flows) exists at the reporting date. Likewise, a liability is booked if the entity is committed to an obligation at the balance sheet date that would result in the payment of future cash flows or other assets. Such an approach would not recognize a DAC as an asset because it cannot be transferred or translated as cash. It would also not recognize an unearned premium liability beyond that needed for future losses, expenses, or returned premiums associated with that contract (profit). The income statement is based on some but not all changes in the values of assets and liabilities over a set period. For example, an increase in **accounts receivable** is reflected as revenue on the income statement, but an increase in the value of a stock investment would not be reflected as a gain on the income statement unless the stock is sold.[13] Therefore, the focus in an asset-liability approach is on the balance sheet instead of the income statement.

Proponents of a deferral-matching approach have commonly focused on the timing of profit emergence. Absent changes in estimates, under a deferral-matching approach, profit emerges in a steady pattern over the insurance policy term.

Proponents of an asset-liability approach have commonly stressed the importance of reliable measures of value at the reporting date. They typically favor the booking of only those assets that have intrinsic value, in contrast with certain assets that can exist under a deferral-matching approach that have no intrinsic value, such as a DAC asset, which cannot be sold, and the immediate reflection of liabilities once they meet recognition criteria.

It is possible for both approaches to produce comparable income statement results, and one would generally expect both to produce comparable equity values, but the actual data available to the user may vary significantly. For insurance contracts, a principal determinant of how similar the income statements would be under the two approaches is the treatment of risk when valuing assets and liabilities. For example, the asset or liability risk margin under an asset-liability approach could be set such that profit is recognized evenly over the coverage period. This could recreate the same profit emergence pattern found under a deferral-matching system. It is also possible for a single accounting framework to combine elements of both these approaches. This is sometimes called a "mixed attribute" framework.

Accounts receivable

A current asset representing monies owed to a business by customers for goods or services rendered.

Impairment

Accounting information may adhere to one framework for income statement purposes and another for balance sheet purposes. This sometimes leads to the use of "impairment" tests and rules to prevent inconsistencies between two valuations from growing too large or problematic. An asset may be considered impaired if it is no longer expected to produce the economic benefits expected when first acquired.

For example, consider an accounting framework that requires an asset to be reported at its fair value with regular remeasurement for balance sheet purposes, but at locked-in historical cost valuation for income statement purposes. A risk under such an approach is that the two values could become significantly disparate, such as when the fair values of assets have dropped significantly below their historical cost. This risk can be mitigated through required testing on a regular basis of any such shortfall to determine whether such a shortfall is permanent (for example, whether a "permanent" impairment exists). When this happens, the extent of permanent impairment would be reflected in the income statement. The result would be a reduction in the discrepancy between the cumulative income statement and cumulative balance sheet changes, without bringing the income statement to a fair value basis.

Revenue Recognition

A key question in some accounting situations is when revenue should be recognized. This is particularly important for those industries where revenue growth is a key performance measure.

Under a deferral-matching approach, revenue is recognized only as service is rendered. In an insurance context, revenue is recognized under the deferral-matching approach over the policy period in proportion to the covered insurance risk. Under an asset-liability approach, revenue is recognized up front, once the insurer gains control of the asset resulting from the revenue. Therefore, the timing of revenue recognition is a function of the chosen accounting framework.

The timing of revenue recognition is a function of the chosen accounting framework.

Reporting Segment

Financial statements that adhere to GAAP are typically produced on a consolidated basis for the reporting entity. The consolidation may include the combined impact of multiple entities with the same ultimate parent company or owner.

Regulatory financial statements for insurers may be required on a nonconsolidated basis, separately for each legal entity, matching the legal entity to the legal authority of the regulator to intervene. For example, an insurance regulator may not have authority over a banking or stock-broking subsidiary, thus it will want to see the insurance entity separately reported.

GAAP accounting rules also require reporting at the reporting segment level, generally defined as the level at which operations are managed and performance measured by senior management.[14] Reporting segments may be defined by product, by geography, by customer, or by other similar criteria, alone or in combination with other factors. The reporting segment selection is based on the way a particular company operates. For example, a company producing one product but in multiple regions, with somewhat autonomous management and functions by region, may be required to define its reporting segments by geographic region. A company with multiple products in one geographic market, with generally autonomous management by product unit, may define its reporting segments by product.

Where the accounting standard defines reporting segment requirements, it typically also includes a list of required items to be reported by reporting segment. Not all items are required to be reported by reporting segment. For example, income statements may have to be disclosed by reporting segment, but not balance sheets.

Liquidation Versus Going Concern

Many GAAP frameworks focus on the assumption that the business is a going concern when valuing an asset or liability. This contrasts with a runoff or liquidation assumption. For example, the value of a factory in use to produce a profitable product may be much greater than the value the factory could be sold for in a liquidation scenario. The factory with its current machinery set-up and purpose has an expected income stream, which gives it value over and above the land, building, and equipment value. A runoff or liquidation assumption may be more appropriate for regulatory accounting purposes, where a solvency focus exists.

Change in Accounting Principle Versus Change in Accounting Estimate

Accounting frameworks may have drastically different reporting requirements for a change in accounting principle than they do for a change in accounting estimate. A change in accounting principle may require special disclosure of the change, with recalculation of prior period results, while a change in accounting estimate generally affects only the latest reporting period and does not involve a prior period recalculation. When recalculation is required, it generally affects only the results for prior periods required to be shown in the financial statement at the time the accounting principle is changed. A cumulative adjustment may also be required for the oldest period shown, equaling the adjustment required to bring the beginning balances in compliance with the new accounting principle being implemented.

For example, a change from undiscounted liability estimates to present value estimates would typically be described as a change in accounting principle, possibly requiring recalculation of prior period results. A change in the estimated amount of undiscounted liabilities would be a change in accounting estimate, requiring no prior period recalculation and affecting only the reporting period during which the estimate was changed. Additional disclosure may be required when the change in estimate is material to the interpretation of the financial reports.

Where the change in accounting principle is due to a change in accounting standard, the new standard itself usually provides the preparer with specific implementation guidance.

Principle-Based Versus Rule-Based

Accounting standards may take the form of general principles, relying on interpretation and judgment by financial statement preparers for implementation, or they may take the form of a series of rules, limiting the flexibility and use of judgment allowed in their implementation. There are advantages and disadvantages to each approach.

Principle-based standards are potentially very flexible with regard to new and changing products and environments. As such, they should also require less maintenance. They do have disadvantages, such as being more difficult to audit relative to compliance, and concern over consistent and reliable interpretations across entities. To the extent that principle-based standards rely on individual judgment to interpret and implement the standards, there is a danger that they can be used to manipulate financial results.

Rule-based standards are generally considered easier to audit for compliance purposes and may produce more consistent and comparable financial reports across entities. Disadvantages may include a lack of flexibility with regard to changing conditions and new products, hence requiring almost continual maintenance. A concern also exists that rule-based standards may be subject to manipulation, as entities may attempt to adhere to the literal wording of the standard while violating its intent. A framework is not exclusively rules based or principle based, but is predominantly one or the other.

FUNDAMENTALS OF INSURER FINANCIAL STATEMENTS

Insurer financial statements have several characteristics that are distinctive from those of organizations in other industries.

Nearly all accounting frameworks require the preparation of a balance sheet, income statement, and cash flow statement. For insurers, the balance sheet and income statement are generally considered the most important statements when analyzing results. Recent changes in accounting rules have increased the importance of notes and disclosures.

Certain elements of the balance sheet and income statement used by insurers to report financial results are unique to insurers, including policyholders' surplus and asset and liability accounts. Insurers also use the cash flow statement to report results and are subject to other qualitative and quantitative disclosure requirements common to most accounting frameworks.[15]

Balance Sheet

For every organization, including insurers, a balance sheet lists, in a single currency, everything the organization owns (its assets) and everything it owes to others (its liabilities) as of a specified date. The currency used depends on the organization's location (for example, in the United States, U.S. dollars; in Europe, Euros; and so forth).

A balance sheet also indicates the difference between an organization's assets and its liabilities. This difference is the organization's net worth (also known as equity or net assets in certain jurisdictions). Net worth is positive if the organization owns more than it owes and negative if the reverse is true. Because net worth is defined as the difference between assets and liabilities (that is, *Net worth = Assets – Liabilities*), the balance sheet will always balance, even if net worth must be a negative number for balance to exist. An organization with negative net worth is probably insolvent.

Conventionally, a balance sheet lists assets in a column on the left side and liabilities in a column on the right side. Net worth is usually listed after liabilities on the right. See the exhibit "General Form of a Balance Sheet."

General Form of a Balance Sheet

Assets	Liabilities
	Net Worth

[DA03446]

From a finance perspective, a balance sheet can be thought of as showing the sources and uses of an organization's funds. The liabilities and net worth of an organization indicate the source of its funding—it obtains funds from those to whom it owes money and from money initially provided by its owners or retained from earnings. This analogy does not work as well for insurers as it does for many other industries. For many other industries, the principal liability is debt, such as bonds or bank loans. For insurers, the principal liabilities are obligations arising from the insurance contracts. Claim liabilities arising from third-party insurance contracts (such as general liability) represent amounts owed by the insurer on behalf of policyholders; and claim liabilities arising from first-party insurance contracts (such as automobile physical damage) represent amounts owed by the insurer to policyholders.

An organization uses funds by investing its assets. A for-profit business hopes to succeed by achieving a higher return on its assets than it must pay for its liabilities.

The balance sheet of an insurer follows the same general form as those of other organizations, but differs from the standard form in some significant ways. First, some jurisdictions use the term "surplus as regards policyholders" as the label for net worth. This distinction is more significant than an arbitrary labeling difference. In some jurisdictions (such as the U.S. and Canada), the whole of the insurer's net worth is available to satisfy policyholder claims before any owner is entitled to compensation. Policyholders' surplus is an appropriate term for mutual or other companies without shareholders where the participating or mutual policyholder owns the residual equity. The other principal difference between the balance sheet of an insurer and another organization is that different elements (accounts) constitute the insurer's primary assets and liabilities.

insurers networth is available to the policyholders before available to any owner

Insurer Assets

Business assets typically include buildings, equipment, and inventory. However, most assets owned by insurers are financial instruments such as bonds and stocks.

A major class of assets owned by property-casualty insurers (and the largest class for U.S. and Canadian insurers) is bonds. Bonds are attractive investments for insurers in many jurisdictions because, compared with other investments, they pay fairly predictable, periodic, secure income. It is important for insurers to generate income from their investments to provide cash flow for payment of future losses.

Bonds are attractive because predictable periodic & secure

Other financial investments that may constitute sizeable portions of insurer assets are stocks, cash, and cash equivalents (for example, money market funds). Insurers also own buildings, equipment (for example, computers), and office furnishings. However, investment in these assets is relatively minor compared with a typical insurer's investments in financial instruments.

Asset accounts that are unique to insurers' balance sheets and are directly related to the writing of insurance contracts include these:[16]

- Premium balances or premium receivables (also known as agents' balances or by other, similar terms)—These are premiums due on policies, either from agents if the agent bills the policyholder or from the policyholder if billed directly. These balances arise from the delay between premium

Reinsurance recoverables

Amounts for losses and loss adjustment expenses owed to an insurer under reinsurance agreements covering paid losses.

DAC

Deferred acquisition costs

The recognition of the cost of acquiring a new customer over the duration of an insurance contract.

Reserve

The amount the insurer estimates and sets aside to pay on an existing claim that has not been settled.

Unearned premium

The portion of policy premium for the unexpired portion of the policy.

This liability is caused by the the deferral of premium revenue under a deferral matching approach

Asset-liability

An accounting approach that focuses on the value of assets or liabilities that exist as of the balance sheet date.

payment by policyholders to the insurer or its agents and the transmittal of these premiums to the insurer.

- **Reinsurance recoverables**—These are amounts due from reinsurers for ceded losses. In some accounting frameworks, the amounts billed and due as a result of ceded paid losses are recorded as an asset (and sometimes called reinsurance receivables), while the amounts to be ceded and billed in the future as a result of incurred but unpaid losses are recorded as a contra-liability and called reinsurance recoverables. For some insurers, reinsurance recoverables can be significant.

- **Deferred acquisition costs**—These represent expense payments that are deferred for income statement purposes under a deferral-matching accounting approach—These expenses are deferred so that they can be recognized in the income statement at the same time as the corresponding revenue.

Insurer Liabilities

Insurer liabilities are even more distinct from the liabilities of other organizations than are their assets. The two principal liability accounts are **claim liabilities** (known as **reserves** in the U.S. and "technical provisions" in certain other jurisdictions) and **unearned premium**,[17] both of which arise from the insurer's operations and both of which are unique to insurers.

These common liability accounts on the balance sheet are directly related to the writing of insurance contracts:

- Policy liabilities—This liability is established for in-force insurance policies for future events, for which a liability exists due to a contract having been established. There is no policy liability for policies that have yet to be written. However, a policy liability may exist for events covered by the renewal of existing policies, under certain situations. For example, a policy liability would exist for level premium renewable term life insurance, but not for possible renewals of property insurance contracts with which the pricing is not guaranteed and either party can decide to non-renew.

- Unearned premiums—This liability is caused by the deferral of premium revenue under a deferral-matching approach. The amount of unearned premium liability generally represents the portion of policy premium for the unexpired portion of the policy. In an **asset-liability** approach, this would be replaced by a policy reserve. This liability account is often referred to as the unearned premium reserve. Liabilities and reserves have similar meanings in the context of insurance, and the unearned premium reserve is listed as a liability on the balance sheet.

- Unpaid claims (also known as loss reserves) —This represents claims on policies for events that have already occurred but have not yet been paid. The Casualty Actuarial Society (CAS) "Statement of Principles Regarding Property and Casualty Loss and Loss Adjustment Expense

Reserves"[18] (Statement of Principles) defines loss reserve as a provision for its related liability. The Statement of Principles states that a total loss reserve is composed of five elements, although the five elements may not necessarily be individually quantified: (1) **case reserves**, (2) provision for future development on known claims, (3) reopened claims reserve, (4) provision for claims incurred but not reported, and (5) provision for claims in transit (incurred and reported but not recorded). Actuaries refer to the sum of the last four components of loss reserves as the broad definition of IBNR. IBNR losses are often further separated into two components: (1) incurred but not yet reported claims (pure IBNR or narrow definition of IBNR) and (2) incurred but not enough reported (IBNER, commonly referred to as development on known claims).[19] IBNER reserves are also sometimes called supplemental or bulk reserves. In most cases, incurred but not reported (IBNR) reserves is used to refer to both IBNYR and IBNER.

- Unpaid adjusting expense—This represents the cost of settling or defending claims on policies for events that have already occurred. It may also include expected adjusting expenses for unreported claims. It includes the cost of defending the insured (for liability policies). It can also include the cost of disputing coverage with the insured. Claim expense liabilities are sometimes included in the claim liability value.

- Insurance expense—This is the liability for expenses incurred but unpaid in conjunction with the insurance policy, other than the claim expenses previously discussed. Typical expenses include commission liabilities (sometimes split into regular and contingent commission liabilities) and premium tax liabilities (where applicable).

Unpaid claim and adjustment expense liabilities must be estimated, and estimates can be inaccurate. Inaccuracies in the claim and adjustment expense liabilities directly affect policyholders' surplus because the balance sheet must always balance. If these liabilities are too low, policyholders' surplus will be overstated (and understated when liabilities are too high). Once inadequate claim and expense liabilities are adjusted upward, policyholders' surplus will be reduced (or increased if liabilities are adjusted downward). This is a critical issue for insurers because policyholders' surplus is vital to an insurer's financial strength and ongoing viability. See the exhibit "Principal Elements of an Insurer Balance Sheet."

Income Statement

While a balance sheet is a snapshot of an organization's assets and liabilities as of a specific date, an income statement portrays financial results over a time period, usually a year or a quarter. An income statement also shows gains or losses from non-operating activities, such as the purchase or sale of assets.

An income statement is structured to calculate an organization's profitability. Generally, an organization is profitable when its revenues exceed its expenses.

Case reserve
A loss reserve assigned to an individual claim.

[handwritten margin notes:]
1) case reserves
2) provision for future development on known claims
3) reopened claims reserve
4) provision for claims incurred but not reported
5) provision for claims in transit (reported but not recorded)

Principal Elements of an Insurer Balance Sheet

Assets	Liabilities
Bonds	Policy Liabilities
Stocks	Unearned Premiums
Cash	Unpaid Claims
Premium Balances	Unpaid Adjusting Expense
Reinsurance Recoverables	Insurance Expense
Deferred Acquisition Costs	**Surplus and Other Funds**
	Surplus (also known as Equity or Net Assets)

[DA03448]

An organization earns revenue by selling its products or services; expenses are the costs incurred in producing that revenue. The general form of an income statement is shown in the exhibit. See the exhibit "General Form of an Income Statement."

General Form of an Income Statement

Revenues
− Expenses
Net Income

[DA03449]

Conventionally, revenues are listed at the top of an income statement and expenses are listed below revenues. The "bottom line" of an income statement is net income, the difference between revenues and expenses, or profit (or loss, if negative).

The general form of an insurer's income statement is similar to that of other businesses' income statements. The revenues from an insurer's underwriting operations are the premiums received from policyholders, and the expenses for an insurer are payments for claims and claim-related expenses (that is, adjustment expenses) covered by the insurer's policies plus the insurer's operating expenses. Additionally, insurers also earn material income from investments. See the exhibit "General Form of an Insurer Income Statement."

General Form of an Insurer Income Statement

Premiums
− Claims and Loss Adjustment Expenses
− Underwriting Expenses
_____

Net Income From Operations

[DA03450]

These common income statement accounts are directly related to the writing of insurance contracts:

- Premiums—Under a deferral-matching approach, insurers record premiums as revenue once they are earned, not when they are written or received. Therefore, **earned premium** is another term for premium revenue under a deferral-matching approach. Earned premiums equal the written premiums less the change in unearned premium liabilities. Earned premiums represent the portion of the charged premium for coverage provided under the reporting period. In contrast, under an asset-liability accounting approach, earned premiums may equal written premiums.

- Claims incurred—These represent claims incurred during the reporting period. Claims incurred represent the amount paid for claims plus the change in claim liabilities.

- Loss or claim adjustment expenses—These represent claim-related expenses incurred on claims resulting from events during the reporting period. A claim expense also can be incurred on a noncovered claim due to the necessary cost to dispute noncovered filed claims. Claim adjustment expenses are sometimes included in "claims incurred."

- Underwriting expenses—These represent expenses incurred that directly relate to the insurance operation. They include sales commission expenses, other acquisition expenses, general expenses, overhead, and various fees and taxes related to the insurance operation.

- Underwriting income—This is calculated as premium revenue less claim adjustment expenses and underwriting expenses.

- Policyholder dividends—These are dividends to policyholders incurred during the reporting period. In some accounting frameworks, these amounts are legally incurred only when declared. In others, historical dividends relating to the policy coverage provided during the reporting period must be estimated and allocated to that reporting period. These amounts are generally included in underwriting income, but may not be for some purposes. It is possible for policyholder dividends to be subtracted from revenue under some accounting frameworks.

- Investment earnings—The results from underwriting operations alone would provide an incomplete picture of the insurer's financial

Earned premiums
The portion of written premiums that corresponds to coverage that has already been provided.

performance. Insurers earn income from invested assets. Investment income arises out of the fundamentals of insurance transactions. Policyholders pay their premiums before insurers pay claims. Between these periods of time, insurers hold funds that are available for investment. Investment earnings include investment income and net capital gains. (Some accounting frameworks include all capital gains in income, others include only realized gains.) Investment income comes principally from interest payments on bonds and dividend payments from stocks. Realized capital gains result when assets, such as shares of stock, are sold for more than the purchase price. The gain is realized upon the sale. Unrealized capital gains on investments result when an asset increases in value but is not sold. "Net" capital gains refers to the net of capital gains over capital losses (also a possibility).

The exhibit presents the important elements of an insurer's income statement prior to policyholder dividends and income taxes. See the exhibit "Principal Elements of an Insurer Income Statement."

Principal Elements of an Insurer Income Statement

Earned Premium
– Claims Incurred
– Claims Adjustment Expenses Incurred
– Underwriting Expenses
_____

Net Underwriting Income (or Loss)
+ Investment Earnings
+ Net Capital Gains (or Losses) – Realized or Unrealized, depending on accounting paradigm
_____

Net Income (Before Dividends or Taxes)

[DA03451]

The remainder of the income statement shows the effect of policyholder dividends and income taxes and may also show the impact of items that directly affect reported surplus (also known as equity or net assets) without going through income. (Examples of such items include unrealized gains under some accounting frameworks, and dividends to the insurer's stockholders.)

Cash Flow Statement

The cash flow statement is typically much less important for a property-casualty insurer than for organizations in other industries. This is due to the nature of insurance, relative to many other businesses, in which insurers receive their revenue before having to meet their contractual obligations. Thus, insurers typically have a large amount of invested assets that are convertible into cash (even when insolvent). In contrast, many other businesses must expend cash before they receive their revenue, making them very dependent on loans for working capital. This dependency on credit makes a cash flow statement important for some industries, even if it is of minor importance for insurers.

Notes and Disclosures

The notes and disclosures sections of financial statements allow for additional information beyond the statements previously mentioned. These include a description of the accounting policies used in preparing the financial statements and a discussion of values that may not be reliably estimable. Such disclosures may include discussion of the risks and uncertainty associated with the insurance liability estimates found in the balance sheet and income statement.

They may also include "forward-looking information," concerning estimates of future financial earnings or events that have yet to occur by the publication date of the financial statements. Note that these are different from possible disclosure of "subsequent events," which are events that occurred after the financial statement or valuation date but before the publication date. For example, a catastrophe that occurred after the statement date but before the publication date would be a subsequent event, not included in the reported equity or income. In contrast, a discussion of future exposure to catastrophes for the coming year would be a "forward-looking" statement.

Another important issue typically addressed in notes and disclosures is the effect of discounting of unpaid loss and loss adjustment expense liabilities. Frequently, the disclosures contain information about the selected discount rate and the total effect of the present value discounting calculations. Similarly, if the estimate of liabilities for claims and claim-related expenses contains a provision for adverse deviation (that is, risk margin), disclosures will generally describe the procedure for the development of the provision and the total value of such provision.

INTERNATIONAL FINANCIAL REPORTING STANDARDS (IFRS)

It is important to understand **International Financial Reporting Standards (IFRS)** and their influence on financial reporting by insurers. Many insurers located outside the United States and operating in the U.S. report under IFRS. Publicly traded U.S. insurers report under U.S. generally accepted accounting principles (GAAP) and, in certain situations, under IFRS as well.

International Financial Reporting Standards (IFRS)
Financial standards developed by the International Accounting Standards Board (IASB).

The increasing globalization of world economies is accelerating the need for a single international accounting standard. Accordingly, standard-setting boards are working to resolve differences between IFRS and U.S. GAAP. Convergence of the two standards would benefit investors, auditors, analysts, and other market participants by making financial statements comparable between U.S. and non-U.S. insurers.

IFRS Compared With U.S. GAAP

The International Accounting Standards Board (IASB) is the independent standard-setting body of the International Accounting Standards Committee Foundation. Similar to the Financial Accounting Standard Board's (FASB's) role for U.S. GAAP, the IASB develops and publishes IFRS. IFRS are intended to be a single set of high-quality, understandable, enforceable, and globally accepted standards designed to meet the financial reporting needs of the global economy. Therefore, they contain elements of generally accepted accounting standards from various countries.

The relatively strict regulatory and legal environment in the U.S. has fostered a rules-based accounting approach. Accordingly, U.S. GAAP include comprehensive guidance and industry-specific interpretations, including those for insurance. IFRS are largely based on principles rather than rules, with less-specific guidance, leaving a greater degree of interpretation of the standards to the reporting organizations.

While international and U.S. accounting standards differ, their general principles, conceptual frameworks, and accounting results are often similar. For example, under both standards, the required financial statements include the balance sheet, income statement, statement of recognized income and expense for IFRS or other comprehensive income for U.S. GAAP, statement of cash flows, and accompanying notes to the financial statements.[20] Furthermore, under both IFRS and U.S. GAAP, financial statements must be prepared using the accrual basis of accounting.

Fair value
The market value, either actual or estimated, of an asset or a liability.

Technological advances, advanced databases of transaction activities, and financial market turmoil have all led to a focus on **fair value** for assets and liabilities. Accounting systems give organizations a greater ability to track all assets and liabilities and mark to market those assets that have well-established trading markets. Similarly, databases of transactions of less-frequently traded assets and liabilities allow organizations to more accurately determine fair value.

IFRS and U.S. GAAP are similar in that they use fair value rather than historical cost reporting for many assets, such as intangible assets and financial instruments, including derivatives, equities, and fixed-income securities.[21] However, they differ in the reported value of property, plant, and equipment assets, with IFRS allowing for fair value and U.S. GAAP using historical cost. There are additional differences between IFRS and U.S. GAAP, including those relating to financial statement presentation, inventory valuation, revenue recognition, foreign currency matters, and treatment of financial instruments and insurance contracts.

Convergence of IFRS and U.S. GAAP

The IASB and the FASB have been working together to promote the international convergence of accounting standards. The boards declared their commitment to convergence of their respective accounting standards at the Norwalk Agreement in 2002.[22] See the exhibit "Convergence of GAAP and IFRS."

Convergence of GAAP and IFRS

"The Norwalk Agreement"

In the Memorandum of Understanding that was issued after the joint meeting of FASB and IASB in Norwalk, Connecticut, both the FASB and IASB pledged to use their best efforts to (a) make their existing financial reporting standards fully compatible as soon as is practicable and (b) to coordinate their future work programs to ensure that once achieved, compatibility is maintained.

Financial Accounting Standards Board, "Memorandum of Understanding: The Norwalk Agreement," September 2002, www.fasb.org/news/memorandum.pdf (accessed January 29, 2014). [DA06136]

Since then, the boards have reaffirmed their commitment to work together on converging accounting standards and have set priorities and various target dates. The boards currently have common standards in areas such as business combinations and noncontrolling interests and are working on additional standards.

Insurer Financial Reporting

Many non-U.S. insurers that operate in the U.S. report under IFRS. A U.S. insurer may need to report using IFRS if it plans to raise capital from other countries, is a subsidiary of a foreign company, or has a large investor that requires IFRS.

All U.S. licensed insurers are required to file quarterly and annual statements using SAP with state insurance regulators. All publicly traded U.S. insurers are required to file quarterly and annual financial reporting with the SEC using U.S. GAAP. Non-publicly traded U.S. insurers, such as mutual and fraternal insurers, are not required to report on a GAAP basis. However, some choose to prepare certain financial information on a U.S. GAAP basis for internal purposes to benchmark with peers and may choose to make portions of this information public.

FASB AND IASB ACCOUNTING STANDARDS FOR INSURANCE CONTRACTS

Insurance contracts have unique characteristics and therefore require specialized accounting treatment.

For all types of insurance, the timing and amount of claims are highly uncertain. Property-casualty policies are generally written for a one-year term; however, claims may not be fully paid until several years after a policy terminates. Life insurance policies and annuity contracts span many years, often decades, and are influenced by many factors, including the general economy and policyholder behavior, so future premiums and benefit payments under a contract are uncertain at any given time. Accounting for insurance contracts should accurately reflect these uncertainties.

Worldwide, insurers' accounting treatments of insurance contracts differ considerably. The International Accounting Standards Board (IASB) and the United States Financial Accounting Standards Board (FASB) have recognized the need to improve insurance contract accounting. Accordingly, they each have worked on standards to address accounting for insurance contracts.

Current FASB Accounting Standards for Insurance Contracts

In June 1982, the FASB issued FASB 60, *Accounting and Reporting by Insurance Enterprises*. This statement addressed the recognition of premium revenue and insurance contract liabilities by separating insurance contracts into short-duration (mainly property-casualty and term life policies) and long-duration (mainly whole life policies and annuity contracts) contracts. Under FASB 60 (which has since been incorporated into Accounting Standards Codification [ASC] Topic 944, *Financial Services—Insurance*), accounting treatment varies significantly depending on contract duration.

- Accounting for property-casualty policies (short duration) is based on the deferral-and-matching concept. An unearned premium reserve is set up at policy inception, and premium is earned over the policy term (generally one year). Claims are recognized when they occur by recording claim payments and accruing an estimated liability for unpaid claims, even for losses that have occurred but have not yet been reported to the insurer. Therefore, the recognition of revenue as premiums are earned and expenses as claims are incurred is based on the matching principle, whereby premium is matched with its associated claims expenses. Property-casualty insurers value the majority of their unpaid claims at their estimated ultimate settlement values on an undiscounted basis, and if there is a range of possible values, they use the most likely value. A change in estimates for incurred losses flows through the income statement in the year the change is made, so underestimating claims reserves can lower future net income as the claims are paid.

- Unpaid claims liabilities for casualty lines of business can be outstanding for several years or even decades after policy expiration.

- Accounting for traditional whole life policies and annuity contracts, which are mostly classified as long duration, is based partly on the deferral-and-matching concept and partly on an economic-model concept, with present-value discounting of future cash flows arising from the contracts. Premium and other considerations are recognized when due from the policyholder. However, the vast majority of these contracts are in effect over a long period of time, even decades, so at any time, a significant portion of the premium and other considerations are not currently due from the policyholder. Similarly, an even larger portion of the benefit payments will be due to policyholders in the future, resulting in a need for benefit reserves. Life insurers accrue a reserve for their future contract liabilities by subtracting the discounted value of estimated future benefit payments from the discounted value of future estimated net premiums at the time current premium revenue is recognized. Insurers' initial assumptions at policy inception regarding investment yield, discount rate, expenses, and mortality are locked in over the life of the contract. However, there is a provision for recognizing premium deficiency if these assumptions prove inadequate.

In December 1987, the FASB issued FASB 97, *Accounting and Reporting by Insurance Enterprises for Certain Long-Duration Contracts and for Realized Gains and Losses from the Sale of Investments*. (FASB 97 has also been incorporated into ASC Topic 944, *Financial Services—Insurance*.) This statement addressed some areas that were under study when FASB 60 was issued, notably the treatment of universal-life-type contracts, which are long-duration contracts in which elements such as premium, mortality, coverage, interest credits, and administration costs are unbundled and not fixed and guaranteed under the contract as they are with traditional whole life policies. The policyholder builds up an account balance, to which premium and interest credits are added and from which expense elements are subtracted. FASB 97 requires that a liability for policy benefits equal to the policyholder account balance be recognized. Premium is not reported as revenue. Instead, the various expense elements assessed against the policyholder are recognized as revenue as the associated services are provided.

Under U.S. generally accepted accounting principles (GAAP), most insurers' invested assets are valued at fair value, which is consistent with the concepts of economic income and economic net worth. However, the recognition of insurer premium revenue and the valuation of insurance liabilities vary by type of contract and, in most cases, are inconsistent with the economic valuation concept. This results in a mixed-attribute accounting model, with inconsistent treatment of insurance contract liabilities and the assets that support them.

Current and Proposed IASB Accounting Standards for Insurance Contracts

The IASB has also been active in the area of insurance contract accounting. In March 2004, it issued Phase I of International Financial Reporting Standard 4 *Insurance Contracts* (IFRS 4) as an interim measure to address some of the divergent international accounting practices until a comprehensive international standard on insurance contracts could be finalized. This was the first time the IASB specifically addressed insurance contract accounting. IFRS 4's objectives were to improve financial-statement disclosure and the understanding of the future cash flows arising from insurance contracts. Furthermore, IFRS 4 provided guidance as to what is considered an insurance contract, and it defined insurance risk. However, IFRS 4 allowed entities to continue to use accounting models from their own jurisdiction, and as a result, there is currently a diverse set of insurance contract accounting standards in use throughout the world.

In June 2013, the IASB issued an Exposure Draft (ED) on insurance contracts to improve transparency and promote international consistency in accounting for insurance contracts. The ED will supersede IFRS 4. A key objective of the IASB proposal is to ensure that financial reporting reflects the economics of insurance contract transactions, consistent with the accounting industry's movement toward fair value reporting and the concepts of economic income and economic net worth. Most insurer assets, notably invested assets, are traded in active markets, and it is therefore easy to establish their fair market value. However, insurance liabilities have no active market, which presents a significant challenge for establishing a fair market value. As an alternative, the IASB proposal values insurance liabilities by estimating the present value of cash flows arising from insurance contracts.

The proposal introduces two models for valuing insurance contract liabilities, the **Building Block Approach (BBA)** and the **Premium Allocation Approach (PAA)**. Both models are based on a "fulfillment" concept, meaning that the cash flows arising from insurance contracts are measured from the insurer's perspective; that is, they are based on the cost to the insurer of fulfilling its obligations to policyholders. This contrasts with the "exit" concept, under which the insurer values its insurance liabilities based on the cost to transfer them to a third party. See the exhibit "IASB Building Block Approach."

Under the BBA, future net cash flows are disaggregated into (a) an expected present value amount for future net cash flows and (b) two margins, one a risk

Building Block Approach (BBA)

A model for valuing insurance contract liabilities arising from a group of insurance contracts that is based on the expected present value of future net cash outflows and a risk margin.

Premium Allocation Approach (PAA)

A model for valuing insurance contract liabilities arising from a group of insurance contracts that is based on the present value of premiums for unexpired coverage and the present value of probability-weighted future payments for incurred losses.

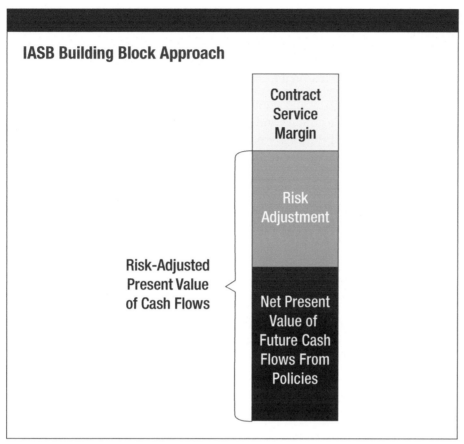

IASB Building Block Approach

Contract Service Margin

Risk Adjustment

Net Present Value of Future Cash Flows From Policies

Risk-Adjusted Present Value of Cash Flows

[DA11118]

adjustment and the other a contract service amount. These are some of the features of the IASB BBA:

- Expected future cash flows are based on a probability-weighted estimate (the expected value) under various scenarios rather than the likely amount, as under FASB 60.

- Cash flows are discounted at a rate that reflects their specific characteristics.

- The expected future cash flows and the discount rate are reevaluated at the end of each reporting period.

- The margins are released into profit over the term of the contracts.

The PAA is less complex than the BBA and employs the deferral-and-matching concept, similar to the accounting for short-duration contracts under FASB 60. Premium is allocated throughout the policy term, similar to the earned/unearned premium concept, and claims are recognized when they are incurred. A key difference between the PAA and FASB 60 is that, under the PAA, cash flows for currently incurred but unpaid claims and unearned premiums are discounted to their present values. (Discounting for incurred claims is not required if the effect is immaterial or the claim is expected to be resolved in one year.) For the PAA, the IASB ED requires a separate risk adjustment margin.

The IASB ED requires the use of the BBA, and it permits use of the PAA when its results are a reasonable approximation of those for the BBA.

The proposed changes would significantly alter the timing of profit recognition for life insurance policies and annuity contracts. Additionally, there is likely to be increased earnings volatility because of the reevaluation of future cash flows and the discount rate at the end of each reporting period.

The IASB has a target date of 2018 for the standards to take effect.

DEPOSIT ACCOUNTING

Accounting frameworks may require the use of deposit accounting for certain insurance contracts. This accounting is generally materially different from the normal accounting required for insurance contracts.

Deposit accounting may be required by a particular accounting framework for an insurance contract under specific conditions. Different accounting frameworks can have materially different rules governing when deposit accounting is to be used for a contract and for determining the deposit accounting approach that should apply to a particular type of contract.[23]

Deposit Accounting Rules

Deposit accounting may be required by an accounting framework for contracts that might otherwise be considered insurance (or reinsurance) contracts under these conditions:

- No risk transfer exists.
- Timing risk exists, but the transfer of amount risk is negligible (for example, when the amount to be paid under the contract is fixed or subject to only minimal uncertainty, but uncertainty exists as to the timing of the payment).
- The reinsurance is considered to be retroactive reinsurance, subject to exceptions.

Whether accounting rules require deposit accounting under these conditions depends on the applicable accounting framework. However, deposit accounting for a contract typically observes these rules:

- The decisions as to whether deposit accounting applies and, if so, how the deposit accounting rules are applied are handled on an individual contract-by-contract basis, not on a portfolio basis. This is true even if the resulting contract-by-contract amounts are reported on a summary basis in financial reports.

- The amount(s) received for a contract is recorded as a deposit liability, with no revenue or expense effect (and therefore, no effect on income).

- The deposit liability is increased by additional receipts and usually by investment income credits of some kind. It is decreased by payments.

- The deposit generally represents a present value of future payment obligations.

Approaches for Deposit Accounting

General approaches to deposit accounting include these:

- Bank deposit approach
- Prospective approach
- Retrospective approach

Bank Deposit Approach

Under the bank deposit approach, the initial deposit grows with interest credited at an interest rate whose calculation is determined in advance (and with possible additional deposits depending on the contract terms) and declines with withdrawals. The defining characteristic of the bank deposit approach is that the ending deposit for a reporting period is dependent solely on the beginning balance, the credited rate for the period, and any deposits or withdrawals during the period. It is not dependent on the particular pattern of cash flows that led to the beginning balance, nor on the projected cash flows for the period beyond the ending balance. The credited rate may be fixed or variable and may be dependent on market rates or based on nonmarket events or rates. Whatever its basis, the method of calculation is generally set in advance.

Prospective Approach

The defining characteristic of the prospective approach is that the current value of the deposit is set equal to the present value of future payments, irrespective of the initial deposit or past payments. The interest rate is generally a market rate, which may be based on risk-free rates and may be locked in at inception so that it does not change over time. Conceptually, it is also possible for a prospective method to use a market rate that is updated for each reporting period.

Under the prospective approach, the deposit value will change with the amortization of interest and with a change in projected future losses. If the discount rate is not locked in by the accounting framework, the deposit value will also change with a change in the discount rate.

Retrospective Approach

The defining characteristic of the retrospective approach is that the deposit is a function of the initial deposit, past payments, and the current estimate of all future payments. Under this method, the interest rate is the rate for which the discounted value of past payments and estimated future payments would equal the initial deposit. The interest rate can change whenever the estimated cash flows under the contract change. This method could conceivably generate a negative rate if applied to a contract in which the projected outflows no longer exceed the initial inflows. Whereas the prospective approach focuses only on the future (except possibly for an interest rate previously locked in), the retrospective approach focuses on all the flows since inception, past and future.

Under the retrospective approach, the deposit value and discount rate are subject to change whenever the projected cash flows since inception are changed.

SUMMARY

Various accounting standard setters have developed qualitative criteria for accounting information to be produced by an accounting framework. For accounting information to be decision-useful, the information should be understandable; relevant; reliable; comparable and consistent; and unbiased. In addition, the accounting rules or requirements must be cost-benefit effective in that the cost to produce the information must be reasonably proportional to the resulting benefit.

Different users of insurer financial statements may develop their own accounting frameworks. These users (and the type of accounting focused on them) can be categorized into four groups:

- GAAP accounting, which focuses on the needs of investors, creditors, and owners (current and potential)
- Regulatory/supervisory accounting, which focuses on the needs of regulators and supervisors, with an emphasis on solvency
- Tax accounting, which focuses on the needs of tax authorities
- Management accounting, which focuses on the needs of insurer management

The sources of the rules that underlie accounting frameworks can vary between GAAP, regulatory/statutory, and tax accounting. Some of these frameworks rely on multiple sources for their rules. Rule hierarchies are established within each accounting framework to resolve conflicts that preparers of financial statements may have when applying the rules.

A variety of accounting concepts that inform accounting rules can affect the values reported on insurer financial statements. Users of financial reports should understand the common accounting concepts that can help explain differences between entities' financial statements and enhance understanding of the debate that occurs as accounting rules are being changed.

Nearly all accounting frameworks require the preparation of a balance sheet, income statement, and cash flow statement. Elements of the balance sheet and income statement insurers use to report financial results are unique to insurers, including policyholders' surplus and asset and liability accounts. Insurers also use the cash flow statement to report results and are subject to other qualitative and quantitative disclosure requirements. For insurers, the balance sheet and income statement are generally considered the most important statements when analyzing financial results.

Throughout the world, IFRS and U.S. GAAP are the most widely recognized accounting standards. The IASB and the FASB are working to converge their standards in many areas. Full convergence would promote consistency in insurer accounting on a global basis and streamline insurer financial reporting. Additionally, it would benefit investors, auditors, analysts, and other market participants.

Although there is worldwide diversity in accounting treatment for insurance contracts, both the IASB and the FASB have created standards. The FASB has issued FASB 60 and FASB 97 to provide guidance for both short-duration and long-duration contracts. The IASB has issued IFRS 4, an ED on insurance contracts, and has proposed BBA and PAA models to value insurance contract liabilities based on a fulfillment value instead of an exit value. The changes will significantly affect life insurers, and they have a target date of 2018.

Some accounting frameworks require deposit accounting for insurance contracts under certain conditions. Three general approaches to deposit accounting are the bank deposit approach, the prospective approach, and the retrospective approach.

ASSIGNMENT NOTES

1. "Exposure Draft of 'An Improved Conceptual Framework for Financial Reporting'," International Accounting Standards Board, May 2008, www.iasb.org/NR/rdonlyres/464C50D6-00FD-4BE7-A6FF-1BEAD353CD97/0/conceptual_framework_exposure_draft.pdf (accessed July 26, 2010).

2. As of 2010, the International Accounting Standards Board (IASB) and the Financial Accounting Standards Board (FASB) were jointly revising their list of qualitative criteria, to be labeled as their Conceptual Framework.

3. Material is adapted with permission from the Casualty Actuarial Society Study Note, "Accounting Concepts for the Actuary" by Ralph Blanchard.

4. The Exposure Draft—Conceptual Framework for Financial reporting of the IASB and FASB has proposed replacing "Reliability" with the concept of Faithful Representation, with the explanation that "[f]inancial reporting information is a faithful representation if it depicts the substance of an economic phenomenon completely, neutrally, and without material error." The draft Framework is

more a reordering of the criteria discussed rather than a change in the criteria. International Accounting Standards Board, "Exposure Draft of 'An Improved Conceptual Framework for Financial Reporting'," May 2008, www.iasb.org/NR/rdonlyres/464C50D6-00FD-4BE7-A6FF-1BEAD353CD97/0/conceptual_framework_exposure_draft.pdf (accessed June 21, 2010).

5. CIA Standards of Practice, 1740.02 and 1740.03.

6. This category grouping for users was chosen due to its close alignment with common types of accounting. It leaves out the rating agency and policyholder user categories. These other users' interests are typically aligned with regulators and supervisors due to the focus on solvency concerns.

7. The term "regulator" is common in the United States, while the term "supervisor" is common in Europe.

8. Material is adapted with permission from the Casualty Actuarial Society Study Note, "Accounting Concepts for the Actuary" by Ralph Blanchard.

9. FASB changed its hierarchy in 2008, and the hierarchy of both the FASB and IASB are subject to change with the Conceptual Framework project. International Accounting Standards Board, "Exposure Draft of 'An Improved Conceptual Framework for Financial Reporting'," May 2008, www.iasb.org/NR/rdonlyres/464C50D6-00FD-4BE7-A6FF-1BEAD353CD97/0/conceptual_framework_exposure_draft.pdf (accessed June 21, 2010).

10. International Financial Reporting Standards, "About the IFRS Interpretations Committee," www.ifrs.org/The+organisation/Members+of+the+IFRIC/About+the+IFRIC.htm (accessed August 16, 2010).

11. (1) Material is adapted with permission from the Casualty Actuarial Society Study Note, "Accounting Concepts for the Actuary" by Ralph Blanchard.

12. International Accounting Standards Board, www.iasb.org/NR/rdonlyres/C4096A25-F830-401D-8E2E-9286B194798E/0/EDFairValueMeasurement_website.pdf (accessed May 9, 2010).

13. Under GAAP, an exception exists for a stock classified as "trading" whereby unrealized gains and losses on the stock would be included in earnings (net income).

14. The IASB standard in reporting segments, IAS 14, defines reporting segments as "organisational units for which information is reported to the board of directors and CEO unless those organisational units are not along product/service or geographical lines, in which case use the next lower level of internal segmentation that reports product and geographical information."

15. Material is adapted with permission from the Casualty Actuarial Society Study Note, "Accounting Concepts for the Actuary" by Ralph Blanchard.

16. These are important, but are not the only asset accounts that are directly related to insurers. Other insurer-related asset accounts are beyond the scope of this content.

17. Copyright Casualty Actuarial Society. Used by permission.

18. Adopted by Casualty Actuarial Society Board of Directors, May 1988.

19. Copyright Casualty Actuarial Society. Used by permission.

20. Ernst & Young, "US GAAP versus IFRS: The basics," November 2012, p. 3, www.ey.com/Publication/vwLUAssets/US_GAAP_versus_IFRS:_The_basics_

November_2012/$FILE/US_GAAP_v_IFRS_The_Basics_Nov2012.pdf (accessed February 19, 2014).

21. Under both IFRS and U.S. GAAP, use of fair value for fixed-income securities depends on how they are classified.

22. Ernst & Young, p. 49.

23. Material is adapted with permission from the Casualty Actuarial Society Study Note, "Basic Insurance Accounting—Selected Topics" by Ralph Blanchard.

Property-Casualty Insurer Financial Statements

Educational Objectives

After learning the content of this assignment, you should be able to:

▷ Compare the contents of a property-casualty insurer's GAAP financial statements to a noninsurer's GAAP financial statements.

▷ Explain how statutory accounting principles differ from generally accepted accounting principles.

▷ Describe the main components of an insurer's NAIC Annual Statement and the information those components contain.

Property-Casualty Insurer Financial Statements

COMPARISON OF PROPERTY-CASUALTY INSURER AND NONINSURER GAAP FINANCIAL STATEMENTS

Historically, property-casualty insurers in the United States have used statutory accounting principles (SAP) for financial reporting. Insurers that are publicly traded are required to report under generally accepted accounting principles (GAAP) as well. Although most property-casualty insurers in the U.S. are not publicly traded, many still choose to fill out GAAP financial statements in addition to their SAP financial statements.

Standards for GAAP were originally developed for commercial and industrial organizations but have been adapted for financial service organizations. The Financial Accounting Standards Board's (FASB's) ASC Topic 944, "Financial Services—Insurance," specifically applies GAAP standards to insurers. Because of the unique nature of the insurance business, the specific items included on insurer GAAP financial statements are substantially different from those included on financial statements for commercial and industrial organizations. These differences can be seen across these statements:

- The balance sheet
- The income statement
- The statement of comprehensive income
- The statement of shareholders' equity
- The statement of cash flows

Differences Between Insurer and Noninsurer Financial Statements

Insurers are financial service organizations that offer products that are produced differently than those of traditional commercial or industrial enterprises. The assets that are used to produce insurance products and the liabilities and income that are generated by these products are substantially different from more tangible products such as consumer electronics or clothing. Insurers do not rely on production facilities, but instead on financial strength, to support their products. This fact results in a substantially different asset mix for insurers.

Once an insurance policy has been sold, liabilities are created over the time it takes to earn the premium and pay all losses. These liabilities are unique to insurers and appear on the liability side of an insurer's balance sheet. The premium income from product sales and the investment income from assets are the most important sources of revenue to insurers, while losses and loss adjustment expenses are unique sources of expenses. All of these differences lead to the unique accounting practices for insurers.

Balance Sheet

An insurer's U.S. GAAP balance sheet retains the same format as the balance sheet of any other organization. The assets of the insurer equal the liabilities plus the shareholders' equity and the balance sheet balances. However, insurers do have different categories of assets and liabilities that appear on the balance sheet.

Assets

An insurer's investment strategy and performance are vital to its success and are stringently reviewed by rating agencies and regulators. Therefore, financial investments dominate an insurer's asset side of the balance sheet. An insurer's financial investments are usually broken down into four categories:

- Short-term investments
- Fixed maturity investments
- Equity securities
- Other invested assets

Short-term investments are investments that will mature in one year or less (similar to current assets). Fixed maturity investments are investments in debt instruments that have a maturity date greater than one year in the future. Examples of fixed maturity investments are U.S. Treasury bonds or long-term bonds issued by other large organizations such as Coca-Cola, Wal-Mart, or General Electric. Because of regulatory restrictions on investments, investments in fixed maturities are usually an insurer's dominant investment and are carried at either amortized cost or fair value. Equity securities are usually common or preferred stock investments in publicly traded organizations, represent an ownership interest in that organization, and are carried at fair value. The other invested assets category is a "catch-all" category representing all other invested assets that do not fall into one of the other three categories.

In addition to the categories of investments, insurers also have these three unique types of assets:

- Premium receivables
- Reinsurance recoverables
- Deferred policy acquisition costs

Premium receivables represent the premiums that have been promised by policyholders in exchange for insurance coverage but have yet to be received by the insurer. The premium receivables category is similar to the accounts receivable category that appears on a noninsurance balance sheet. Reinsurance recoverables represent loss payments that are due to an insurer from a reinsurer for losses that have occurred that were covered by reinsurance contracts. When a policyholder incurs a loss, the insurer may pay the claim and then be reimbursed by a reinsurer (if the loss is covered by the reinsurance contract). The amount that is owed by the reinsurer is an asset for the insurer. Again, reinsurance recoverables are analogous to accounts receivable on a noninsurance balance sheet. Deferred policy acquisition costs represent prepaid expenses relating to premium revenue that has not yet been earned. They are categorized as an asset because they have been incurred during the current period but will not be recognized as an expense until the associated premium revenue is earned during a subsequent period.

Liabilities

On the liability side of the balance sheet, an insurer has two unique categories of reserves:

* Unpaid losses and loss adjustment expenses
* Unearned premium

Reserves are accounts that insurers set up to represent payments that they are likely to have to make in the future. The unpaid losses and loss adjustment expenses entry on the balance sheet represents an estimate of liabilities that an insurer is responsible for from a variety of sources, including these:

* Losses and loss adjustment expenses that have been incurred but have not yet been paid
* Incurred but not reported losses and loss adjustment expenses
* Losses and loss adjustment expenses from claims that may be reopened

Property-casualty insurers are not allowed to set aside reserves for losses that do not occur during the policy period being covered. For example, insurers cannot reserve for hurricane or other catastrophic losses during the current policy period for an event that will likely occur in a policy period in the near future but that has not yet happened.

The insurer's other principal liability is the unearned premium reserve. This liability represents the amount of premiums received from policyholders but not yet earned. Policyholders pay premiums before the period for which they are covered and sometimes pay the entire premium before the policy period begins. Although insurers receive cash for the premium at the start of the policy period, they earn premium proportionately as the policy period transpires. For example, on an annual policy, the insurer earns 1/365th of the annual premium as each day of the policy period passes. At the end of the policy period, all premiums received will be earned. However, in the meantime, insurers must recognize as a liability the unearned premium amounts they have received from policyholders.

Shareholders' Equity

If an insurer is organized as a stock company, there will be common and sometimes preferred stock shares outstanding. Common and preferred stock is carried on the balance sheet at par value, and, if the stock is originally issued for an amount above par value, the additional amount appears in the shareholders' equity section as additional paid-in capital. Retained earnings represent accumulated net income retained in the business. Accumulated Other Comprehensive Income (Loss) represents other comprehensive income (explained in the next section) reported on an accumulated basis. See the exhibit "Cooper Insurance, Inc., GAAP Balance Sheet."

Income Statement

An insurer's GAAP income statement retains the same format and general categories as the income statement for any other organization. All of the relevant revenues and expenses incurred by the insurer during the time period covered by the income statement must be included. Insurers have different categories of revenues and expenses from noninsurer organizations.

Revenues

The primary revenues generated by property-casualty insurers are premiums earned and income from investments. Investments generate two types of income for insurers that appear on the income statement: investment income and net realized investment gains or losses. Premiums earned are the premium income generated by coverage provided by the insurer on the policies in force during the time period covered by the income statement. Investment income consists of the coupon payments on fixed income securities, the dividend payments on equity holdings, and any income generated by real estate holdings less the insurer's investment expenses. Any investment gains or losses realized on the sale of investments[1] are included in the net realized investment gains (losses) category of revenues. Unrealized gains on investments are recognized in the statement of comprehensive income. While insurers have other income, usually listed on the income statement as other income, it is not usually a major revenue source for insurers.

Expenses

The primary expenses of property-casualty insurers included in the income statement are losses and loss adjustment expenses. In addition to these claims expenses, insurers incur expenses acquiring and underwriting policies (policy acquisition costs and other underwriting expenses), paying interest expenses on any debt they have outstanding (interest expense), and paying administrative and other expenses. The expense categories that are related to

Cooper Insurance, Inc., GAAP Balance Sheet

Cooper Insurance, Inc.
Balance Sheet (000s omitted)
12/31/20X1

Assets		Liabilities	
Investments		Unpaid Losses and Loss Adjustment Expenses	$27,000
Short-Term Investments	$1,500	Unearned Premiums	6,000
Fixed Maturity Investments	35,000		
Equity Securities	10,000	Long-Term Debt	12,000
Other Invested Assets	2,000		
Total Investments	$48,500	Dividends Payable to Shareholders	0
		Other Liabilities	5,000
		Total Liabilities	$50,000
Cash	$2,500		
Accrued Investment Income	750	Common Stock	$384
Insurance Premium Receivables	1,000	Additional Paid-In Capital	616
Reinsurance Recoverables	1,750	Retained Earnings	22,750
Deferred Policy Acquisition Costs	1,250	Accumulated Other Comprehensive Income	1,420
		Total Shareholders' Equity (Owners' Equity)	$25,170
Intangible Assets and Goodwill	17,740		
Other Investments	1,680		
Total Assets	$75,170	Total Liabilities and Shareholders' Equity	$75,170

Cooper Insurance, Inc., has more than half of its total assets in financial investments. It also has more than half of its total liabilities in its loss and loss adjustment expense reserve and unearned premium reserve.

[DA06141]

the policies (loss and loss adjustment expenses, policy acquisition costs, and other underwriting expenses) are matched to the policies as the premiums are earned. See the exhibit "Cooper Insurance, Inc., GAAP Income Statement."

Net Income

The net income calculation for a property-casualty insurer is identical to that used by noninsurers. The total revenues minus the total expenses calculation yields the income before taxes. Once income tax expense is taken into account, the resulting balance is the net income. As is true for noninsurers, certain categories of income do not appear on the income statement. Those categories appear on the statement of comprehensive income.

Cooper Insurance, Inc., GAAP Income Statement

Cooper Insurance, Inc.
GAAP Income Statement (000s omitted)
For the Year Ended December 31, 20X1

Revenues	
Premiums Earned	$28,000
Investment Income	4,800
Other Revenues	2,100
Realized Investment Gains (Losses)	4,500
Total Revenues	**$39,400**
Expenses	
Loss and Loss Adjustment Expenses	$18,000
Policy Acquisition Costs	7,500
Administrative Expenses	3,500
Interest Expense	1,200
Other Expenses	1,500
Total Expenses	**$31,700**
Income Before Taxes	**$7,700**
Income Taxes	2,695
Net Income	**$5,005**

The majority of income for Cooper Insurance, Inc., is generated by premiums earned. The second most important income source is its investments. Loss and loss adjustment expenses are its largest expenses, and policy acquisition costs are the second largest.

[DA06140]

Statement of Comprehensive Income

Similar to noninsurance organizations, property-casualty insurers have the option of reporting comprehensive income on the income statement or on a separate statement of comprehensive income. The components of the statement of comprehensive income for insurers are the same as those for other organizations; the statement reports net income from the income statement, the unrealized appreciation or depreciation of investments, gains or losses in foreign currency translations, or changes in minimum pension liabilities. See the exhibit "Importance of Comprehensive Income to Insurers."

The statement of comprehensive income for insurers may contain significant amounts of income not reported on the balance sheet because of the importance of investments. Because insurers have a significant percentage of their

Importance of Comprehensive Income to Insurers

Unrealized net capital gains or losses on investments may be substantial for insurers. For example, on its 20X1 Statement of Comprehensive Income, XYZ Insurance Co. reported net income of $945 million from its income statement. It also had more than $5.2 billion in unrealized net capital gains, resulting in a comprehensive income of over $6 billion, more than six times its net income.

[DA06139]

assets in investments, the unrealized appreciation or depreciation of those investments may be substantial. See the exhibit "Cooper Insurance, Inc., Statement of Comprehensive Income."

Cooper Insurance, Inc., Statement of Comprehensive Income

Cooper Insurance, Inc.
Statement of Comprehensive Income (000s omitted)
For the Year Ended December 31, 20X1

Net Income (after tax)	$5,005
Other Comprehensive Income (net of taxes)	
Change in unrealized appreciation (depreciation) of investments	$4,426
Foreign currency translation gains (losses)	(585)
Changes in minimum pension liability	(950)
Comprehensive Income (loss)	$7,896

During the reporting period, Cooper Insurance, Inc., had a change in unrealized investment appreciation that almost equaled its net income.

[DA06142]

Statement of Shareholders' Equity

The statement of shareholders' equity is the financial statement that explains any changes that have occurred in the insurer's capital accounts over the fiscal period being examined. Any activity affecting the value of shareholders' equity, such as the issuance of common stock, is shown and used to reconcile the changes in shareholders' equity between the beginning and the end of the period. Comprehensive income (loss) also appears in the statement and is used to reconcile the difference between beginning and ending accumulated comprehensive income.

Statement of Cash Flows

Insurers, like other organizations, generate cash flows from three main sources: operating activities, investing activities, and financing activities. The operating activities include all cash flows associated with the marketing, underwriting, and servicing of insurance policies, and related services (insurer operations). On the statement of cash flows, the net income, changes in reserves, changes in accounts receivable (premiums receivable, reinsurance recoverables), depreciation, and other activities all appear under the cash flows from operating activities section.

Activities related to investments appear in the cash flow from investing activities. These activities include the proceeds from sales or maturities of fixed maturity investments or equities. They also include the purchase of securities, fixed maturities, other investments, and property and equipment. The cash flows from investing activities also include an "other" category just like the operating activities and financing activities sections.

If an insurer has issued debt or equity securities of its own, the cash flows from that activity appear in the cash flows from financing activities. The activities can include new issues or repayment of long-term debt, or new issues or buy-backs of stock. At the end of the statement of cash flows, the net cash position over the time period is summarized.

STATUTORY ACCOUNTING PRINCIPLES (SAP) COMPARED WITH GAAP

Insurers are required to prepare financial statements using statutory accounting principles (SAP) but may also be required to prepare a second set of financial statements using generally accepted accounting principles (GAAP). These different accounting approaches often produce significant differences in the reported value of assets, liabilities, equity, and earnings.

SAP and GAAP are similar in many ways. They differ in terms of how they value many assets and liabilities and recognize many revenues and expenses. Major areas in which they differ include these:

- Nonadmitted and admitted assets
- Bond investments
- Premium balances due from agents
- Reinsurance recoverables
- Provision for reinsurance
- Policy acquisition costs
- Reporting of subsidiaries and affiliates
- Pension accounting

- Statement of comprehensive income
- Specific life insurance and annuity accounts

These valuation disparities arise from a fundamental difference in the objectives of GAAP and SAP. GAAP treat a business as a going concern and focus on measuring earnings from period to period. SAP are primarily focused on solvency and the ability of the insurer to meet its obligations to policyholders.

Nonadmitted and Admitted Assets

SAP impose a strict valuation rule that excludes certain assets that cannot be readily converted to cash (that is, those assets that are not liquid). These are referred to as **nonadmitted assets**.

By contrast, GAAP count all assets, regardless of their liquidity. These are examples of nonadmitted assets:

- Furniture
- Fixtures
- Equipment
- Supplies
- Automobiles
- Uncollected premiums over ninety days due
- Prepaid expenses
- Loans or advances to certain company personnel

Because assets on a SAP balance sheet are reduced by the value of the nonadmitted assets, surplus is reduced by an amount equal to the value of the nonadmitted assets. An enhanced accounting equation represents the exclusion of nonadmitted assets from a balance sheet:

Total assets - Nonadmitted assets = Liabilities + Policyholders' surplus

Rearranging the equation and placing policyholders' surplus on the left side results in:

Policyholders' surplus = [Total assets - Nonadmitted assets] - Liabilities

Excluding nonadmitted assets from both total assets[2] and surplus, as presented in this equation, exemplifies the SAP liquidation-valuation criterion because these assets are not liquid assets. This approach is a conservative method of evaluating an insurer's policyholders' surplus and helps to assess insurer solvency.

Insurers report a variety of **admitted assets** on their statutory balance sheets, including investments and other types of assets. Invested assets constitute the bulk of assets and include items such as cash, stocks, bonds, and real estate investments. Other assets include items such as premiums receivable.

Nonadmitted assets

Types of property, such as office furniture and equipment, that regulators do not allow insurers to show as assets on financial statements because these assets cannot readily be converted to cash at or near their market value.

Admitted assets

Assets meeting minimum standards of liquidity that an insurer is allowed to report on its balance sheet in accordance with statutory accounting principles.

Bond Investments

A key difference between SAP and GAAP involves bond valuation. Bond prices rise and fall with changes in market interest rates for comparable bonds. A bond is usually purchased at a premium or discount from the face amount that will be paid to the investor at the bond's maturity. See the exhibit "Effect of Nonadmitted Assets on Policyholders' Surplus Under SAP and GAAP."

Effect of Nonadmitted Assets on Policyholders' Surplus Under SAP and GAAP

An insurer that purchases $100,000 of office furniture, a nonadmitted asset, would see its policyholders' surplus reduced by that same amount under SAP. By contrast, its GAAP balance sheet would simply show a shift in assets from one category to another and no change in total assets or policyholders' surplus. To simplify the analysis, assume the insurer starts with no nonadmitted assets.

	SAP Balance Sheet		GAAP Balance Sheet	
	Before Purchase	After Purchase	Before Purchase	After Purchase
Cash	$1,000,000	$900,000	$1,000,000	$900,000
Office Furniture	0	100,000	0	100,000
Other Assets	14,000,000	14,000,000	14,000,000	14,000,000
Total Assets	15,000,000	15,000,000	15,000,000	15,000,000
Nonadmitted Assets	0	100,000	n/a	n/a
Net Admitted Assets	15,000,000	14,900,000	n/a	n/a
Total Liabilities	10,000,000	10,000,000	10,000,000	10,000,000
Policyholders' Surplus/ Shareholders' Equity	$5,000,000	$4,900,000	$5,000,000	$5,000,000

[DA06257]

Under SAP, most bonds are valued at an adjusted cost amount called amortized cost, which evenly amortizes any premium or discount over the remaining life of a bond. Under GAAP, amortized cost valuation is permitted only if the insurer is able and intends to hold the bond to maturity; otherwise, bonds are classified as "available for sale" or "trading" and reported at market value.

Amortized-cost valuation benefits the insurer because it shields the value of its invested bond assets, and therefore its policyholders' surplus, from short-term fluctuations in market bond prices. Allowing bond investments to be valued at amortized cost is based on a going-concern perspective. This is a notable exception to most SAP asset-valuation practices, which are based on a liquidation perspective. See the exhibit "Effect of Bond Valuation on Policyholders' Surplus."

Effect of Bond Valuation on Policyholders' Surplus

The use of amortized cost in valuing bonds helps to prevent large fluctuations in surplus from year to year. To illustrate the difference between using amortized cost and market value, assume that in 20X1, an insurer paid $1,020,000 for U.S. government bonds, a $20,000 premium over their par value of $1,000,000. The following year, market interest rates rose significantly, causing the market value of the bonds to fall to $900,000. The amortized cost of the bonds fell to only $1,010,000.

Valuing the bonds at amortized cost rather than market value stabilizes the insurer's reported policyholders' surplus. Upon maturity, the market value of the bonds will equal their amortized cost, eliminating any temporary differences in their valuations.

Market Valuation

	20X1	20X2
Bonds at Market Value	$1,020,000	$ 900,000
All Other Assets	625,000	625,000
Total Assets	1,645,000	1,525,000
Liabilities	1,175,000	1,175,000
Policyholders' Surplus	$470,000	$ 350,000

Amortized Cost Valuation

	20X1	20X2
Bonds at Amortized Cost	$1,020,000	$1,010,000
All Other Assets	625,000	625,000
Total Assets	1,645,000	1,635,000
Liabilities	1,175,000	1,175,000
Policyholders' Surplus	$ 470,000	$ 460,000

[DA06258]

Premium Balances Due From Agents

Under SAP, premium balances more than ninety days past due are nonadmitted. GAAP require that premium balances due from agents be offset with a reserve for amounts that are deemed uncollectible.

Reinsurance Recoverables

Under SAP, reinsurance recoverables for unpaid losses and loss adjustment expenses are netted (subtracted) from loss and loss-adjustment expense reserves, so there is no need to show these recoverables as an asset. Under GAAP, these same reinsurance recoverables are shown as an asset and are not netted (subtracted) from loss and loss-adjustment expense reserves.

Provision for Reinsurance

Unauthorized reinsurer

A reinsurer that is not licensed or otherwise authorized to do business in the primary insurer's state of domicile.

SAP require creation of a liability for a portion of overdue reinsurance recoverables and reinsurance recoverables from **unauthorized reinsurers**, unless the recoverables are collateralized. This is called the provision for reinsurance and supports SAP's liquidation perspective. GAAP do not have this same requirement. However, under GAAP, reinsurance recoverables deemed uncollectible must be subtracted from the reinsurance recoverables asset.

Policy Acquisition Costs

Under SAP, insurers are required to recognize the full amount of policy acquisition costs, including underwriting expenses, commissions, and taxes, at policy inception, even though the matching principle would require those expenses to be spread evenly over the term of the policy as the associated premium revenue is earned. Immediately recognizing policy acquisition costs while deferring recognition of the associated revenue causes surplus to decrease. This is often referred to as "a drain on policyholders' surplus." GAAP allow policy acquisition costs to be capitalized (thereby creating an asset called "deferred policy acquisition costs") and amortized over the policy's life, correctly matching premium revenues with expenses.

SAP's treatment of policy acquisition costs is consistent with its liquidity perspective; GAAP's treatment is consistent with the going-concern perspective. Deferring the recognition of revenue but not the associated expenses is consistent with SAP's conservative approach to valuation. See the exhibit "Policy Acquisition Costs Under SAP and GAAP."

Reporting of Subsidiaries and Affiliates

Under SAP, investments in subsidiaries, controlled, or affiliated entities (SCAs) are considered admitted assets and must be shown on the parent company's balance sheet. Under GAAP, the financial statements of majority-owned subsidiaries are consolidated into the parent company's financial statements.

Statutory accounting has various rules for valuing SCAs, depending on their characteristics. For example, if a subsidiary's stock is publicly traded, its market value can be used. However, most subsidiaries are not publicly traded. In these cases, parent companies are required to account for their equity in

Policy Acquisition Costs Under SAP and GAAP

An insurer incorporates on 6/30/X1 with $1 million in cash, no liabilities, and total policyholders' surplus of $1 million. The next day, the insurer writes a policy for $210,000 in premium, which is immediately paid in full. Underwriting expenses, including the agent's commission and premium taxes, are 15 percent of premium, or $31,500, and are immediately paid out. Expected losses are 82 percent of premium, or $172,200. Assuming that the loss experience turns out as expected, the insurer will realize a profit on this policy of $6,300 (3 percent of premium) by the end of the policy period. Assets go up immediately by $178,500 (the $210,000 premium received less the $31,500 expenses paid).

Under SAP, policyholders' surplus immediately declines by the amount of the policy acquisition expenses. Halfway through the policy period, the insurer's policyholders' surplus has recovered somewhat, and by the end of the policy period, policyholders' surplus has increased by the amount of the underwriting profit, which is $6,300.

Under GAAP, an asset called "deferred policy acquisition costs" is set up at the beginning of the policy period. These deferred costs are recognized as policy acquisition expenses on the income statement throughout the year. Note that shareholders' equity does not decline at the beginning of the year and increases evenly throughout the year. At the end of the year, policyholders' surplus under SAP equals shareholders' equity under GAAP, with both including the underwriting profit of $6,300.

the SCA by using either SAP or GAAP accounting, depending on the characteristics of the SCA.

Pension Accounting

Under SAP, contributions made for nonvested employees under both defined-benefit plans and defined-contribution plans are not recognized when made and are therefore not a deductible expense on the income statement. Such contributions qualify as a prepaid expense, but, under SAP, a prepaid expense is a nonadmitted asset because it is not readily convertible to cash. GAAP recognize pension contributions as expenses as they are incurred for all employees, whether vested or nonvested.

Statement of Comprehensive Income

GAAP require a statement of comprehensive income, which shows unrealized appreciation (depreciation) of investments, foreign currency translation gains (losses), and changes in minimum pension liability, none of which are included in the GAAP income statement. The statement of comprehensive income adds these amounts to net income to determine comprehensive income.

SAP do not require a statement of comprehensive income. However, the capital and surplus account in the annual statement shows similar types of items that are not included in net income and are entered directly as an adjustment to policyholders' surplus. Included are the changes in net unrealized capital gains (losses), net unrealized foreign exchange capital gain (loss), the provision for reinsurance, and nonadmitted assets.

SAP Treatment

	6/30/20X1	7/1/20X1	12/31/20X1	6/30/20X2
Premium Written	$ 0	$ 210,000	$ 0	$0
Premium Earned	0	0	105,000	210,000
Losses (82%)	0	0	86,100	172,200
Policy Acquisition Expenses (15%)	0	31,500	31,500	31,500
Revenue	0	0	105,000	210,000
Expenses	0	(31,500)	(117,600)	(203,700)
Net Income (Loss)	$ 0	($ 31,500)	($ 12,600)	$ 6,300
Assets:				
Cash	1,000,000	1,178,500	1,092,400	1,006,300
Liabilities:				
Unearned Premiums	0	210,000	105,000	0
Contributed Capital	1,000,000	1,000,000	1,000,000	1,000,000
Unassigned Surplus	0	(31,500)	(12,600)	6,300
Policyholders' Surplus	$1,000,000	$ 968,500	$ 987,400	$1,006,300

GAAP Treatment

	6/30/20X1	7/1/20X1	12/31/20X1	6/30/20X2
Premium Written	$ 0	$ 210,000	$ 0	$ 0
Premium Earned	0	0	105,000	210,000
Losses (82%)	0	0	86,100	172,200
Policy Acquisition Expenses (15%)	0	0	15,750	31,500
Revenue	0	0	105,000	210,000
Expenses	0	0	101,850	203,700
Net Income (Loss)	$ 0	$ 0	$ 3,150	$ 6,300
Assets:				
Cash	1,000,000	1,178,500	1,092,400	1,006,300
Deferred Policy Acquisition Costs	0	31,500	15,750	0
Liabilities:				
Unearned Premiums	0	210,000	105,000	0
Contributed Capital	1,000,000	1,000,000	1,000,000	1,000,000
Retained Earnings	0	0	3,150	6,300
Shareholders' Equity	$1,000,000	$1,000,000	$ 1,003,150	$1,006,300

Life Insurance and Annuities

Despite some similarities between GAAP and SAP, there are several key differences that uniquely apply to life insurance and annuities.

SAP methods for accounting for traditional life insurance and annuity contract reserve liabilities are similar to GAAP. Both GAAP and SAP state that benefit reserves for traditional contracts should be determined as the excess of the present value of future benefits less the present value of future net premiums. However, the actuarial methodology is more conservative for SAP than GAAP.

SAP policy reserves are determined using prescribed methods, such as the commissioners' reserve valuation method (CRVM), commissioners' annuity reserve valuation method (CARVM), or net level premium method, which are based on prescribed statutory morbidity, mortality, and interest rate assumptions. GAAP reserves are determined using the net level premium or estimated gross margin method with estimates of future morbidity, mortality, interest, and **persistency** based on the company's experience.

Another key difference is that SAP use a method similar to the method for traditional contracts to calculate the policy reserve liabilities for universal-life-type contracts, unlike the method provided in GAAP by FAS 97. Under SAP, payments received for nontraditional (universal-life-type) contracts are reported as premium revenue, and changes in policy reserves are reported as expenses. In contrast, GAAP treat these payments as deposits to policyholder account balances.

Additionally, two reserves are required under SAP that are not required under GAAP. The first is the **asset valuation reserve (AVR)**, a contingency reserve against potential fluctuations in the statement value of common stocks and real estate investments or credit-related declines in the value of bonds, mortgage loans, and certain derivatives. Positive or negative change in the AVR for any reporting period is applied directly to surplus. The AVR is not recorded under GAAP.

The second reserve required under SAP is the **interest maintenance reserve (IMR)**. IMR spreads over time the recognition of interest-rate-related **realized capital gains** (losses) on fixed income investments, net of taxes; these gains are amortized into net income over the estimated remaining periods until the maturity of the investments that were sold. These fixed income investments consist mainly of bonds and mortgage loans. Under GAAP, these realized gains (losses) are reported as revenue.

Persistency

A measurement of retained policies or accounts over a long period of time.

Asset valuation reserve (AVR)

A reserve account required by the National Association of Insurance Commissioners (NAIC) for the purpose of offsetting credit-related investment gains and losses.

Interest maintenance reserve (IMR)

A reserve account required by the National Association of Insurance Commissioners (NAIC) for the purpose of offsetting realized capital gains and losses resulting from interest rate fluctuations.

Realized capital gain

The profit earned by an insurer when an asset, such as a bond or stock, is sold for more than its cost.

COMPONENTS OF THE NAIC ANNUAL STATEMENT

Regulators, financial analysts, customers, and competitors use the information reported in an insurer's National Association of Insurance Commissioners (NAIC) Annual Statement to gauge the insurer's financial strength.

NAIC Annual Statement

The primary financial statement prepared by insurers and required by every state insurance department.

Insurers must file an **NAIC Annual Statement** with the insurance department of the state in which they are domiciled and, directly or through the NAIC, in every state in which they do business. Similar to financial statements prepared using generally accepted accounting principles (GAAP), the Annual Statement contains a balance sheet, an income statement, a statement of changes in capital and surplus (shareholders' equity under GAAP), and a statement of cash flows. However, the Annual Statement provides much more supporting detail than a GAAP financial statement.

General Organization of the Annual Statement

In an Annual Statement, detail to support the primary financial statements is provided through supplementary exhibits, schedules, notes, and interrogatories. See the exhibit "Key Components of the Annual Statement."

Assets and Liabilities (Balance Sheet)

The balance sheet portion of the Annual Statement is a summary of the insurer's financial position on December 31 of the calendar year. Assets are what the insurer owns, liabilities are what the insurer owes, and policyholders' surplus is the difference between the two.

Note that the Annual Statement refers to policyholders' surplus (often called "surplus") rather than the GAAP-preferred term "shareholders' equity." This reflects the focus of statutory accounting, which reports on the insurer's ability to meet its obligations to policyholders.

The asset side of the balance sheet shows both the admitted assets and non-admitted assets for each major asset class. Asset classes are organized into two broad categories: invested assets and noninvested assets.

Invested assets are income-producing assets such as bonds, stocks, real estate, and mortgages. In addition to the summary value reported on the balance sheet, the supporting schedules report details on individual stocks, bonds, real estate, and mortgages.

Noninvested assets are those that support the generation of income but do not directly earn income. The two largest categories of noninvested assets are receivables for reinsurance and receivables for premiums.

Reinsurance contracts typically require the primary insurer to pay for a loss before being reimbursed by the reinsurer. The lag between when the reinsurer

Key Components of the Annual Statement

The Annual Statement blank contains more than 200 pages of financial statements and supporting exhibits and schedules. Many of the schedules and exhibits themselves have subschedules and supplemental addenda.

> Balance Sheet
> > Assets
> >
> > Liabilities, Surplus and Other Funds
>
> Statement of Income
>
> Cash Flow
>
> Details on Underwriting and Investment Results:
> > Underwriting and Investment Exhibits
> >
> > Exhibit of Premiums and Losses
> >
> > Insurance Expense Exhibits
>
> Details on Investment Holdings:
> > Schedule A—Real Estate
> >
> > Schedule B—Mortgage Loans
> >
> > Schedule BA—Other Long-Term Invested Assets
> >
> > Schedule D—Bonds and Stocks
> >
> > Schedule DA—Short-Term Investments
> >
> > Schedule DB—Derivative Investments
> >
> > Schedule E—Cash and Cash Equivalents
> >
> > Schedule F—Reinsurance
> >
> > Schedule P—Losses and Loss Expenses
>
> Notes to Financial Statements
>
> General Interrogatories
>
> Five-Year Historical Data

[DA06249]

is asked for payment and when the reinsurer actually pays generates a receivable that falls into a category called reinsurance recoverables. Although some credit risk is associated with these receivables, they are generally carried at face value.

Premium receivables include amounts due but not yet received from agents, deferred premiums, and accrued retrospective premiums.

The Liabilities, Surplus and Other Funds page is the second page of the balance sheet. Liabilities are the amounts the insurer owes to others, and policyholders' surplus is the difference between the assets and the liabilities.

Loss reserve

An estimate of the amount of money the insurer expects to pay in the future for losses that have already occurred and been reported, but are not yet settled.

Loss adjustment expense reserves

Estimates of the future expense that an insurer expects to incur to investigate, defend, and settle claims for losses that have already occurred.

The principal liabilities are **loss reserves**, **loss adjustment expense reserves**, and the unearned premium reserve. Reinsurance recoverables for unpaid losses and loss adjustment expenses are netted from the loss reserves and loss adjustment expense reserves. Unsecured recoverables and penalties for over-due recoverables from reinsurers are included under a liability account called "provision for reinsurance."

Surplus can be classified into three major parts: contributed surplus, unassigned surplus, and treasury stock. Contributed surplus is money that has been invested in the firm by outside parties. See the exhibit "Principal Elements of an Insurer Annual Statement (SAP) Balance Sheet."

Statement of Income

The Statement of Income (income statement) measures the insurer's earnings over the course of the year and serves as the basis for determining the insurer's federal income tax liability. The summary values reported in the income statement are supported by numerous pages of detail on the source of the premiums, expenses, and investment income for the year. The income statement breaks down earnings into three main categories:

- Underwriting income
- Investment income
- Other income

Underwriting income is measured as the difference between premiums earned and losses and expenses incurred during the period. If the number is positive, it is a net underwriting gain; otherwise, it is a net underwriting loss.

Changes in premium and loss reserves from prior years affect the current-year results. Earned premium is reported on a calendar-year basis and calculated as the sum of this year's written premiums plus the unearned premium reserve at the beginning of the year, less the unearned premium reserve at the end of the year. Losses and loss adjustment expenses are also reported on a calendar-year basis as the sum of losses and loss adjustment expenses paid during the year, plus ending reserves, minus beginning reserves.

Investment income has two components: net investment income and net realized capital gains. Net investment income is the interest, dividends, and real estate income earned on invested assets during the year, minus expenses incurred in conducting investment operations. Net realized capital gains are the gains or losses realized from selling invested assets during the year. The value of an invested asset held by the insurer through the year may rise or fall during the year, but until an investment is actually sold, these changes in value do not flow through the income statement.

Other income consists of revenues and expenses that are not related to either underwriting or investment activities. Examples include charge-offs of outstanding receivables from agents, dividends to policyholders, and finance and

Principal Elements of an Insurer Annual Statement (SAP) Balance Sheet

Assets	Current Year		
	Assets	Nonadmitted Assets	Net Admitted Assets
Bonds (Schedule D)	33,525,000		33,525,000
Preferred stocks (Schedule D)	265,000		265,000
Common stocks (Schedule D)	3,750,000	50,000	3,700,000
Real estate (Schedule A)	1,900,000		1,900,000
Cash (Schedule E)	5,250,000		5,250,000
Other invested assets (Schedule BA)	310,000	190,000	120,000
Subtotal cash and invested assets	45,000,000		44,760,000
Uncollected premium	4,200,000	150,000	4,050,000
Amounts recoverable from reinsurers	1,750,000	25,000	1,725,000
Furniture and equipment	415,000	415,000	0
Other assets	2,050,000		2,050,000
Totals	53,415,000	830,000	52,585,000

Liabilities, Surplus, and Other Funds	Current Year
Losses	22,165,000
Loss adjustment expenses	2,250,000
Reinsurance payable (Schedule F)	2,510,000
Commissions payable	1,800,000
Unearned premiums	8,400,000
Provision for reinsurance (Schedule F)	1,200,000
Total liabilities	38,325,000
Common capital stock	2,000,000
Gross paid in and contributed surplus	5,250,000
Treasury stock	(1,500,000)
Unassigned funds (surplus)	8,510,000
Surplus as regards policyholders	14,260,000
Totals	52,585,000

Note: The above illustration does not include all the information contained in the NAIC Annual Statement blank.

Adapted from the NAIC Annual Statement blank. [DA06251]

service charges not included in premiums. See the exhibit "Principal Elements of an Insurer Annual Statement (SAP) Income Statement."

Principal Elements of an Insurer Annual Statement (SAP) Income Statement

Statement of Income	Current Year
Underwriting Income	
Premiums earned	10,000,000
− Losses incurred	5,960,000
− Loss adjustment expenses incurred	1,210,000
− Other underwriting expenses incurred	2,500,000
Net underwriting gain (loss)	330,000
Investment Income	
+ Net investment income earned	900,000
+ Net realized capital gains (losses)	(59,000)
Net investment gain (loss)	841,000
Other Income	
+ Other income (expense)	220,000
− Policyholder dividends	360,000
Net income before income taxes	1,031,000
− Federal and foreign income taxes	231,000
Net income	800,000

Note: The above illustration does not include all the information contained in the NAIC Annual Statement blank.

Adapted from the NAIC Annual Statement blank. [DA06252]

Capital and Surplus Account

The Capital and Surplus Account exhibit, which is included in the Statement of Income, provides details of changes in the policyholders' surplus during the year. Net income directly affects the level of policyholders' surplus. Other surplus changes flow from changes in balance sheet accounts. The principal balance sheet-related elements leading to changes in policyholders' surplus are changes in nonadmitted assets, net unrealized capital gains, net unrealized foreign exchange capital gains, net deferred income taxes, changes in the provision for reinsurance, and contributions to and withdrawals from contributed capital accounts.

Increases in nonadmitted assets are a direct charge to surplus. For example, if a premium receivable became overdue, net admitted assets would decline by the amount of the receivable, but liabilities would remain the same. Because policyholders' surplus is the balancing figure, it would decline by the nonadmitted amount.

Unrealized capital gains or losses on invested assets occur when an asset increases or decreases in value during the year, but the asset is not sold during the year. Those changes in value are not reported in the income statement until the asset is sold. However, the statutory principle of valuing an insurer at liquidation value requires an adjustment to policyholders' surplus to reflect the change.

Similarly, unrealized foreign exchange capital gains or losses are charged against surplus. A United States insurer might purchase a British subsidiary and pay for it in British pounds or may have established reserves on losses payable in euros rather than in dollars. Those assets and liabilities are converted to dollar equivalents when they are first entered on the balance sheet; however, subsequent changes in foreign exchange rates can alter the current dollar value.

Timing differences between when income tax obligations are recorded on an insurer's books and when the tax is paid create deferred tax assets and liabilities. Deferred tax assets arise when tax payments will be lower in the future, and deferred tax liabilities occur when tax payments will be higher in the future. Net deferred income tax is the difference between deferred tax assets and deferred tax liabilities, and changes in the relative balance are charged to surplus.

Contributed capital is equity capital from outside sources. A mutual insurer could issue a **surplus note** to raise additional capital, or a stock insurer could issue additional shares of stock to new investors. An insurer could also repurchase some of its outstanding shares from existing investors, reducing its policyholders' surplus. Dividend payments to shareholders also reduce policyholders' surplus. See the exhibit "Principal Elements of an Insurer Capital and Surplus Account."

Surplus note

A type of unsecured debt instrument, issued only by insurers, that has characteristics of both conventional equity and debt securities and is classified as policyholders' surplus rather than as a liability on the insurer's statutory balance sheet.

Cash Flow

The purpose of the insurer's cash flow statement is to show the actual cash, as opposed to accounting earnings, that flows through the business in the course of the year. Cash, not earnings, is what pays policyholders' claims and underwriters' salaries. The cash flow statement also shows whether investments as well as financing and miscellaneous sources are generating positive or negative cash flows. It is divided into three sections:

• Cash from Operations
• Cash from Investments
• Cash from Financing and Miscellaneous Sources

Principal Elements of an Insurer Capital and Surplus Account

	Capital and Surplus Account	Current Year	Prior Year
	Policyholders Surplus, End of Prior Year	14,061,000	14,000,000
+	Net Income	800,000	91,000
+	Change in Net Unrealized Capital Gains (Losses)	(250,000)	25,000
+	Change in Net Unrealized Foreign Exchange Capital Gain (Loss)	(121,000)	(1,000)
+	Change in Net Deferred Income Tax	10,000	7,000
+	Change in Nonadmitted Assets	(200,000)	(15,000)
+	Change in Provision for Reinsurance	50,000	12,000
+	Dividends to Stockholders	(85,000)	(83,000)
+	Contributed Capital (Capital Withdrawals)	(5,000)	25,000
	Policyholders' Surplus, Current Year	14,260,000	14,061,000

Note: The above illustration does not include all the information contained in the NAIC Annual Statement blank.

Adapted from the NAIC Annual Statement blank. [DA06253]

The Cash Flow from Operations section shows the cash generated from the insurer's core business function: selling and servicing insurance policies and earning investment income from the funds held to service the insurer's obligations. Unlike the income statement, the values reported in the cash flow statement are actual dollar flows that occur during the period. Premiums received increase the amount of cash in the insurer's checking account, regardless of whether those premiums have been earned. Examples of cash outflows that reduce the insurer's cash account include loss payments, agents' commission payments, and dividends to policyholders.

The Cash from Investments section shows the cash inflows and outflows from the sale and purchase of investment assets. Sales of assets increase cash, while purchases of assets decrease cash. Separate lines are shown for bonds, stocks, mortgages, real estate, other invested assets, and cash and short-term investments. A miscellaneous category is used for all investment assets that do not fit into these six categories.

The Cash Flow from Financing and Miscellaneous Sources section includes changes in borrowed funds and contributed capital. Cash inflows include income from the issuance of surplus notes or capital notes and sale of new shares of stock. Cash outflows include payment of dividends to stockholders (but not dividends to policyholders), repayment of borrowed funds, and repurchase of shares of the insurer's own outstanding stock.

The subtotal values for the three sections should equal the change in the cash account for the firm over the course of the year. Negative values are common in each of the categories, but in the long run, an insurer must be able to consistently generate positive cash flow from its operations. See the exhibit "Principal Elements of an Insurer Annual Statement Cash Flow Statement."

Principal Elements of an Insurer Annual Statement Cash Flow Statement

	Cash Flow	Current Year	Prior Year
	Cash at Beginning of Year	3,421,000	2,513,000
+	Cash from Operations	758,000	(150,000)
+	Cash from Investments	900,000	1,258,000
+	Cash from Financing and Miscellaneous Sources	171,000	(200,000)
	Cash at End of Year	5,250,000	3,421,000

Note: The above illustration does not include all the information contained in the NAIC Annual Statement blank.

Adapted from the NAIC Annual Statement blank. [DA06254]

Other Exhibits and Schedules

Several different schedules are prepared to provide details on the assets and liabilities reported on the balance sheet and the income statement. These include Schedule D, which provides detail on an insurer's investment portfolio; Schedule F, which addresses reinsurance; and Schedule P, which covers loss development.

Schedule D is a series of schedules that describe an insurer's investments in bonds, preferred stocks, and common stocks. The schedules can be classified into two types: detail schedules and summary schedules.

Detail schedules provide specific information on each bond, preferred stock, and common stock bought, sold, or owned by an insurer during the past year. Schedule D, Part 1, lists all bonds owned and provides complete identification information, including the name of the issuer, the Committee on Uniform Security Identification Procedures (CUSIP) identifier, maturity date, coupon rate, and NAIC quality classification. Financial information includes the statement value, purchase price, premium or discount amortization, and amount of interest earned during the year. Because each individual bond issue is reported on a separate line, this schedule can be spread over more than 100 pages in a large insurer's Annual Statement. Similar information for each equity security owned by the insurer is provided in Schedule D, Part 2, Section 1 (preferred stocks) and Schedule D, Part 2, Section 2 (common stocks).

In addition to the detailed information on the individual stocks and bonds owned as of the statement date, three separate detail schedules are provided to list all stocks and bonds bought during the year (Schedule D, Part 3), sold during the year (Schedule D, Part 4), or bought and then sold during the year (Schedule D, Part 5). Thus, an analyst can follow the trail of any stock or bond that the insurer owned at any time during the course of the year.

Summary schedules are used to aggregate the stocks and bonds in a variety of categories so that an analyst can evaluate the overall investment strategy. The summary schedules collate the investment holdings into various categories, such as affiliated versus unaffiliated, foreign versus U.S., issuer type, and NAIC quality classification. Ultimately, single summary values for bonds, preferred stock, and common stock are each carried forward to the balance sheet.

Schedule F is a nine-part schedule that provides expanded information on an insurer's reinsurance arrangements, including reinsurance ceded to **authorized reinsurers**, unauthorized reinsurers, and **certified reinsurers** (an unauthorized reinsurer with which a primary insurer may claim credit for reinsurance, without the reinsurer posting full collateral, depending on an analysis of the reinsurer's financial strength). The schedule is also used to calculate the provision for reinsurance located on the liabilities side of the primary insurer's balance sheet. When an insurer posts a liability to the balance sheet without a corresponding increase in assets, its **policyholders' surplus** is reduced. Therefore, an insurer will want to minimize its provision for reinsurance.

These are the nine parts of Schedule F:

- Part 1—Assumed Reinsurance
- Part 2—Premium Portfolio Reinsurance
- Part 3—Ceded Reinsurance
- Part 4—Aging of Ceded Reinsurance
- Part 5—Provision for Unauthorized Reinsurance
- Part 6—Provision for Reinsurance Ceded to Certified Reinsurers (Section 1) and Provision for Overdue Reinsurance Ceded to Certified Reinsurers (Section 2)
- Part 7—Provision for Overdue Authorized Reinsurance
- Part 8—Provision for Overdue Reinsurance
- Part 9—Restatement of Balance Sheet to Identify Net Credit for Reinsurance

Parts 1 through 3 provide the supporting data for the insurer's assumed and ceded reinsurance accounting entries. Parts 3 through 7 provide data for the provision for reinsurance appearing in Part 8, which sums up the penalties calculated in Parts 5 through 7. Part 9 restates the statutory balance sheet from a net to a gross basis.

Part 6, which the NAIC added in 2012, reduces collateral requirements for unauthorized reinsurers that qualify as certified reinsurers. The amount of

Authorized reinsurer
A reinsurer that is authorized to do business in the primary insurer's state of domicile.

Certified reinsurer
An unauthorized reinsurer that meets certain qualifications and is approved by the state insurance regulator of the ceding company's state of domicile.

Policyholders' surplus
Under statutory accounting principles (SAP), an insurer's total admitted assets minus its total liabilities.

collateral required is based on the financial strength rating of the reinsurer. Part 6, Section 1 calculates the provision for reinsurance for certified reinsurers due to collateral deficiencies, which then becomes part of the overall provision for reinsurance that a primary insurer reports on the liabilities side of the balance sheet. Part 6, Section 2 establishes the provision for overdue reinsurance recoverables from certified reinsurers.

The purpose of Schedule P is to provide information to analyze loss reserve levels and incurred loss development. Losses are reported on a calendar-year basis in the income statement, but Schedule P reports them on an accident-year basis for each of the last ten years and includes interim valuations to show how losses for each accident year have developed over time. Hypothetically, incurred losses and loss reserves for any given year should be set at their ultimate value as of December 31 of that year and then never change. The reality is that incurred losses and reserves are estimates that may or may not be accurate.

Schedule P has seven major sections that provide up to ten accident years of data, and subschedules are prepared for each of twenty-two separate lines of insurance:

- Part 1—Current Estimate of Premiums and Losses
- Part 2—Incurred Loss Development
- Part 3—Paid Loss Development
- Part 4—IBNR Reserve Development
- Part 5—Claim Count Development
- Part 6—Earned Premium Development
- Part 7—Summary Information on Loss-Sensitive Insurance Products

SUMMARY

GAAP accounting standards were originally developed for commercial and industrial organizations but have been adapted for financial service organizations. While the general format of financial statements remains unchanged, the specific items included on the statements are substantially different for property-casualty insurers.

Insurers may be required to prepare two sets of financial statements, one based on SAP and the other based on GAAP. SAP are primarily focused on solvency and the ability of the insurer to meet its obligations to policyholders. GAAP treat a business as a going concern and focus on measuring earnings from period to period. Differences in these two accounting methods may lead to significant differences in the reported financial position of an insurer.

The NAIC Annual Statement is a lengthy and complex document that includes not only a balance sheet, an income statement, and a statement of cash flows, but also hundreds of pages of supporting documentation that explains in detail where the figures in the primary pages of the statement come from.

ASSIGNMENT NOTES

1.   There are exceptions whereby losses on investments deemed to be "impaired" are included in net realized gains (losses), even though the investments have not been sold.

2.   On a SAP balance sheet, total assets minus nonadmitted assets are called "net admitted assets."

3

Life Insurer Financial Statements

Educational Objectives

After learning the content of this assignment, you should be able to:

▷ Compare the contents of a life insurer's GAAP financial statements with a property-casualty insurer's GAAP financial statements.

▷ Describe the main components of the NAIC Annual Statement for life insurers.

▷ Explain the operation and valuation of separate accounts for life/annuity insurance companies.

Life Insurer Financial Statements

3

LIFE INSURER GAAP FINANCIAL STATEMENTS

United States life insurers that are publicly traded are required to report under U.S. generally accepted accounting principles (GAAP). Many life insurers that are not publicly traded, including mutual insurers, voluntarily complete GAAP financial statements. In addition, all U.S. licensed insurers must complete financial statements based on statutory accounting principles (SAP).

The format of life insurers' GAAP financial statements is the same as that for property-casualty insurers in many respects. However, because of the unique types of products life insurers offer, there are significant differences in the specific accounts life insurers use.

Life Insurer GAAP Balance Sheet

Compared with a property-casualty insurer's balance sheet, the asset and liability accounts on a life insurer's GAAP balance sheet reflect the investment component of many life insurance and annuity contracts as well as the long terms over which life insurance premiums and annuity considerations are received and benefits are paid. See the exhibit "Rockport Life Insurance, Inc., GAAP Balance Sheet."

The root of the differences lies in the essence of each type of insurance. Property-casualty insurance contracts are typically issued for a one-year term and provide coverage for various risks of loss that are uncertain in their timing and amount. By contrast, the vast majority of life insurance policies and annuity contracts are issued for longer periods of time, often decades, to provide coverage for mortality or longevity, both of which are somewhat predictable for a group of individuals with similar characteristics. However, at any time, future premium and consideration receipts and benefit payments under a life insurance policy or an annuity contract are uncertain because they are influenced by additional factors, including the general economy and policyholder behavior.

Because life insurance premiums and annuity considerations are usually paid over time and well before most benefits are paid out, the contracts accumulate a future benefit obligation to the contract holders. Additionally, some types of life insurance and annuities maintain an investment that directly benefits the insured, which is not the case with property-casualty insurance contracts.

Rockport Life Insurance, Inc., GAAP Balance Sheet

Rockport Life Insurance, Inc.
GAAP Balance Sheet (000s omitted)
12/31/20X1

Assets		Liabilities and Shareholders' Equity	
Fixed-maturity investments		Future policy benefits	$18,300
Available for sale, at fair value	$20,000	Policyholders' account balances	15,200
Trading securities, at fair value	5,000	Policy claims	350
Equity securities	1,200	Dividends payable to shareholders	400
Mortgage loans, net of allowances	11,000	Debt	2,300
Policy loans	9,000	Other liabilities	700
Other invested assets	7,000	Separate account liabilities	5,400
Total Investments	53,200	Total Liabilities	42,650
Cash and cash equivalents	2,000	Common stock	300
Accrued investment income	1,500	Additional paid-in capital	600
Premiums and fees receivable	200	Retained earnings	23,850
Reinsurance recoverables	1,800	Accumulated other comprehensive income	1,500
Deferred policy acquisition costs	3,300	Total Shareholders' Equity	26,250
Intangible assets and goodwill	1,100		
Other assets	400		
Separate account assets	5,400		
Total Assets	$68,900	Total Liabilities and Shareholders' Equity	$68,900

[DA11116]

Assets

Reflecting the investment purpose of many life insurance policies and annuities, there are two entries on the asset side of life insurer balance sheets that do not appear on property-casualty insurer balance sheets: policy loans and separate account assets. Separate accounts are addressed later in this discussion.

Policy loan

A loan by an insurer to a policyholder with the cash value of the policyholder's life insurance policy as collateral.

Life insurance policyholders with policies that accrue a cash value over time have a provision in their contracts, required by all states, that gives them the right to a **policy loan**. This loan accrues interest and is valued on the balance sheet at the unpaid principal balance. Upon policy termination, whether through lapse, surrender, or death, the unpaid principal balance is subtracted from the policy benefit.

Although mortgage loans may be an asset on property-casualty insurers' balance sheets, they are usually a larger asset for life insurers. Most of these loans are for commercial mortgages.[1]

Liabilities

The majority of the differences between life insurer and property-casualty insurer balance sheets are on the liability side of the balance sheet. Both life and property-casualty insurers have reserves for estimated claims. However, the type and valuation of those reserves are different for life insurers.

There are two major categories of policy reserves for a life insurer:

- Future policy benefits
- Policyholders' account balances

Future policy benefits are the reserves for traditional life insurance and annuity contracts, which include whole life, guaranteed renewable term life, and most fixed annuities. Traditional contracts are characterized by level premiums or considerations and guaranteed death benefits. The liability for future benefits is valued as the "excess of the present value of future promised benefits expected to be paid over the present value of the future net benefit premiums."[2] The net benefit premiums are the portion of premiums allocated for paying the promised benefits and exclude expense loadings.

A reserve is necessary because in the early years of a traditional life insurance policy or annuity contract, insureds pay a premium or consideration that covers more than the projected mortality costs for their age group. The excess is available to fund future benefit payments and, therefore, needs to be reserved for on the balance sheet.

Life insurer actuaries use several assumptions in calculating reserves for future policy benefits, including these:

- **Mortality rates**— percentage rate of death among a defined group of people for a defined period, such as one year
- Interest rate—rate of investment earnings (net of investment expenses) on invested assets
- Surrender rate—percentage rate of policies that are voluntarily surrendered in a specific time period, such as one year
- Lapse rate—percentage rate of policies that are terminated for failure to pay sufficient premium

Mortality, surrender, and lapse rates are based on company experience. Actuaries must also take into account expected policy dividends and maintenance expenses as well as build in provisions to their assumptions for adverse deviation.

The **lock-in concept** applies to the assumptions used to value future policy benefits. The Financial Accounting Standards Board's (FASB's) 1982

Mortality rates
Probabilities of death at specific ages.

Lock-in concept
A GAAP accounting concept in which certain assumptions are fixed over the policy term in valuing future policy benefits for traditional life insurance and annuity contracts.

Statement of Financial Accounting Standards No. 60 (now incorporated as part of the FASB's ASC Topic 944) provides guidance regarding GAAP reporting for traditional life insurance products and contains this statement addressing the lock-in concept:

The liability, which represents the present value of future benefits to be paid to or on behalf of policyholders and related expenses less the present value of future net premiums..., shall be estimated using methods that include assumptions, such as estimates of expected investment yields, mortality, morbidity, terminations, expenses, applicable at the time the insurance contracts are made. ... The assumptions shall include provision for the risk of adverse deviation. Original assumptions shall continue to be used in subsequent accounting periods to determine changes in the liability for future policy benefits (often referred to as the "lock-in concept") unless a premium deficiency exists.[3]

The second major category of policy reserves, policyholders' account balances, is for universal-life-type contracts, which are nontraditional contracts. Universal-life-type contracts consist of life insurance and annuity contracts in which one or more of the elements, such as premium and mortality charges, are not fixed and guaranteed. Examples are universal life insurance, variable universal life insurance, and variable annuities. Universal-life-type contracts are usually characterized by a policyholder fund to which premium payments and interest are credited and amounts are assessed for mortality, coverage, and administrative costs. Life insurance policies and annuity contracts in which no mortality risk is transferred are accounted for as investment contracts rather than insurance contracts.

Policyholder account balances for nontraditional contracts are required by FASB 97. As nontraditional life insurance and annuity contracts became more common in the 1980s, the FASB decided that the accounting method specified under FASB 60 did not adequately recognize revenue and reflect the liabilities for these contracts. In 1987, the FASB issued FASB 97 (also now incorporated as part of ASC Topic 944), which addressed these issues:[4]

> The liability for policy benefits for universal-life-type contracts shall be equal to the sum of:
>
> a. The balance that accrues to the benefit of policyholders at the date of the financial statements
>
> b. Any amounts that have been assessed to compensate the insurer for services to be performed over future periods
>
> c. Any amounts previously assessed against policyholders that are refundable on termination of the contract
>
> d. Any probable loss (premium deficiency)

The liability for policy claims is the amount due for benefits that has not yet been paid.

Separate Accounts

For life insurers, there are accounts called **separate account** assets and separate account liabilities, with the same balance in each. The investment of separate account assets is directed by the contract owner, who bears the investment risk. Separate account assets are segregated from an insurer's **general account**. Insurers that provide only property-casualty products do not have separate account entries on their balance sheets because they do not issue policies that provide investment benefits to policyholders.

Life Insurer GAAP Income Statement

The revenues and expenses included on a life insurer's GAAP income statement have some similarities with those on a property-casualty insurer's income statement. However, as on the balance sheet, there are several important differences. See the exhibit "Rockport Life Insurance, Inc., GAAP Income Statement."

Separate account

An account maintained by an insurer that is distinct from its general account and established solely to enable variable insurance product owners to participate directly in the account's investment performance.

General account

The invested assets of a life insurer that support interest-rate guarantees for which the insurer bears the investment risk.

Rockport Life Insurance, Inc., GAAP Income Statement

Rockport Life Insurance, Inc.
GAAP Income Statement (000s omitted)
For the Year Ended December 31, 20X1

Revenues	
Premiums	$4,300
Fees—Universal life policies and annuity contracts	500
Investment income	3,750
Realized investment gains (losses)	10
Other income	250
Total Revenue	8,810
Benefits and Expenses	
Policyholder benefits	2,100
Increase in liability for future policy benefits	774
Interest credited to policyholders' account balances	800
Operating expenses	1,900
Dividends to policyholders	500
Total Benefits and Expenses	6,074
Income Before Taxes	2,736
Income taxes	275
Net Income	$2,461

[DA11117]

Revenue

Two major sources of revenue for property-casualty and life insurers are premium and investment income. However, life insurers also receive significant revenue from fees for nontraditional life insurance and annuity contracts.

As stipulated in FASB 60, premiums and considerations for traditional life and annuity contracts are recognized as revenue when due. Under FASB 97, which applies to nontraditional life and annuity contracts (universal-life-type contracts), premiums are not recognized as revenue. Premiums are treated like bank deposits, with no revenue recorded when premium is received. Instead, revenue from nontraditional products consists of fees assessed against the contracts for policy administration, surrenders, and mortality and expense risk. These fees are recognized as revenue when the associated services are provided.

Expenses

Property-casualty insurers' major expense consists of loss and loss adjustment expenses. By comparison, life insurers' major expense is policy benefits under traditional life insurance policies and annuity contracts. This expense is recognized as incurred.

Life insurers are expected to periodically review their liability for future policy benefits. FASB 60 states: "Changes in the liability for future policy benefits that result from its periodic estimation for financial reporting purposes shall be recognized in income in the period in which the changes occur."[5] Therefore, any change in the liability for future policy benefits is recognized in the current period.

For universal-life-type contracts in which the policyholder account balance is backed by the general account, interest credited to policyholders is recognized as an expense.

Net Income

Net income is determined similarly for a property-casualty insurer and a life insurer. Total revenues minus total expenses equals income before taxes. After accounting for income taxes, the resulting balance is the net income. However, as for property-casualty insurers, certain categories of income appear on the statement of comprehensive income.

Life Insurer Statement of Comprehensive Income

The components of other comprehensive income for life insurers are similar to those for property-casualty insurers. FASB 97 states that insurers should report the results of all investment operations in operating income.[6] Insurers, similarly to other financial institutions, use FAS 115 guidelines for valuing and reporting both realized and unrealized investment gains and losses.[7]

Life Insurer Statement of Cash Flows

Life insurers' statement of cash flows, similar to that of property-casualty insurers, reports the company's cash flow in three parts:

- Cash flow from operations, including investment income from existing investments
- Cash flow from investing operations, including proceeds from maturity or sale of investments and the reinvestment of these proceeds
- Cash flow from financing, including sale of stocks or bonds by the company, repurchase of outstanding stocks or bonds, and payments of shareholder dividends.[8]

COMPONENTS OF THE LIFE INSURER NAIC ANNUAL STATEMENT

All insurers must file a National Association of Insurance Commissioners (NAIC) Annual Statement with the insurance department of the state in which they are domiciled and, directly or through the NAIC, with that of each state in which they do business. This requirement applies to both property-casualty and life insurers.

As in generally accepted accounting principles (GAAP) financial statements, there are significant differences as well as similarities between property-casualty and life insurers' NAIC Annual Statements. See the exhibit "Key Components of the Annual Statement for Life-Health Insurers."

Balance Sheet

The major differences between property-casualty and life insurers' balance sheets under statutory accounting principles (SAP), similar to their differences under GAAP, lie in the reserves listed on the liability side and in separate accounts on both the asset and liability sides of the balance sheet. Another important difference is that contract loans, which do not apply to property-casualty insurers, are included as an asset for life insurers.

The aggregate reserve for life contracts on the liability side of the balance sheet is taken from the exhibit for aggregate reserves and includes any changes in reserve valuation during the year. These reserves are established for all general account guaranteed benefits using actuarial assumptions regarding interest rates, mortality, and morbidity. These statutory reserves are calculated as "the excess of the present value of future benefits to be paid to or on behalf of policyholders less the present value of future net premiums." They include reserves for universal-life-type contracts maintained in the insurer's general account.[9]

Key Components of the Annual Statement for Life-Health Insurers

Balance Sheet

    Assets

    Liabilities, Surplus and Other Funds

Summary of Operations

Cash Flow

Details on Underwriting and Investment Results:

    Exhibit of Premiums and Annuity Considerations for Life and Accident and Health Contracts

    Exhibit of Aggregate Reserve for Life Contracts

    Insurance Expense Exhibits

    Exhibit of Claims for Life and Accident and Health Contracts

    Interest Maintenance Reserve

    Asset Valuation Reserve

Details on Investment Holdings:

    Schedule A—Real Estate

    Schedule B—Mortgage Loans

    Schedule BA—Other Long-Term Invested Assets

    Schedule D—Bonds and Stocks

    Schedule DA—Short-Term Investments

    Schedule DB—Derivative Investments

    Schedule E—Cash and Cash Equivalents

    Schedule F—Contested and Compromised Claims

    Schedule S—Reinsurance

    Schedule T—Premiums and Annuity Considerations, Allocation by States and Territories

    Schedule Y—Information on Holding Company Members

Notes to Financial Statements

General Interrogatories

Five-Year Historical Data

[DA11160]

The reserve for deposit-type contracts is the insurer's liability for waived premiums in the event of the death or disability of a contract owner of an investment-type contract. These contracts contain no morbidity or mortality risk. Examples of these types of contracts include structured settlements and deposit funds that include waiver of premium conditions.[10]

Two liabilities that apply to life insurers are the interest maintenance reserve (IMR) and the asset valuation reserve (AVR). The amounts recorded on the balance sheet are taken from the forms in the Annual Statement blank for calculating these reserves. These forms are discussed in the subsequent section on exhibits and schedules.

Contracts under which the contract owner bears the investment risk are maintained in the insurer's separate account. Separate account assets equal separate account liabilities and are reported on individual lines under the total assets and liabilities on the balance sheet.[11] Amounts received from contract holders for management fees on these contracts flow through the Statement of Operations as income. Any guarantees provided by the insurer related to these contracts, such as a guaranteed death benefit, are included in the insurer's aggregate policy reserve liabilities based on regulatory valuation guidelines. See the exhibit "Principal Elements of a Life Insurer Annual Statement (SAP) Balance Sheet."

The other balance sheet entries for life insurers are similar to those for property-casualty insurers. Most investment entries are similar and supported by the same schedules. Admitted and nonadmitted assets are also defined and treated in a similar manner.

Summary of Operations

Instead of the Income Statement in the property-casualty Annual Statement, the life-health Annual Statement blank contains a Summary of Operations. Despite the difference in name, many of the accounts on both the SAP Income Statement and Summary of Operations are similar. However, there are significant differences between the two. See the exhibit "Principal Elements of a Life Insurer's Annual Statement (SAP) Summary of Operations."

Premiums for life contracts and considerations for annuity contracts in the life insurer's general account are recognized as income when due from policyholders or contract owners in the amounts and under the terms specified in the contracts.[12]

Net investment income is determined similarly to its determination on the property-casualty insurance Income Statement. It includes the interest, dividends, real estate, and mortgage income earned on invested assets during the year, minus expenses incurred in conducting investment operations.

Other income for life insurers includes the amount amortized from the IMR, which is discussed later in this section, and income from management and other fees incurred in separate accounts.

Principal Elements of a Life Insurer Annual Statement (SAP) Balance Sheet

Assets	Current Year		
	Assets	Nonadmitted Assets	Net Admitted Assets
Bonds (Schedule D)	25,350,000		25,350,000
Stocks (Schedule D)			
Preferred stocks (Schedule D)	150,000		150,000
Common stocks (Schedule D)	2,900,000		2,900,000
Mortgage loans on real estate (Schedule B)	4,250,000		4,250,000
Real estate (Schedule A)	2,325,000		2,325,000
Cash (Schedule E)	4,900,000		4,900,000
Contract loans	25,000		25,000
Subtotals, cash and invested assets	39,900,000		39,900,000
Uncollected premiums and agents' balances	375,000	25,000	350,000
Amounts recoverable from reinsurers	3,800,000		3,800,000
Furniture and equipment	350,000	350,000	0
Receivables from parent, subsidiaries and affiliates	1,200,000		1,200,000
Total assets, excluding Separate Accounts	45,625,000	375,000	45,250,000
From Separate Accounts Statement	3,315,000		3,315,000
Total	48,940,000	375,000	48,565,000

Liabilities, Surplus, and Other Funds	Current Year
Aggregate reserve for life contracts	26,162,900
Liability for deposit-type contracts	1,575,000
Contract claims	17,320
Interest maintenance reserve	225,000
Commissions to agents due on accrued-life and annuity contracts	500,500
Asset valuation reserve	320,000
Payable to parent, subsidiaries and affiliates	75,000
Total Liabilities excluding Separate Accounts Business	28,875,720
From Separate Accounts Statement	3,315,000
Total Liabilities	32,190,720
Unassigned funds (surplus)	3,000,000
Treasury stock	-500,000
Surplus	13,874,280
Totals	48,565,000

Note: The illustration above does not include all the information contained in the NAIC Annual Statement blank. An actual Annual Statement blank would include a prior-year column.

Adapted from the NAIC Annual Statement blank. [DA11161]

Principal Elements of a Life Insurer's Annual Statement (SAP) Summary of Operations

	Current Year
Premiums and annuity considerations for life and accident and health contracts (Exhibit 1)	$8,340,000
Net investment income	950,000
Amortization of Interest Maintenance Reserve (IMR) (Line 5)	78,000
Miscellaneous income	
Income from fees associated with investment management, administration and contract guarantees from Separate Accounts	175,000
Charges and fees for deposit-type contracts	20,300
Totals	9,563,300
Death benefits	1,450,000
Annuity benefits	320,000
Surrender benefits and withdrawals for life contracts	905,000
Increase in aggregate reserves for life and accident and health contracts	2,730,000
Totals	5,405,000
Commissions on premiums, annuity considerations and deposit-type contract funds (direct business only)	550,000
General insurance expenses	800,000
Insurance taxes, licenses and fees, excluding federal income taxes	156,000
Net transfers to or (from) Separate Accounts net of reinsurance	250,000
Dividends to policyholders	7,800
Federal and foreign income taxes incurred (excluding tax on capital gains)	14,000
Net gain from operations after dividends to policyholders and federal income taxes and before realized capital gains (losses)	2,380,500
Net realized capital gains (losses) excluding gains (losses) transferred to the IMR less capital gains tax of $ 85,000	155,000
Net income	$2,535,500

Adapted from the NAIC Annual Statement blank. [DA11162]

These are expenses recorded on the Summary of Operations related to contracts in the life insurer's general account:[13]

- Death benefits—This line is for death benefits due to beneficiaries of life insurance policies during the reporting period. It excludes death benefits under annuity contracts, which are reported on a separate line recording all benefits incurred under annuity contracts.

- Surrender benefits and withdrawals for life insurance contracts—This line includes all benefits connected with surrender or withdrawal of funds from life contracts. It excludes premium and annuity considerations for these contracts, which are deducted from line 1, premium and annuity consideration income.

- Increase in aggregate reserves for life and accident and health contracts—This line includes an increase in reserves because of a deficiency in the reserves reported in a prior period. It excludes any increase in reserves that result from a change in valuation basis.

The remainder of the Summary of Operations for life insurers is similar to the Income Statement of the Annual Statement blank for property-casualty insurers. Expenses are subtracted from income to produce a total net income before realized capital gains (losses). Capital gains (losses) are then added or subtracted, and the result is the insurer's net income for the reporting period.

Capital and Surplus Account

The Summary of Operations for life insurers also contains the report of the insurer's Capital and Surplus Account. This report is essentially the same for both life and property-casualty insurers, with the exception of a line on the life-health statement to report changes in the AVR.

Cash Flow

The purpose and organization of the cash flow statement are the same for life insurers and property-casualty insurers. However, life insurers report cash from operations differently. Similar to the statement for property-casualty insurers, the entry for premiums collected net of reinsurance is the sum of all the premiums and considerations collected by the insurer during the reporting period. Considerations for separate accounts are deducted from this total. Additionally, the amounts paid for benefits during the period are deducted.

Reporting for cash from investments and cash from financing and miscellaneous sources is the same for life insurers and property-casualty insurers.

Other Exhibits and Schedules

Many of the NAIC Annual Statement exhibits and schedules are similar for both life and property-casualty insurers. However, it is important to note that Schedule F for property-casualty insurers, which concerns reinsurance, is Schedule S for life insurers; Schedule F for life insurers identifies contested and compromised claims during the reporting period.

Other significant forms in life insurers' Annual Statements include the IMR and AVR, which were mentioned earlier regarding the Balance Sheet and Summary of Operations.

Interest Maintenance Reserve

The purpose of the IMR exhibit is to record the realized capital gains (losses) resulting from interest rate changes on fixed-income investments and amortize these into income over the life of investments that have been sold. All of these gains (losses) are net of capital gains taxes. Realized gains (losses) on preferred stocks, debt securities, and mortgage-backed securities are included in the IMR according to rules outlined by the NAIC. Called bonds, tendered bonds, and **sinking fund provision** payments are also included. Mortgages may be included in the IMR as well.

For derivatives, determining whether the capital gains (losses) should be allocated to the IMR or AVR is based on how the underlying interest or covering asset is treated. Derivative transactions that were made for the purpose of hedging the interest rate on the insurer's assets should be allocated to the IMR and amortized over the life of the hedged asset.

The insurer must complete a separate IMR for separate accounts. The amortization of general accounts' IMR for the current period is recorded on the summary of operations. The remaining IMR is recorded as a liability on the balance sheet.[14]

Sinking fund provision
A provision that requires a bond issuer to set aside money at periodic intervals for the specific purpose of repaying a portion of its existing bonds each year.

Asset Valuation Reserve

The purpose of the AVR is to address credit and equity risks of the insurer's assets. All capital gains (losses) reported in the AVR should be net of capital gains taxes. United States government securities are exempt from the AVR.

Realized gains (losses) on any security that result from changes in its classification by the NAIC or the Securities Valuations Office, as outlined in NAIC rules, from the date of purchase to the date of sale must be reported in the AVR. Permanent impairment write-downs should be reported as credit-related losses. Certain mortgage loans are also reported. Unrealized gains and losses net of deferred tax assets are also included in the AVR according to NAIC instructions. The total AVR is reported as a liability on the balance sheet, and any changes are charged directly to surplus.

SEPARATE ACCOUNTS FOR LIFE/ANNUITY INSURANCE COMPANIES

Separate accounts insurance products were first created in the 1950s to allow annuity customers greater flexibility in managing the investment returns of their insurance contracts. From those humble beginnings, separate accounts have experienced tremendous growth in size and scope. In 2012, life insurers held $5.8 trillion of invested assets, with more than $2 trillion of that amount segregated into separate accounts.[15]

A life insurer's balance sheet has two types of investment accounts. The general account includes the assets used to fund the benefits and guarantees included in the insurer's products, as well as the noninsurance promises made by the insurer, such as those to creditors and employees. The assets in the general account are available to all creditors. The second type of investment account is the separate account. Assets held in separate accounts are not available to the insurer's creditors. Instead, these assets are available only to back the promises made to the separate accounts' policyowners.

Purpose of Separate Accounts

Unit-linked insurance products

Insurance products under which the investment performance of a segregated bundle of assets is passed through to the policyowners.

The most common use of separate accounts is in conjunction with **unit-linked insurance products** such as variable life insurance (including universal life insurance), variable annuities, and certain pension products. The separate accounts have different levels of risk and return, depending on the type of assets in the separate account. Because gains and losses are passed directly to those policyowners, the policyowners assume the investment risk of the separate account assets.

This gives the policyowner greater control over a product's investment risk and long-term investment performance. Policyowners can allocate their equity in their insurance policies in and out of separate accounts with varying levels of risk and return at their discretion. Common stock makes up about 80 percent of separate account assets. By comparison, stocks make up only about 2 percent of the general account invested assets. Insurers often restrict the number of transactions between separate accounts over the course of a year or charge fees for reallocations to discourage excessive trading between separate accounts.

The assets in the separate account are not subject to state laws restricting insurer investments. A key advantage of unit-linked insurance products is that the policyowner can choose from among different bundles of assets and thus assume, from the available investment options, the level of investment risk with which he or she is most comfortable. Although common stock makes up the bulk of separate account assets, other types of invested assets include hedge funds, corporate bonds, unaffiliated mutual funds, mortgages, and derivatives.

Structure of Separate Accounts

Unit investment trust

A regulated investment company that issues a fixed number of shares representing an investment in a specific bundle of securities.

Separate accounts must be registered with the Securities and Exchange Commission (SEC). Most separate accounts are configured as **unit investment trusts**. The separate accounts are then subdivided into smaller subaccounts that register as mutual funds. The separate accounts and the subaccounts are registered and regulated as investment companies under the Investment Company Act of 1940. A policyowner who purchases a product linked to the separate accounts receives a prospectus from both the unit investment trust and the underlying mutual fund. Because these products are a combination of an insurance policy and a registered security, life insurance sales agents must be licensed both as insurance agents and as investment advisers.

A key advantage of cash value life insurance is that the investment earnings are tax deferred. The separate accounts structure is integral to maintaining this tax advantage because the insurance company continues to own the assets in the separate accounts. If the policyowner owned the assets directly, the tax advantage would be lost. Instead, the policyowner buys units or shares in the separate account, and this structure protects the deferred tax status of these products.

Some separate accounts are actively managed, which means that the fund manager picks the individual stocks and bonds for the pool and attempts to outperform a market benchmark. Others are passively managed, which means that the fund manager simply purchases stocks and bonds based on an established index.

Apply Your Knowledge

The most common method of registering a separate account with the Securities and Exchange Commission is to register it as

a. A unit investment trust.

b. An investment pooling club.

c. An exchange-traded fund.

d. A registered investment adviser.

Feedback: a. The most common method of registering a separate account with the Securities and Exchange Commission is to register it as a unit investment trust.

Financial Reporting

Under generally accepted accounting principles (GAAP), assets and liabilities are reported as separate accounts when all of these conditions are met:

- The separate accounts meet the legal and regulatory requirements under state and federal law, including the registration requirements dictated by the SEC.

- The assets supporting the contract liabilities are legally protected from the insurer's general account creditors, meaning that they are segregated and dedicated to the separate accounts policyowner.

- The investment allocation decisions are made by the policyowner, meaning that the policyowner decides where the separate account assets are invested, such as into stocks or into a money market fund.

- The investment performance, net of fees and assessments, is passed through to the policyowner. Although contracts may include floors that provide minimum investment performance on the separate account funds, the insurer cannot place a cap on the investment returns earned by the policyowner.

Both GAAP and statutory accounting principles (SAP) allow the insurer to report the summary total of separate account assets separately from the general account assets. Assets in separate accounts are typically carried at fair value. However, some institutional separate accounts may be reported at book value. Separate account liabilities are typically equal to separate account assets but can be lower. If separate account assets exceed separate account liabilities, the excess equity is available to satisfy general account creditors.

The investment performance of unit-linked products directly affects the value of the policyowner's benefits under the contract because the investment results are passed through. However, some contracts include guaranteed minimum death benefits, guaranteed minimum annuity payments, or guaranteed minimum accumulation values. If the fair value of the separate account assets is insufficient to meet those guarantees, the difference is made up from the general account.

Because investment risk is borne by the policyowner, the separate account investment performance flows through to the policyowner rather than through the insurer's income statement. However, insurers earn fees for managing the underlying assets. The larger the separate account balance, the greater the potential to generate fee income. These separate account management fees flow through the insurer's income statement.

Under SAP, in addition to reporting the total separate account assets and liabilities in the statutory annual statement, life insurers file a separate account annual statement with the state regulator that shows the specific assets that support their unit-linked insurance products held by policyowners in separate accounts. The separate account annual statement includes details on how the funds are invested. Insurers that do not offer separate accounts are not required to file the separate accounts annual statement.

Under GAAP, separate account assets and liabilities are separated from those of the general account. See the exhibit "U.S. GAAP Balance Sheet Reflecting Separate Accounts."

U.S. GAAP Balance Sheet Reflecting Separate Accounts

In U.S. GAAP statements, separate account assets are segregated from the general account, and a summary total is reported at the bottom of the assets page. An equal amount is recorded as a separate account liability. Policy minimum benefits or guarantees that exceed the value of the separate account assets would be recorded as a liability in the general account.

Primature Life Insurance Company GAAP Balance Sheet

Assets	12/31/20X1	Liabilities & Equity	12/31/20X1
Fixed Maturities–Available for Sale	16,300	Policyholders' Account Balances	9,000
Fixed Maturities–Trading	750	Future Policy Benefits	8,500
Equities–Available for Sale	250	Dividends Payable to Policyowners	110
Equities–Trading	350	Policy Claims	140
Mortgage Loans	2,900	Debt	500
Policy Loans	1,000	Other Liabilities	750
Other Investments	1,750	General Account Liabilities	19,000
Total Investments	23,300		
Cash and Cash Equivalents	500	Separate Account Liabilities	3,200
Deferred Policy Acquisition Costs	350		
Investment Income Due & Accrued	200	Total Liabilities	22,200
Other Assets	450		
General Account Assets	24,800	Total Equity	5,800
Separate Account Assets	3,200		
Total Assets	28,000	Total Liabilities & Equity	28,000

[DA11141]

SUMMARY

Although many similarities exist between the financial statements of life insurers and of property-casualty insurers, there are major differences in how life insurers account for premium and benefits, as well as certain items that apply only to life insurers, such as policy loans and policyholders' account balances.

There are many similarities between property-casualty and life insurer Annual Statements under SAP. However, significant differences include liabilities for reserves on the balance sheet, separate accounts, surrender benefits and withdrawals, the interest maintenance reserve, and the asset valuation reserve.

Life insurers use separate accounts to segregate the investment assets supporting a specific group of insurance products from the assets in the general account. The investment returns from separate account assets are passed through to the policyowners themselves, who bear the investment risk. Assets held in separate accounts are typically exempt from state laws limiting insurance company investment risk. Separate account assets and liabilities are reported separately from other insurer assets and liabilities.

ASSIGNMENT NOTES

1. National Association of Insurance Commissioners and Center for Insurance Policy and Research, "The Insurance Industry's Exposure to Commercial Mortgage Lending and Real Estate: A Detailed Review of the Life Insurance Industry's Commercial Mortgage Loan Holdings (Part II)," Capital Markets Special Report, www.naic.org/capital_markets_archive/121220.htm (accessed February 10, 2014).

2. "GAAP Accounting," Life and Accident and Health Insurance Accounting (Durham, N.C.: Insurance Accounting & Systems Association, Inc., 2001) p. 15-25.

3. Financial Accounting Standards Board, Statement of Financial Accounting Standards No. 60, Norwalk, Conn., June 1982, p. 9.

4. Financial Accounting Standards Board, Statement of Financial Accounting Standards No. 97, Norwalk, Conn., December 1987, p. 9.

5. Financial Accounting Standards Board, Statement of Financial Accounting Standards No. 60, Norwalk, Conn., June 1982, pp. 9-10.

6. Financial Accounting Standards Board, Statement of Financial Accounting Standards No. 97, Norwalk, Conn., December 1987, p. 24.

7. Financial Accounting Standards Board, Statement of Financial Accounting Standards No. 115, Norwalk, Conn., May 1993.

8. Edward E. Graves, ed., McGill's Life Insurance, 8th ed. (Bryn Mawr, Pa.: The American College, 2011), pp. 24-28.

9. National Association of Insurance Commissioners (NAIC), Accounting Practices and Procedures Manual, Vol. I (Kansas City, Mo.: NAIC, 2013), pp. 51–4.

10. Accounting Practices and Procedures Manual, Vol. I, p. 52–3.

11. Accounting Practices and Procedures Manual, Vol. I, p. 56–4.

12. Accounting Practices and Procedures Manual, Vol. I, p. 51–3.

13. National Association of Insurance Commissioners (NAIC), Official NAIC Annual Statement Instructions: Life, Accident & Health (Kansas City, Mo.: NAIC, 2008), pp. 49–50, http://student.bus.olemiss.edu/files/liebenberg/blanksandinstructions2008/08%20Life%20Instructions.pdf (accessed March 12, 2014).

14. Official NAIC Annual Statement Instructions: Life, Accident & Health, pp. 201-214.

15. American Council of Life Insurers, Life Insurers Fact Book 2013, pp. 7-8, www. acli.com/Tools/Industry%20Facts/Life%20Insurers%20Fact%20Book/Documents/ FB13%20Chapter%202_Assets.pdf (accessed February 18, 2014).

Property-Casualty Premium Accounting

Educational Objectives

After learning the content of this assignment, you should be able to:

▷ Explain how and when insurers recognize premium revenue in their financial statements under deferral-matching and asset-liability approaches.

▷ Distinguish between the various types of written premium and policy transactions that may not be classified as premium.

▷ Summarize the implications of these premium accounting issues:

- Financing—premiums versus service charges

- Earning premium before it is written

- Extended reporting endorsements (definite versus indefinite periods)

- Reinsurance lags

- Large deductible credits

▷ Summarize the purpose of unearned premium and these issues associated with how premiums are earned over time:

- Pro rata and non-pro rata approaches to earning premium

- Multiyear policies

- Liability adequacy test and the premium deficiency reserve

▷ Explain the relationship between loss reserves and the unearned premium reserve.

Property-Casualty Premium Accounting

PREMIUM ACCOUNTING—REVENUE RECOGNITION

Premiums are the principal source of revenue for insurers. Therefore, an understanding of how insurers account for premium revenue is necessary in the use of insurers' financial statements.

Income statements focus on revenue as a function of company volume and as a measure of company growth. For insurers, the principal sources of revenue are premium from insurance sales and investment income.

The point at which a company can recognize revenue in its income statement is an important consideration for most accounting frameworks. Although improper revenue recognition has not historically been a major issue for insurers, it has occasionally been a source of fraud or unethical earnings management in other industries, such as those involved in the sales of consumer goods or in the sales of services. Some companies in those industries facing perceived growth targets from investors have tried to accelerate the recognition of sales revenue or manage its timing to "bank" high-growth periods that can be released into income during future times of low growth. This practice has raised concern within the accounting world regarding when revenue (such as insurance premiums) should be recognized on an entity's financial statements.

Within an insurance accounting framework, several rules may be used to determine when policy premium may be recognized as revenue. These rules have been considered in the International Accounting Standards Boards' (IASB's) deliberations on insurance contract accounting:

- When the insurance contract is signed
- When the premium is due from the policyholder
- When the premium is received
- When the insurance policy becomes effective
- When the risk covered by the policy runs off (or expires)[1]

Deferral-Matching

Many life insurance accounting frameworks recognize premium revenue as income based on when premium is due. In contrast, most property-casualty insurance accounting frameworks recognize premium revenue as coverage is provided for underlying insurance events. The approach most commonly used by property-casualty insurers is called a deferral-matching approach, as it attempts to defer recognition of any revenue or expenses so that they can be matched with the timing of the incurred losses. (This is the same approach common in accounting for service contracts, such as maintenance contracts, where the intent is to recognize revenue as the service is provided.)

As an example of a deferral-matching approach, assume an insurer writes a $400 commercial liability policy lasting one year, effective October 1, 20XX. By December 31, 20XX, only one-quarter of the policy term would have expired. Under a deferral-matching approach, only one-quarter, $100, of the premium would be recognized as income on the year-end income statement.

Deferral-matching approaches generally utilize an account known as written premiums. Written premiums for a policy during a reported period are generally defined as the amount of premium charged for that policy during the reporting period. This assumes that the policy in question has already become effective. Any premium charged on a policy before its effective date will be deferred and not recognized as written premium until the effective date. The portion of the policy's written premium for the unexpired policy risk is called the unearned premium, a liability set up to defer recognition of the premium revenue. As the coverage period runs off, the unearned premium liability is proportionally reduced.[2]

Premium revenue for a particular policy during a particular period equals the written premium during the period plus the beginning unearned premium liability less the ending unearned premium liability. See the exhibit "First Single-Policy Example."

The "Second Single-Policy Example" exhibit addresses treatment of the actual premium billing process on accounting results. The actual billing of the premium under many accounting frameworks does not affect certain premium revenue accounts on the balance sheet or income statement until the policy effective date. If the billed premium is received before the effective date, that amount is treated as a deposit until the effective date. See the exhibit "Second Single-Policy Example."

Alternatively, the premium for the policy could have been paid after the effective date. In this case, an asset account, called "premiums receivable" or "agents' balances," is established once the premium is booked as written. The asset is retained until the premium is paid. The term "premiums receivable" is more generic than "agents' balances," allowing the insurer to either bill the customer directly or bill the agent (who is then responsible for collecting the premium from the customer). The two terms are sometimes treated synonymously.

The two billing methods can have materially different effects on commission payments. Generally, the amount due from agents is net of commission, as agents take their commission out of the funds they receive directly from the policyholders. When an insurer bills a policyholder directly, it collects the full

First Single-Policy Example

Policy is sold March 1, 20X1, with a May 1, 20X1, effective date. Assume a twelve-month policy term and that the premium charged is $120.[a]

For simplicity, also assume no losses, expenses, or taxes.

1st quarter 20X1
Balance sheet at 3/31/20X1

Assets	Liabilities	
	Unearned Premium	0 (referred to later as UPR)

Written premium for 1st quarter 20X1
Written Premium   0 (referred to later as WP)[b]

Income statement for 1st quarter 20X1
Earned Premium (revenue)   0 (referred to later as EP)

2nd quarter 20X1
Balance sheet at 6/30/20X1

Assets	Liabilities	
	UPR	100

Written premium for 2nd quarter 20X1
WP   120

Income statement for 2nd quarter 20X1
EP (revenue)   20 (equals WP + beginning UPR – ending UPR)
                  120 + 0 – 100

3rd quarter 20X1
Balance sheet at 9/30/20X1

Assets	Liabilities	
	UPR	70

Written premium for 3rd quarter 20X1
WP   0

Income statement for 3rd quarter 20X1
EP (revenue)   30 (equals WP + beginning UPR – ending UPR)
                  0 + 100 – 70

Full Year 20X1
Balance sheet at 12/31/20X1

Assets	Liabilities	
	Unearned Premium	40

Written premium for year 20X1
WP   120

Income statement for year 20X1
EP (revenue)   80 (equals WP + beginning UPR – ending UPR)
                  120 + 0 – 40

The remaining portion of the policy's unearned premium in this example would become earned (revenue) in 20X2, as the policy expires and UPR runs off to zero.[c] Risk is expected to be even over the coverage period.

[a] This example also assumes that the premium is earned evenly over each month of the twelve-month policy period.

[b] Note that the WP is zero during the 1st quarter, even though premium was charged the policyholder during the period. This is because the policy had yet to become effective in that quarter.

[c] For policies longer than twelve months, the time until the UPR runs off to zero would be even longer. In some countries, policies lasting longer than twelve months are the norm, while for other countries such policies are rare.

Second Single-Policy Example

Policy is sold March 1, 20X1, with a May 1, 20X1, effective date. Assume a twelve-month policy term and that the premium charged is $120. The premium is received as cash on March 15.

1st quarter 20X1

Balance sheet at 3/31/20X1

Assets		Liabilities	
Cash	120	Deposit	120
		UPR	0

2nd quarter 20X1

Balance sheet at 6/30/20X1

Assets		Liabilities	
Cash	120	Deposit	0
		UPR	100

3rd quarter 20X1

Balance sheet at 9/30/20X1

Assets		Liabilities	
Cash	120	Deposit	0
		UPR	70

[DA06360]

amount, including commissions, and addresses payment of the agents' commissions separately.

The third single-policy example assumes ultimate collection of the premium. Billed premium that is subsequently determined to be uncollectible may be written off in several different locations, based on the particular accounting framework in use. For example, regulatory accounting in the United States treats such uncollectible amounts as negative other income, while they may be accounted for as underwriting expenses under GAAP. They also may be considered negative premium in other accounting frameworks. See the exhibit "Third Single-Policy Example."

The third single-policy example focuses on premium revenue on a calendar-period basis. Sometimes, actuaries focus on policy year or underwriting year instead. For such approaches, the focus is either on the ultimate revenue for the policy/underwriting year or on the amount of revenue recognized to date.

When ultimate premium revenue for a policy/underwriting year is the focus, unearned premium liability is not recognized. Ultimate premium revenue for that policy/underwriting year equals total written premiums to date, with

Third Single-Policy Example

Policy is sold March 1, 20X1, with a May 1, 20X1, effective date. Assume a twelve-month policy term and that the premium charged is $120. The premium is received as cash on July 15.

1st quarter 20X1

Balance sheet at 3/31/20X1

Assets		Liabilities	
Premium receivable	0		
Cash	0		
		UPR	0

2nd quarter 20X1

Balance sheet at 6/30/20X1

Assets		Liabilities	
Premium receivable	120		
Cash	0		
		UPR	100

3rd quarter 20X1

Balance sheet at 9/30/20X1

Assets		Liabilities	
Premium receivable	0		
Cash	120		
		UPR	70

[DA06361]

the possible adjustment for written premium amounts expected in the future for that policy/underwriting year. (Examples of such future written premium transactions are late bookings, policy cancellations, and endorsements.)

When policy/underwriting year premium revenue to date is the focus, the calculation is generally written premium to date less unearned premium for that policy/underwriting year as of the desired accounting date. See the exhibit "Policy Year Premium Example."

Sometimes an actuary will want to examine premium revenue for a past calendar period after adjustment for reporting lags and other distortions. This is especially useful when the actuary is trying to compare estimates of incurred losses to premium revenue. If the incurred loss estimate is at an ultimate level but the premium revenue amount is distorted due to booking lags, the actuary may produce erroneous indications of profitability, especially during periods of change such as periods of rapid growth.

Policy Year Premium Example

Assume annual policies are written at a stable level through the year 20X1, with the initial amount charged equaling $2 million for each month. Assume the only adjustment necessary is to reflect the fact that half any month's premium is booked one month late.

Policy year 20X1 at 12/31/20X1

Written premium (WP)	$23 million
WP adjustment	$1 million (anticipated amount of premium from December 20X1 effective month that will be booked in January 20X2)
Total ultimate WP	**$24 million**
WP through 12/31/X1	$23 million
UPR at 12/31/X1	$11 million[a]
EP through 12/31/X1	**$12 million[b]**

[a] The UPR was calculated by assuming that the average policy for each month was written in the middle of the month, such that only 1/24 was still unearned for the January 20X1 policies, 3/24 for the February 20X1 policies, and so forth, with $2 million for each effective month except for $1 million for December 20X1 (due to the booking lag).

[b] Notice that the booking lag in this example had no effect on earned premium. This is because the booking lag was small, and applied only to a portion of premium that was mostly unearned at the time of the valuation. When carried out to more decimals, the earned premium in this example is $11.96 million.

[DA06362]

Asset-Liability

During preliminary discussions of a new accounting standard for insurance contracts, the IASB discussed using an asset-liability approach for all insurance contracts rather than a deferral-matching approach. Under an asset-liability approach, revenue is recognized up front once the insurer gains control of the asset resulting from the revenue.

When the full amount of premium charged is recognized upon the policy taking effect, there is no unearned premium. Instead, other liabilities must be established for losses and expenses expected for the unexpired portion of the policy. Deposit or similar liabilities must still be established for any premiums received before the effective date. When the full premium is recognized even earlier, at date of sale (such as when the contract is signed) or date of premium receipt even if before the effective date, then no deposit liability is called for. Instead, the insurer would establish loss and expense liabilities for future cash outflows under the policy even before the coverage became effective.

These approaches do not employ the earned premium concept. Therefore, any income statement or other performance measures that rely on earned premium (such as loss ratio) would need to be adapted to reflect the different premium revenue recognition treatment. Policy or underwriting year concepts may fit this premium accounting approach better than calendar/accident year.

PREMIUM ACCOUNTING—TYPES OF WRITTEN PREMIUM

Premium represents the most significant source of revenue for most insurers and is a principal measure of insurer size and growth. An understanding of the types of premium transactions included in reported written premium, and policy transactions that may be included in reported written premium, is beneficial in the analysis of an insurer's financial statements.

Written premium is commonly used in the property-casualty insurance industry as a measure of business growth. Therefore, an understanding of the types of written premium transactions (and certain transactions similar to written premium) is necessary to evaluate growth correctly. Absent this understanding, a user of written premium information may misinterpret the true growth rate of an insurer, especially during periods of rapid change (such as a change in processing systems or transition to a different type of business).[3]

Written premiums
The total premium on all policies written (put into effect) during a particular period.

Written Premium Transactions

In the simplest case, a policy's premium is known and fixed in advance when the policy is sold. The policy is never changed by an endorsement or cancellation and is allowed to run its course. In such a case, it is easy to interpret the amount of business an insurer has sold based on the written premium reported in the financial statements. Other scenarios, however, present complexities.

Many complications can arise that deviate from the simple model of premiums fixed in advance. Where ceded reinsurance exists, these direct and assumed premium transactions may also trigger corresponding ceded premium transactions.

Deposits

Policies may be bound, or formally agreed to, before all of the contract details have been finalized. This can result in a binder premium, or an initial **deposit premium**. Policies for which the pricing exposure is not initially known can also be sold, also requiring an initial deposit premium until an estimate of the ultimate premium can be obtained. Deposit premiums are also sometimes used for reinsurance treaties when the final premium is a function of the subject business during the treaty effective period.

Deposit premium
The amount a policyholder pays at the beginning of a policy period, pending the determination of the actual premium owed.

Estimates

When the pricing exposure is not initially known, it may sometimes be estimated. Estimated written premiums generally require a premium adjustment once the actual pricing exposure level is determined. Examples of estimated premiums include a commercial liability policy for which the premium is a function of the insured's business sales during the policy period, or a reinsurance treaty with a premium that is a function of the final subject premium.

Audits

In cases where the pricing exposure is not known at contract inception, audits may be used to determine the actual final exposure. These audits can occur during the policy term or at the end of the policy term, depending on the pricing exposure base characteristics. For example, a policy with a final premium that is based on the insured's sales (such as a commercial liability policy for a retail store) or payroll (such as a workers compensation policy) during the policy period will require an audit after the policy has expired to determine the final premium.

Endorsements/Cancellations

Policies may be changed mid-term through endorsements, which can potentially generate positive or negative written premium. Policies may even be canceled mid-term, an extreme form of endorsement. A common example of such a situation is one in which a new car is purchased, with the existing auto policy endorsed to reflect the purchase of the new car in addition to or in place of the car(s) already covered by the in-force policy.

Reinstatement Premiums

Reinstatement premium

A premium that applies to reinsurance contracts or primary policies to reinstate the original policy limit after it has been exhausted by the covered event in order to cover another possible event under the reinsurance or primary policy.

Many catastrophe or per-event excess-of-loss reinsurance treaties require the payment of a **reinstatement premium** in the event of a covered catastrophe. In general, such a ceded premium must be accounted for when the endorsement is triggered.

Retrospective Premium Adjustments

For some policies, the final premium is determined based on the losses incurred under the contract. Such retrospectively rated policies result in an initial premium, followed by a series of adjustment premium entries based on the covered losses under the policy (subject to limitations such as minimums and maximums). These adjustments can sometimes continue for many years after the original policy term has expired. For example, large workers compensation or commercial liability contracts in the United States can be written on a retrospectively rated basis so that premium adjustments continue for five years or more after the original effective date. Reinsurance contracts are also sometimes written so that future premium adjustments are made as incurred losses under the contract change.

Earned Premium Implications

Under a deferral-matching approach, the portion of the written premium from the previously described transactions that relate to past coverage periods is earned immediately. The portion that relates to future coverage periods is earned over time through the establishment of an unearned premium liability. For example, an audit premium transaction that occurs after a policy has expired is immediately earned. As another example, the adding of another driver to an automobile [4] policy prospectively would result in written premium that initially affects only unearned premium, not earned premium. A retroactive endorsement generating additional written premium that is processed in the middle of a policy period would affect both earned premium and unearned premium, as the portion relating to the already expired portion would be earned immediately.

Earning of Deposit Premium and Other Premium Adjustments

There may be multiple approaches for earning items such as deposits, audit premiums, and other types of revenue that are classified as premium. Interim premium audits are audits that modify the premium charged and are performed before policy expiration. The audits performed after expiration are generally not an issue, as premiums resulting from these audits are immediately earned when booked as written. In general, any written premium is wholly earned immediately if it relates wholly to a period that has expired.

When the accounting framework does not dictate the earning approach, the goal would normally be to choose an approach that focuses on the total earned premium, with as simple an approach as possible for the types of revenue that contribute to the total premium. This may be a function of the individual processing systems and policies that the company uses.

Installment Premiums

Installment premiums are not considered written premium transactions under certain accounting frameworks (such as those in the U.S.). Instead, under those frameworks, the full policy premium is recorded up front in a written premium transaction. The decision as to whether to collect this full amount up-front or via installments is treated solely as a billing issue and does not affect written premium. Installments billed and due but not yet collected are categorized in one type of premium receivable account, while those yet to be billed and not yet due are included in a different premium receivable account.

Policy Transactions That May Be Considered Premiums

Certain policy transactions may or may not be considered premiums, depending on the context and the accounting framework in place, including these:

- Policyholder dividends
- Tax surcharges

Policyholder Dividends

Under some property-casualty policies, the policyholder is eligible for discretionary dividends paid by the insurer. The accounting for such dividends relative to premium can vary based on the rules of the jurisdiction or even the preference of management (for management accounting purposes). Possible accounting treatment includes negative premium or positive expense. See the exhibit "Example—Impact of Varying Policyholder Dividend Treatment."

Example—Impact of Varying Policyholder Dividend Treatment

Written Premium:	$ 110
Earned Premium:	$ 100
Incurred Losses:	$ 60
Underwriting Expense	$ 18
Policyholder Dividends	$ 4

Loss ratio: (incurred losses divided by earned premium)

Policyholder Dividend treated as expense   60/100 = 60%

Policyholder Dividend treated as premium   60/96 = 62.5%

Expense ratio: (underwriting expense divided by written premium)

Policyholder Dividend treated as expense   (18+4)/110 = 20%

Policyholder Dividend treated as premium   18/106 = 17%

[DA06363]

Tax Surcharges

In some jurisdictions, the insurer is used as a tax collector for special purpose taxes levied on the policyholder as a function of premium. While billed as a function of premium, some of these taxes may not be included in reported premium. Instead, they are characterized separately and may not even be reported as part of income or expense.

The decision as to whether to include such tax surcharges as premiums may be based on law, regulation, or accounting rules, depending on the jurisdiction and the particular tax surcharge. In the U.S., the criteria for such treatment are that the surcharge is shown separately on the premium bill sent to the policyholder and that the insurer is not liable for the portion of such amounts not collected. The only effects of these taxes on the balance sheet are a temporary entry in the cash asset account and in the noninsurance liability account, which is greater than zero until the actual payments are remitted to the taxing authority.

OTHER PREMIUM ACCOUNTING ISSUES

Users of insurer financial statements should be aware of special premium accounting issues.

These special premium accounting issues may have significant implications for insurer financial statements:

- Financing—premiums versus service charges
- Earning premium before it is written
- Extended reporting endorsements (definite versus indefinite periods)
- Reinsurance lags
- Large deductible credits[5]

Financing—Premiums Versus Service Charges

Some premium payment plans allow the payment of premiums to be spread over a period of time. These payment plans may include additional payments that exceed the amount required if the premium was paid in full at policy inception. Depending on the applicable payment terms and the jurisdiction and/or accounting framework, these additional payments may be recorded as additional premium, as service charges, or as financing charges.

For example, for United States regulatory accounting, additional payments that are fixed per payment date, regardless of the amount of premium paid, are treated as service charges rather than as part of premium. Those that are a function of the amount of payment are treated as finance charges rather than as part of the premium. (The distinction between service charge and finance charge could potentially help determine which rules or regulations apply, depending on the jurisdiction.) See the exhibit "Example—Service Charge Versus Finance Charge—U.S. Regulatory Accounting."

Earning Premium Before It Is Written

Some components of premium revenue are not known with certainty, can be reliably estimated only on an aggregate basis, or do not lead to billing of the

> ## Example—Service Charge Versus Finance Charge—U.S. Regulatory Accounting
>
> Two insureds with annual policies want to pay their premium quarterly rather than paying one amount up front.
>
> > Insured A: Annual premium $200
> >
> > Insured B: Annual premium $400
>
> If insured A is offered the ability to pay $55 per quarter and B is allowed to pay $105 per quarter, where the rule is to add a $5 per billing fee, then the additional amounts charged are treated as service fees.
>
> If insured A is offered the ability to pay $55 per quarter and B is allowed to pay $110 per quarter, where the rule is to add 10 percent to the amounts, then the additional amounts charged are treated as finance charges.

[DA06364]

amount due until some time after the exposure period. These are examples of premium earned before it is written:

- Audit premium—The amount of additional premium generated by premium audits may be reasonably estimable during the coverage period in the aggregate (that is, across all policies subject to audit), but may not be assignable and/or billable to individual customers until some time after the exposure period, once the audit is complete.

- Reinstatement premium—A reinstatement premium obligation may be likely or nearly certain given the current loss reserves, but the actual payment is not due until paid losses breach the attachment point (which could be many years in the future).

These amounts can be sizable for some products and in some situations (such as during an economic expansion for audit premium or after a major catastrophe for reinstatement premium). Therefore, delaying recognition of this revenue until the premium is charged could result in distorted earnings reports.

How can these premiums be reflected in revenue, when the amount, timing, and/or assignment to individual policies are uncertain? One way is to record an estimate of these amounts as written premium. This requires a slight deviation from the definition of written premium as the amount of premium charged during the period. This is because no premium would be charged to a party (or payable to a party in the case of reinstatement premiums on ceded contracts) as a result of these written premium bookings.

As the actual audits are performed or the reinstatement premium is triggered, the actual audit or reinstatement is booked and recorded as written premium and the estimated amount previously booked is reversed. This approach also requires additional financial controls because written premium generally results in either a cash receipt or the establishment of a premium receivable. No cash is actually received when these estimates are booked, and there may be no clearly identified counterparty from whom the receivable will be collected.

The written premium approach could be used either under a deferral-matching approach or under an approach that recognizes revenue when premium is written. Another approach exists for recording premium revenue for these situations under a deferral-matching approach. This approach starts with the basic equation for premium revenue under a deferral-matching approach:

Earned premium = Written premium + Beginning unearned premium − Ending unearned premium

Rather than affecting premium revenue through the written premium component (and possibly the unearned premium component, to the extent that some of these amounts are for the unexpired portion of policies) of this equation, as the previous approach does, premium revenue can be affected through only the unearned premium component.

For example, if an audit premium of $100 is expected to be booked in the future on existing or past policies with 75 percent of it related to exposure periods that have already occurred, the desired earned premium effect can be produced by adjusting unearned premium down by $75. Given that earned premium equals written premium plus beginning unearned premium less ending unearned premium, a $75 decrease in ending unearned premium results in $75 additional premium revenue. Under this approach, the unearned premium adjustment is continually updated, just as other reserve items are updated (such as loss reserves). An advantage of this approach is that it eliminates the need to continually reverse written premium estimates booked a year or more in the past. Hence, it should require fewer steps to implement.

Two terms sometimes used to represent premium that has been earned but not yet billed are earned but unbilled (EBUB) and earned but not reported (EBNR).

Extended Reporting Endorsements (Definite Versus Indefinite Periods)

Some policies cover only claims reported during the policy term (for example, claims-made policies). This is common in some markets for directors and officers liability and for professional liability policies. These policies sometimes allow for an extension of such claim-reporting timeframes, sometimes for no additional cost if a certain event occurs, and sometimes for a fixed cost determined at policy inception. The accounting for these extended reporting periods can vary. In the U.S., the regulatory accounting system requires the liability for extended periods to be recorded as unearned premium reserves when the extension is for a definite period into the future and as loss reserves when the extension is for an indefinite period.

Reinsurance Lags

Some reinsurance contracts (especially those involving reinsurance pools) result in material lags in the reporting of premiums and losses. This can cause misleading results, particularly if the late reported losses are subsequently reported to the correct accident, policy, or underwriting year. The net effect can be distortion in loss development or historic calendar/accident year measures.

One way of correcting these distortions is to require companies to book estimates of the premiums and losses that are reported late. These estimates are then replaced with the actual values as those values become known. See the exhibit "Example—Reinsurance Lag."

Example—Reinsurance Lag

A company writes workers compensation business in the state of Connecticut, thereby requiring it to participate in the state's residual market pool for that line of business. Participants share in pool results, with results reported with a three-month lag.

At year-end 20XX, the company has received reports from the pool administrators covering only periods through September 30, 20XX. The company would have to estimate the written and earned premium expected from the fourth quarter 20XX report not yet received. (Accruals would also have to be estimated for the corresponding losses and expenses from pool participation.)

[DA06365]

Large Deductible Credits

In some contracts with deductibles, the insurer pays the full claim and then seeks reimbursement from the insured for the deductible portion of the contract. In some jurisdictions, such arrangements are known as "large deductibles." The resulting policy premium for such large deductible policies is expected to be smaller than if no deductible existed. Different accounting systems may choose to treat the premium reduction due to the deductible credit differently. For example, regulatory accounting systems may wish to gross up the reported premiums for such deductible credits, with regard to premium assessment systems.

For example, assume that a state is using the insurance industry's premium for liability coverage to fund ancillary benefits for society. Examples of such benefits could include safety programs to reduce the types of accidents that trigger such liability. Assume the total industry premium is $10 billion, with 20 percent, or $2 billion, coming from the largest insureds. Assume that these insureds can reduce their premium by 50 percent by using "large deductibles." If no adjustment is made, the assessable premium will drop to $9 billion, shifting some of the burden of funding the safety program to smaller insureds. To prevent the assessment burden from shifting, the state may include the deductible credits, to some degree, in the assessable premium base.

UNEARNED PREMIUM

Under a deferral-matching approach, an insurer's unearned premium reserve reflects revenue associated with the unexpired portion of its in-force policies. A liability adequacy test is applied to the unearned premiums to determine whether the liability is sufficient to provide for the losses and expenses associated with the runoff of the unexpired policies.

Under a deferral-matching approach, pro rata or non-pro rata approaches may be used for revenue recognition of unearned premium. The method used to calculate the unearned premium reserve may vary depending on whether the associated coverage is evenly spread over the policy term. The unearned premium reserve is subject to a liability adequacy test. If it is determined that the unearned premium reserve is insufficient to meet its liabilities, a premium deficiency reserve may be required. Issues related to unearned premium that must be considered in conjunction with multiyear policies are inflation, the assignment of written premium, and the year to which premium is assigned.[6]

Pro Rata and Non-Pro Rata Approaches to Earning Premium

Unearned premium is most frequently viewed as a means of deferring revenue so that the revenue is earned as the insurance coverage is provided. Unearned premium may also be viewed as a reflection of the refund liability in the event of policy cancellation. This view of the unearned premium reserve does not apply to noncancelable policies (such as some warranty contracts).

The calculations of unearned premium under these two views may result in different values, such as when a penalty would be charged to the policyholder for early policy cancellation, although in practice, such differences are generally ignored. Ideally, the accounting framework will specify the view to use in quantifying the unearned premium reserve when the two views result in different values.

With regard to the deferral-matching view of unearned premium reserves, the current United States GAAP guidance (for property-casualty insurance) is to recognize premiums as revenue over the period of the contract in proportion to the amount of insurance protection provided. In practice, it is common to use a pro rata over time method of calculation, which assumes that the insurance protection is evenly spread over the policy term.

In some policies, the insurance protection is not evenly spread over the policy term. Examples include these:

- Policies that cover seasonal risks, such as snowmobile policies, for which the risk is concentrated in the winter months.

- Aggregate excess policies that insure losses above a specified amount over the policy period. The risk on these policies is greater toward the end of the policy term than at the beginning.

- Warranty policies, under which warranty claims (and mechanical breakdowns) usually increase as the product under the warranty ages.

- Financial guarantee and other performance bonds, where initial underwriting should make it unlikely for immediate nonperformance, resulting in greater likelihood of nonperformance as the contract ages.

For policies in which the insurance risk is not evenly spread throughout the policy period, it may be necessary (and may be required) to calculate a non-pro rata earning pattern for the premium. This may involve an actuarial calculation for how the risk of loss varies over the contract period. See the exhibit "Exhibit 1."

Exhibit 1

Example—Aggregate Excess Policies

Assume a policy with a $2 million premium that reimburses the policyholder when aggregate losses for the calendar year exceed $10 million. Assume that the losses covered by the policy are generally low-severity/high-frequency, with minimal catastrophe potential (for example, the policy is not meant to cover the risk of large losses but instead the risk that the expected losses were misestimated). Also assume that the expected losses are $8 million, and that the expected losses normally occur evenly throughout the year.

After one quarter, losses would have to be 500 percent of expected for attachment to occur. After two quarters, losses would have to be 250 percent of expected for attachment to occur. After three quarters, losses would have to be 167 percent of expected for attachment to occur. For the full year, losses would need to be 125 percent of expected for attachment to occur. As such, attachment is much less likely early in the year then later. If premium is earned evenly, then the earnings would be biased high early in the year, to the detriment of earnings later in the year.

In this example, first quarter losses of $4.5 million may make ultimate attachment more likely, but they do not trigger a loss. In most accounting systems, such greater probability of loss might be recognized as an unearned premium reserve deficiency, not necessarily as a loss reserve need.

[DA06377]

Non-pro rata earning approaches are generally more complex and involve more estimation than pro rata approaches. As such, accounting rules may allow the more simplistic pro rata methods to be used when the effect is not material to the financial statements. See the exhibit ""Material" Defined in the Context of Financial Statements."

"Material" Defined in the Context of Financial Statements

According to the Canadian Institute of Actuaries (CIA) Standards of Practice 1340.03, "'Material' has its ordinary meaning, but judged from the point of view of a user, having regard for the purpose of the work. Thus, an omission, understatement, or overstatement is material if the actuary expects it materially to affect either the user's decision making or the user's reasonable expectations."

Canadian Institute of Actuaries (CIA) Standards of Practice 1340.03 [DA06547]

Example—Auto Extended Warranty Coverage

Assume a company provides coverage that effectively extends the original warranty on an automobile. (Legal reasons may prevent the issuer from labeling such coverage as "warranty," but for simplicity purposes this example will call this coverage "extended warranty coverage.") How should premium of $100 be earned that extends a manufacturer's three-year warranty for two more years? Assume an expected loss ratio of 50 percent, no expenses, and that 20 percent of losses are expected in year 4 and 80 percent in year 5 (in the last year of the extended warranty). The following compares the possible results of earning the premium evenly over time versus earning the premium based on expected losses.

	Pro rata over time			Based on expected losses		
Year	EP	Loss	Loss Ratio	EP	Loss	Loss ratio
1	20	0	0 percent	0	0	–
2	20	0	0 percent	0	0	–
3	20	0	0 percent	0	0	–
4	20	10	50 percent	20	10	50 percent
5	20	40	200 percent	80	40	50 percent
Total	100	50	50 percent	100	50	50 percent

The danger is that management under the pro rata method will overestimate the underlying profitability, decreasing the price and growing the business. When carried to the extreme, such decision making can result in significant losses being locked in for several years before the company is aware of the mistake.

[DA06378]

Multiyear Policies

The risks covered by multiyear policies may be less likely to be spread evenly over the policy term, especially in a high-inflation environment. As such, multiyear policies may be candidates for non-pro rata earned premium recognition. For example, if inflation is 20 percent a year, then for a three-year policy with expected losses of $100 the first year, the expected losses would be $120 the second year and $144 the third year. This would imply that only about 27 percent, or 100 ÷ $364, of the three-year premium should be recognized the first year.

Issues may also arise when written premium is assigned for multiple-year policies. Some frameworks account for multiple-year policies with annual premium payments as a series of annual policies, with only the premium for the current year treated as "written." This is especially common for policies of indefinite term, such as reinsurance treaties that are automatically renewed annually unless canceled before a new year begins. (These policies are sometimes called "continuous.") In the extreme, a written premium definition for a continuous policy based on estimated ultimate premium for the policy's life could result in an infinite value, hence the desire to book only one year of premium at a time.

Liability Adequacy Test and the Premium Deficiency Reserve

The primary concept underlying the premium deficiency reserve is that any liability established should be subject to a liability adequacy test to determine whether the liability is expected to be sufficient at runoff. If the liability is expected to be insufficient, the financial statements are generally considered to be biased in that a future earnings loss (such as negative income) would be expected from the liability runoff. To prevent such a bias, a premium deficiency reserve is calculated.

The unearned premium reserve is generally considered deferred revenue. A liability adequacy test is used to determine if deferred revenue is sufficient to cover corresponding losses and expenses. If unearned premium is determined to be inadequate, most accounting frameworks require the booking of an additional liability, sometimes called a premium deficiency reserve.

The premium deficiency reserve is generally equal to the difference between the expected losses and expenses underlying the unearned premiums and the unearned premium reserve reported on the financial statements. The accounting framework in place may also reflect the time value of money and/ or provisions for adverse deviation in this calculation. For example, Canadian actuarial Standards of Practice and regulatory financial reporting requirements specify that the analysis of premium liabilities includes adjustments for both present value discounting and provisions for adverse deviation. This calculation results in a positive liability only if the unearned premium is not expected to be sufficient to cover the runoff of claims and expenses. If this calculation results in a zero or negative value, no liability is established.

The concern about bias is somewhat one-sided in many accounting frameworks. Most accounting frameworks find the booking of a liability that is expected to be insufficient almost totally unacceptable; however, these same accounting frameworks sometimes accept the booking of a liability that is expected to be excessive.

While it is a function of the unearned premium liability, the actual location of the premium deficiency reserve in the balance sheet can vary significantly by accounting framework. A portion of it may even be accounted for as a negative asset. In U.S. GAAP accounting, any premium deficiency reserve is first established as a contra-asset that reduces the corresponding deferred acquisition cost (DAC), with a liability established only for the remainder after the DAC has been reduced to zero. See the exhibit "Example—Auto Premium Deficiency Reserve."

Example—Auto Premium Deficiency Reserve

Assume:
Unearned premium liability of $100
Estimated losses from the unearned premium runoff of $95
Estimated expenses remaining from the runoff of the unearned premium liability of $15

Also assume no investment income or time value of money potential.

Premium deficiency reserve = (95 + 15) − 100 = $10.

If instead the expected losses were $75, then no premium deficiency reserve would be set up.

[DA06375]

An evaluation of the premium deficiency reserve can be quite involved, but these basic concepts are of particular importance:

• The premium deficiency reserve is an estimate of expected deficiency in the unearned premium liability at the balance sheet date. It should not reflect conditions that did not exist at the balance sheet date. For example, the unearned premium reserve for property insurance on December 31 should not reflect the effect of an earthquake that occurred January 15 of the following year, even if the calculations for the liability adequacy test were performed after the earthquake occurred. The earthquake would not be reflected in the calculation unless it was anticipated in advance of the balance sheet date.

• The accounting framework may include only the marginal expenses that are directly related to the runoff of the contract in the premium deficiency reserve calculation, and not fixed expenses and general overhead expenses. This is the case for current U.S. GAAP and statutory accounting.[7] These marginal expenses are typically much lower than the overall expense level used in pricing. Alternatively, the accounting framework may include average direct costs (such as underwriting), but not indirect costs (such as allocations of human resource departments), or may include all costs.

• The level of aggregation is important in the premium deficiency reserve calculation, given that indicated negative values are established as zero. The more detailed the level at which the premium deficiency reserve is calculated, the more likely a positive reserve will result (and the higher any positive reserve will be).

Example—Premium Deficiency Reserve—Aggregation Issue

Assume:

The premium deficiency reserve is calculated in two pieces. One piece is operation A and another piece is operation B.

The premium deficiency reserve on a stand-alone basis is as follows, before any application of minimum values:

Operation A:	–$20
Operation B:	$10

If the premium deficiency reserve is calculated for the combination of A and B, then the result is:

$$[-20 + 10] = -10 \text{ before applying the minimum}$$

0 after applying the minimum

If the premium deficiency reserve is calculated by piece, then added, the result is:

Operation A:	–20 before minimum, or 0 after minimum
Operation B:	10 before and after minimum
Total:	0 plus 10 = 10

In this example, the premium deficiency reserve is 0 if calculated on an overall aggregate basis, and $10 if calculated on an operation basis separately, then added together.

[DA06376]

THE RELATIONSHIP BETWEEN LOSS RESERVES AND THE UNEARNED PREMIUM RESERVE

In order to properly evaluate insurance contract liabilities under a deferral-matching approach, it is necessary to know which policy obligations are meant to be covered by the unearned premium liability and which are meant to be covered by the claim liability (that is, loss reserves).

The relationship between loss reserves and the unearned premium reserve entails these special considerations:

- While both cover claim obligations under policies, loss reserves and unearned premium reserve cover different portions of these claim obligations with no overlap.
- Deficiencies to either loss reserves or the unearned premium reserve can occur.
- Any deficiencies must be reflected in the appropriate reserve figure.

Under a deferral-matching approach, losses are recognized and reserved for only after the event triggering coverage has occurred. Loss reserves are established for events that occur during the expired portion of the policy period. Losses potentially arising from the unexpired portion of the policy are not covered by the loss reserves but instead are covered by the unearned premium reserve.

Either reserve may become deficient:

- The recorded liability for loss reserves may become a deficient estimate of the ultimate cost of incurred but unpaid losses. This may be due to new information having emerged since the original estimate was made or to a changing economic or legal environment.
- The recorded liability for the unearned premium reserve may be determined to be deficient with regard to the expected losses over the unexpired policy term. Possible reasons include new information regarding pricing and/or underwriting decisions or changes in the legal interpretation of policy language since the policy was sold.

Deficiency in one reserve does not necessarily indicate a deficiency in the other reserve. In general, any expected deficiency in the reserves for events that have not yet occurred will be reflected in the unearned premium reserve (and/or the premium deficiency reserve), and any deficiency in the reserves for events that have occurred will be reflected in the loss reserves. However, in some cases, deficiencies in loss reserves may result in a reevaluation of the adequacy of the unearned premium reserve.[8]

SUMMARY

Currently, most property-casualty insurer accounting frameworks use a deferral-matching approach to recognize premium revenue. These approaches employ written premium, unearned premium, and deposit liability accounts. Discussions at the IASB could result in a very different approach for revenue recognition for insurance contracts in the near future.

Because written premium is used in the property-casualty industry as a measure of growth, it is important that users of financial statements understand the many types of written premium transactions, including deposits, estimates, audits, endorsements and cancellations, reinstatement premiums, and retrospective rating adjustments. Installment premium billings are not considered written premium transactions in certain accounting frameworks. Depending on the circumstances and the accounting paradigm, policyholder dividends and tax surcharges may or may not be considered premiums.

Numerous factors can affect the timing, classification, and reporting of premiums. When analyzing financial statements, users should be aware of the implications of these special premium accounting issues:

- Financing—premiums versus service charges
- Earning premium before it is written
- Extended reporting endorsements (definite versus indefinite periods)
- Reinsurance lags
- Large deductible credits

Under a deferral-matching accounting framework, pro rata or non-pro rata approaches may be used for revenue recognition of unearned premium. The risks covered by multiyear policies may be less likely to be spread evenly over the policy term, especially in a high-inflation environment. As such, they may be candidates for non-pro rata earned premium recognition. A liability adequacy test is used to determine if the unearned premium reserve is sufficient to cover corresponding losses and expenses. If unearned premium is determined to be inadequate, most accounting frameworks require the booking of an additional liability, sometimes called a premium deficiency reserve.

In order to properly evaluate insurance contract liabilities under a deferral-matching approach, it is necessary to know which policy obligations are meant to be covered by the unearned premium liability and which are meant to be covered by the claim liability. Unearned premium reserves cover claims expected from the unexpired portion of in-force policies, while loss reserves cover unpaid claims from events occurring during the expired portion of policies. A deficiency may develop in one or the other reserve, or both, but a deficiency in one does not necessarily indicate a deficiency in the other.

ASSIGNMENT NOTES

1. Material is adapted with permission from the Casualty Actuarial Society Study Note, "Premium Accounting" by Ralph Blanchard.
2. Some jurisdictions commonly use the term "unearned premium reserve (UPR)" rather than "unearned premium liability." Some jurisdictions also commonly use the term "technical provisions" rather than "reserves." As the coverage period runs off, the unearned premium liability is proportionally reduced.
3. Material is adapted with permission from the Casualty Actuarial Society Study Note, "Premium Accounting" by Ralph Blanchard.
4. (1) Also known as a motor policy in some jurisdictions.

5. Material is adapted with permission from the Casualty Actuarial Society Study Note, "Premium Accounting" by Ralph Blanchard.

6. Material is adapted with permission from the Casualty Actuarial Society Study Note, "Premium Accounting" by Ralph Blanchard.

7. At the time this was drafted, the comparable rule for International Financial Reporting Standards (IFRS) was under development, with the outcome uncertain.

8. Material is adapted with permission from the Casualty Actuarial Society Study Note, "Premium Accounting" by Ralph Blanchard.

Direct Your Learning ▶▶

5

Property-Casualty Loss Accounting

Educational Objectives

After learning the content of this assignment, you should be able to:

▷ Describe the role of loss reserves, including the relationship over time between incurred losses, paid losses, reserves, and policyholders' surplus.

▷ Explain how case reserves are established for the following categories of loss reserves:

- Reported losses—payment certain

- Reported losses—payment uncertain

- Allocated loss adjustment expenses (ALAEs)

▷ Explain how bulk reserves are established for the following categories of loss reserves:

- Reported losses—payment uncertain

- IBNR reserves

- Loss adjustment expenses, both allocated and unallocated

▷ Describe the following issues related to loss and loss adjustment expense (LAE) accounting:

- Loss accounts

- Loss cycle

- Paid loss versus cash payment

- Recoverable amounts

- Accounting for discounted reserves

- Self-insurer issues

Property-Casualty Loss Accounting

LOSS RESERVES

Loss reserves are an important factor in determining the financial condition of insurers. Accurate reserving practices are critical to the stability and solvency of insurers.

Because insurers rely on estimates called loss reserves, they have difficulty establishing amounts that accurately reflect future loss and expense payments. However, because losses are a large portion of the liabilities recorded on an insurer's balance sheet, reserve amounts directly affect policyholders' surplus and insurer profitability.

Loss and Loss Adjustment Expense Reserves

Insurers must establish loss reserves to cover the delay between the time a loss occurs and the time the loss is settled and the claim is paid. Once a claim has been reported to the insurer, time is required to investigate the loss to determine whether the incident is covered under the policy and then to negotiate an appropriate settlement. This delay is shorter for most property claims and is usually longer for third-party liability claims, which often involve litigation. For example, a products liability or medical malpractice claim may take several years to settle and close, while a kitchen fire under a homeowners policy is usually closed within a few months.

Loss reserves also include **loss adjustment expense (LAE)** amounts, related either to individual claim files or to the overall claim operation, that cannot be allocated to a specific claim file. The National Association of Insurance Commissioners (NAIC) categorizes these expenses as either Defense and Cost Containment (DCC) or Adjusting and Other (AO).[1] DCC includes expenses related to the defense and litigation of claims. AO includes all other expenses, such as adjusters' salaries and other fees and expenses. Previously, the terms **allocated loss adjustment expense (ALAE)** and **unallocated loss adjustment expense (ULAE)** had been used to categorize loss expenses.

Despite the change in terminology, many insurance professionals continue to use the former terms. DCC expenses are often related to ALAE, and AO expenses are related to ULAE. Because actuarial techniques used to estimate unpaid LAE consider whether an expense can be directly associated with a particular claim, most actuarial literature continues to categorize loss adjustment expenses as either ALAE or ULAE. Loss adjustment expense reserves

Loss adjustment expense (LAE)

The expense that an insurer incurs to investigate, defend, and settle claims according to the terms specified in the insurance policy.

Allocated loss adjustment expense (ALAE)

The expense an insurer incurs to investigate, defend, and settle claims that are associated with a specific claim.

Unallocated loss adjustment expense (ULAE)

Loss adjustment expense that cannot be readily associated with a specific claim.

are related to loss reserves and represent estimates of future expenses for settling outstanding claims.

Loss reserve amounts are only one component of an insurer's total loss amount. Loss and LAE reserves are combined with **paid losses** to arrive at an **incurred losses** amount.

Paid losses

Losses that have been paid to, or on behalf of, insureds during a given period.

Incurred losses

The losses that have occurred during a specific period, no matter when claims resulting from the losses are paid.

Incurred but not reported (IBNR) reserves

A reserve established for losses that reasonably can be assumed to have been incurred but not yet reported.

Incurred losses = Paid losses + Loss reserves + Loss adjustment expense reserves

Insurers also establish bulk (or aggregate) reserves to estimate (1) the growth in reported case reserves or an amount for reported losses for which case reserves are inadequate, (2) losses that are assumed to have happened but have not yet been reported, and (3) additional costs of claims that have been reopened after previously being settled and closed. These bulk reserve components are collectively known as **incurred but not reported (IBNR) reserves**.

Establishing reserves for losses that have not yet been reported is more difficult than establishing reserves for known cases. IBNR reserves are generally estimated based on past experience and then modified for current conditions, such as increased claims costs and the current frequency and severity of reported claims.

Life Cycle of Incurred Losses

Loss reserves amounts must be reviewed and updated to reflect changes in paid losses and loss expense amounts over time. Insurers periodically update their estimates of incurred losses for past years using different methods. One approach is to update losses using an **accident-year method**, which aggregates incurred losses for a given period (such as twelve months) using all incurred losses for insured events that occurred during that period. Any losses that occurred in previous periods are not included.

Accident-year method

A method of organizing ratemaking statistics that uses incurred losses for an accident year, which consist of all losses related to claims arising from accidents that occur during the year, and that estimates earned premiums by formulas from accounting records.

For example, accident-year data for the calendar year 20X6 would include all events that occurred in that year. Loss amounts for events that occur in subsequent years would not be included in this amount. As loss payments are made during the accident year, paid losses increase and reserves decrease by an equal amount. Therefore, incurred losses are unchanged. However, incurred losses do change when a reserve is increased or decreased because of new information on a claim or because a new claim is reported. An accident year's accounts can be kept open for many years until all losses that occurred in that year are fully paid.

Ultimate loss

The final paid amount for all losses in an accident year.

Insurers attempt to estimate accurate loss reserves as soon as possible after the end of an accident year. If loss reserves have been accurately estimated, then incurred losses should equal ultimate losses at that point in time. In practice, an accident year's incurred losses are often less than **ultimate loss** amounts for some time after the end of the accident year. Information received after the end of an accident year usually causes loss reserves to increase, also causing incurred losses to increase for the accident year. This situation might occur when an insurer has to make a large payment as a result of a court judgment many years after the date of loss. This payment may not have been anticipated when reserves were originally established, and this causes incurred losses to increase for the accident year. The increase or decrease of incurred losses over time is called **loss development**.

For example, actuaries can review the life cycle of incurred losses related to a single accident year. Based on this review, it is determined that incurred losses increased from zero months to seventy-two months after the start of the accident year, at which point incurred losses equaled the ultimate loss amount. The review also indicates that losses for the accident year were not fully paid until 108 months after the start of the accident year. See the exhibit "Life Cycle of Incurred Losses for a Single Accident Year."

Loss development

The increase or decrease of incurred losses over time.

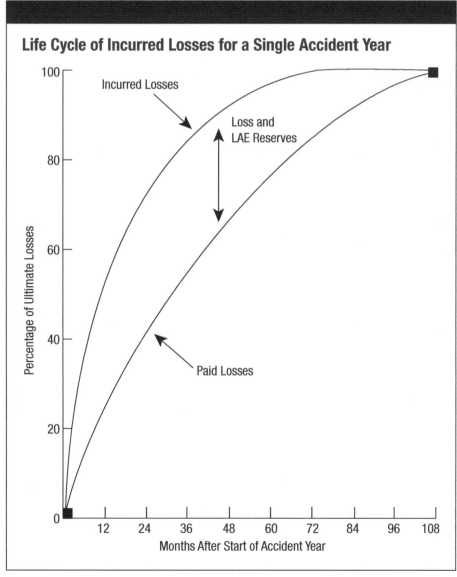

Life Cycle of Incurred Losses for a Single Accident Year

[DA06229]

Implications of Inadequate Loss Reserves

Loss amounts are a key element on insurers' financial statements, and accurate claim reserving is critical to maintaining the insurer's financial strength. Underestimating or overestimating the final cost of claims can distort an insurer's financial condition. Continued underreserving of claims over several years can lead to insolvency or bankruptcy for an insurer. Establishing and maintaining adequate loss reserves is important for the insurer's financial health because reserves directly affect the insurer's ability to maintain existing business and to grow in the future.

In their review of insurer financial statements, state regulators focus on the continued solvency of the insurer and its ability to pay claims in the future. Regulators are, therefore, also concerned about the adequacy of loss reserves and about insurers with a history of understating loss reserves. Insurers that consistently overstate loss reserves may also be of concern to regulators because doing so may lead to unwarranted rate increases over time and to overpriced insurance products. Continued overstating of loss reserves could result in tax penalties relating to the taxes that would otherwise apply to the resulting deferred income.

Past claims payments are also the basis of future rates. As part of ratemaking, actuaries base future rates not only on the amount paid on both open and closed claims, but on the amount reserved for open claims and IBNR claims. Consistent and accurate loss reserving translates into insurance rates that accurately reflect future loss potential.

Challenges to Establishing Adequate Loss Reserves

One internal cause of inadequate loss reserves is errors on the part of claims personnel. These errors can occur in several ways, such as when initial reserves are determined based on incomplete or inaccurate information. Reserve inaccuracy can also be the result of a lack of expertise on the claims representative's part or an unwillingness to reevaluate the claim and adjust the loss reserve amount where appropriate. Lack of training for claims representatives or frequent turnover in the claims department can result in underreserving or overreserving of losses as well. Furthermore, management changes, changes in reserving guidelines, or restructuring of reinsurance programs can affect the adequacy of loss reserves.

Because reserves should reflect the ultimate cost of a claim and not the claim's present value, they should account for the claim's future settlement value. For example, a medical malpractice claim could take many years to settle and close. During that time, external factors such as inflation may increase medical costs, or new and expensive medical technology may be developed. Whenever possible, the reserves for such claims should anticipate those increased costs.

Other external causes of inadequate loss reserves include changes in legislation or regulation, which could, for example, increase workers compensation benefits. Judgments in court cases can lead to new case law and open emerging areas of coverage, such as environmental or construction defects claims. Because related claims would not previously have been contemplated under existing coverage forms, claims personnel would need to review claims files to determine whether to establish reserves.

Relationship Between Loss Reserves and Surplus

The difference between any organization's assets and its liabilities indicates its net worth. For insurers, this net worth is designated as policyholders' surplus. This means that all of an insurer's net worth is available to satisfy claims before any owner is entitled to funds. Loss reserves are one of the largest liabilities on an insurer's balance sheet and are shown under the "Losses" element. Loss adjustment expense reserves are included within the "Loss Adjustment Expenses" element of the balance sheet.

If reserves are too low, the difference between assets and liabilities will result in an overstated policyholders' surplus amount. Underreserving will also result in an overstated underwriting profit for that year. As claims are settled in the future and reserves are adjusted, future underwriting profits may decrease. Once inadequate reserves are properly recognized and the liabilities amount is corrected on the balance sheet, policyholders' surplus will be reduced. When reserve amounts are set too high, policyholders' surplus will be understated and will need to be increased once the reserves are properly recognized. This is a critical issue for insurers because policyholders' surplus is vital to insurer financial strength. See the exhibit "Principal Elements of an Insurer Balance Sheet."

Principal Elements of an Insurer Balance Sheet

Assets	Liabilities
Bonds	Losses
Stocks	Loss Adjustment Expenses
Cash	Unearned Premiums
Premium Balances	**Surplus and Other Funds**
Reinsurance Recoverables	Surplus as Regards Policyholders

[DA06230]

For example, an insurer with $10 million in reserves and policyholders' surplus of $5 million has a ratio of reserves to policyholders' surplus of 2 to 1. An error of 10 percent in estimating reserves would cause an error of 20 percent in the stated policyholders' surplus. If reserves were initially established at $10 million and later adjusted to $11 million, the effect on policyholders' surplus would be a 20 percent decrease, from $5 million to $4 million. See the exhibit "Effect of Understated Reserves on Policyholders' Surplus."

Effect of Understated Reserves on Policyholders' Surplus

Table 1—Primary Insurer Balance Sheet

Assets		Liabilities	
Cash	$25,000,000	Unearned Premiums	$10,000,000
		Reserves	10,000,000
		Policyholders' Surplus	5,000,000
Total Assets	$25,000,000	Total Liabilities and Surplus	$25,000,000

Table 2—Primary Insurer Balance Sheet With 10 Percent Adjustment to Reserves

Assets		Liabilities	
Cash	$25,000,000	Unearned Premiums	$10,000,000
		Reserves	11,000,000
		Policyholders' Surplus	4,000,000
Total Assets	$25,000,000	Total Liabilities and Surplus	$25,000,000

[DA06231]

METHODS FOR ESTABLISHING CASE RESERVES

To accurately report their financial position, insurers must estimate reserves as precisely as possible. However, estimating reserves is difficult because, in most cases, the amount that the insurer will eventually pay for a claim is uncertain. For example, the insurer may not know all the facts about the underlying claim when estimating its reserves.

Bulk reserves

Reserves established for the settlement of an entire group of claims.

There are two general methods for establishing reserves for losses and loss adjustment expenses—case reserves and **bulk reserves**. For some categories of claims, reserves can be set using either the case or bulk reserve method. For example, in instances in which the amount of payment is uncertain for reported losses, loss reserves could be set for each individual loss (case) or for the whole group of losses (bulk).

With case reserves specifically, the primary insurer's claims department usually sets reserves. A claims file is established for each reported loss and includes an estimate of the ultimate loss that will be paid to the claimant. The claims representative's estimate of the ultimate loss, less any payments already made, makes up the case loss reserve for the file. Allocated loss adjustment expense reserves can also be established for each individual claim.

Case reserves can be established for these categories of loss reserves:

- Reported losses–payment certain
- Reported losses–payment uncertain
- Allocated loss adjustment expenses (ALAEs)

Reported Losses—Payment Certain

The reserve for reported losses for which the amount of payment is certain is the easiest of the loss reserves to calculate. Because the claimant and the insurer have already agreed on the amount of the payment, calculating this type of reserve is simply a matter of adding the agreed settlement amounts for all claims. Calculating reserves in the other categories is more complex.

Reported Losses—Payment Uncertain

More expertise is necessary to determine the amount to reserve for reported losses for which the amount of payment is uncertain. The insurer must estimate the ultimate loss using known information about the claim, historical loss data for similar claims, and the judgment of the individual making the estimate. If the claimant later reports additional facts that will affect the value of the claim, the insurer must adjust the reserve accordingly.

Three methods are commonly used to determine the case loss reserves for reported losses when the amount of payment is uncertain:

- Judgment method
- Average method
- Tabular method

Judgment Method

The first method of determining case loss reserves is the judgment method. With the **judgment method**, a claims representative estimates the value of each claim based mostly on professional experience. This method does not involve any statistical analysis.

One weakness of the judgment method is that the accuracy of its results depends on the quality and extent of the claims representative's experience. Two people may estimate vastly different figures for the same loss. Even reserves established by the same person for similar losses could vary from time to time.

Average Method

The second method for determining case loss reserves is based on statistical data and is generally called the **average method** or the factor method. Through this method, the case reserve for specific categories of claims is set at

Judgment method
A method to establish a case loss reserve based largely on experience with similar claims.

Average method
A method to establish a case reserve by using an average amount for specific categories of claims.

an average amount that is based on an analysis of past claims and is trended for inflationary changes, changes in amounts insured, and other factors that may cause future payments to differ from past payments.

The average method is most suitable for types of insurance in which claims are relatively frequent, reported and paid promptly, and not subject to extreme variations. Automobile physical damage is an example of a type of insurance with these characteristics. For example, every auto collision claim may be reserved at a value of $1,500, and that value is not changed until the claim is paid. The insurer may feel that setting more accurate reserves on this type of claim is not worth the expense associated with the extra effort.

Under the average method, reserves for some individual claims are inadequate, and reserves for other claims are excessive. However, if the average is accurate, the aggregate loss reserve accurately reflects the ultimate loss amounts for all outstanding claims.

If used alone, the average method may produce inadequate reserves for those types of liability insurance that have a wide variation in claims amounts and long delays in settlements (such as medical malpractice insurance and product liability insurance). In these cases, the average method and the judgment method are sometimes used together. Using this combined reserving approach, an average value is assigned to each claim as soon as it is reported. For example, every auto bodily injury claim may initially be reserved for an average value of $10,000. In sixty days, or as soon as additional information becomes available on the claim, the reserve is adjusted, based on judgment.

Tabular Method

Tabular method

A case reserving method that establishes an average amount for all claims that have similar characteristics in terms of the claimant's age, health, and marital status.

The third method of determining case loss reserves is the **tabular method**. This method is useful for calculating case loss reserves for lost income benefits under workers compensation insurance or for calculating structured settlement amounts under liability insurance.

The tabular method uses rates and factors from one or more actuarial tables to calculate the present value of future loss payments. This present value amount becomes the case loss reserve for those payments. These tables are examples of those that can be used:

- Morbidity tables, showing the likelihood of sickness or injury
- Mortality tables, showing the likelihood of death
- Annuity tables, showing the likelihood of survival
- Remarriage tables, showing the likelihood of remarriage by a widow or widower [2]

Each case loss reserve calculated by the tabular method can be considered an average reserve for all claims with the same characteristics (for example, claimants with the same age, health, and marital status). Consequently, the tabular method is likely to yield an appropriate total reserve for a large number of individual claims—even though the case reserve for any given claim can vary substantially from the amount ultimately paid for that claim. The primary weakness of the tabular method is that its applicability is limited to situations in which a fixed amount of benefits is paid over a period of time, such as a person's life; however, in these types of situations, it is the preferred method. See the exhibit "Calculating Case Reserves by Using the Tabular Method: An Example."

Calculating Case Reserves by Using the Tabular Method: An Example

Suppose a lost income benefit of $300 per week for life is payable to a fifty-year-old permanently disabled male worker. A case loss reserve for this benefit can be calculated by using mortality tables and present value factors. Mortality tables can be used to derive one-year probabilities of survival at each age. Because this person is disabled, the factors in the mortality table may need to be adjusted to reflect the mortality rates for disabled persons. Special mortality tables for this purpose have been developed. Using present value factors and the results of the mortality table values, actuaries can calculate the present value factor for an annual annuity of $1 payable to this person for life. Assume this present value factor is 16.412. The case reserve is calculated by multiplying the present value factor by the annual benefit amount. In this example, the case reserve would be $256,027 ($300 per week × 52 weeks × 16.412).

[DA09061]

Allocated Loss Adjustment Expenses (ALAEs)

Case reserves for ALAE can be established by using the judgment method or by adding a fixed percentage to each case loss reserve. The judgment method of establishing case reserves for ALAE suffers from the same weaknesses as the judgment method of establishing case loss reserves. For some types of insurance, simply adding a percentage to each loss reserve can produce accurate aggregate reserves for ALAE.

Correcting Case Reserves

At any point in time, the total case reserves for reported losses are likely to be inadequate because they tend to develop, or increase, over time.

One method for correcting inadequate total case reserves is to increase the case reserve for each claim. The simplest way to do this is to add the same percentage to each. These increases are often called "additional case reserves."

A more time-consuming method of correcting understated case reserves is to review each open claims file, increasing only those reserves that are inadequate. This approach assumes that either the reviewers can more accurately determine loss reserve amounts than those who established the original claim reserve or more information has become available on the claim.

For their own financial reporting purposes, reinsurers may supplement the primary insurer's case reserves. A reinsurer's claims personnel may review the primary insurer's claim files and add amounts that they feel are necessary to account for loss development. The reinsurer's total case reserves would then consist of the primary insurer's case reserves and the reinsurer's additional case reserves.

METHODS FOR ESTABLISHING BULK RESERVES

An insurer usually cannot identify specific claims with inadequate or excessive case reserves or predict which claims will reopen. Therefore, insurers make a general provision for additional reserves, called bulk reserves. For some types of insurance, the bulk reserves can be a substantial part of an insurer's total liabilities.

Typically determined by an actuary, bulk reserves can be established for these categories of loss reserves:

- Reported losses—payment uncertain
- Incurred but not reported (IBNR) reserves
- Loss adjustment expenses, both allocated and unallocated

Reported Losses—Payment Uncertain

Reserves for reported losses when the amount of payment is uncertain can be calculated on a bulk basis by subtracting the amount already paid for losses from a certain percentage of total earned premium. For example, an actuary may estimate general liability losses at 70 percent of an earned premium of $13 million, or $9.1 million. However, if $3 million has already been paid on these losses, then this amount is subtracted from the reserve, reducing the reserve from $9.1 million to $6.1 million.

IBNR Reserves

Incurred but not reported (IBNR) losses are losses that have occurred but have not yet been reported to the insurer. Because these losses have occurred, IBNR reserves are established and reflect estimates of unknown future loss payments. The IBNR loss category also includes a reserve for reported losses that are expected to develop; that is, the final payment for these losses is expected to exceed the amount for which they are currently reserved. (This component of IBNR is sometimes called IBNER: incurred but not enough reserved.)

For liability insurance, IBNR reserves are difficult to estimate because tremendous uncertainty exists regarding the number and size of losses yet to be reported and the development of reported losses.

A primary insurer usually has a liability for IBNR losses. Because estimating the number and average size of individual claims that may be reported late is difficult, IBNR reserves are, by their nature, a bulk reserve. IBNR reserves are residual reserves because, at any point in time, they equal the difference between incurred losses and ultimate losses. This formula shows the relationship:

IBNR reserves = Ultimate losses − Reported incurred losses

Three basic methods of estimating IBNR reserves exist, along with many acceptable alternative approaches:

- Loss ratio method
- Percentage method
- Loss triangle method

Loss Ratio Method

The first method of estimating IBNR reserves is the loss ratio method. This method assumes that the ultimate loss ratio will equal the loss ratio that was considered when calculating premium rates. Therefore, if the premium rates assumed a loss ratio of 80 percent, the ultimate losses are assumed to equal 80 percent of earned premiums. Deducting paid and reserved amounts for reported losses from the ultimate loss amounts yields the IBNR reserve.

The loss ratio method may be useful in the early stages of developing IBNR reserves for long-tail liability insurance. However, the loss ratio method should be used only for the first year or two after losses are incurred. More sophisticated and responsive methods should be used as soon as the actual reported losses provide an adequate basis for projecting IBNR reserves.

One weakness of the loss ratio method is that the actual loss ratio seldom equals the anticipated loss ratio. In fact, the difference between them can be substantial. If the actual loss ratio is less than the anticipated loss ratio, the loss ratio method results in redundant reserves. If the actual loss ratio is greater than the anticipated loss ratio, the method results in inadequate reserves. Furthermore, if the premium rates charged were inadequate (as evidenced by an underwriting loss), the reinsurer needs to recognize the inadequate subject premium rates used by the primary insurer when calculating the anticipated loss ratio.

Despite these weaknesses, the loss ratio method is often used in the early stages of development for long-tail liability insurance because, during this time, the loss triangle method is not completely reliable. After twenty-four months, the loss triangle method is likely to be more reliable than the loss ratio method.

Percentage Method

The second method of estimating IBNR reserves is the percentage method. This method uses historical relationships between IBNR reserves and reported losses to develop percentages that are used in IBNR forecasts. For example, if the IBNR losses were 30 percent of total incurred losses over a period of years, IBNR losses for a particular year may be estimated at 30 percent of incurred losses for that year. In its application, the percentage method develops a separate percentage for each accident year. If the trend (upward or downward) in the percentage of IBNR losses is measurable, the percentage used for projecting IBNR losses should reflect that trend.

The number of months necessary for losses to develop to their ultimate level varies depending on the type of insurance. The percentage method is acceptable for estimating property loss reserves because they can be estimated with reasonable accuracy soon after they are reported. It is likely to be less accurate for liability loss reserves, which typically take longer to develop.

The exhibit shows an IBNR calculation using the percentage method. In this example, IBNR losses are assumed to equal 20 percent of reported losses for the most recent accident year—twelve months of development (twelve months after the start of the policy year), 10 percent for the prior accident year—twenty-four months of development, and 5 percent for the next prior accident year—thirty-six months of development. Losses are assumed to be fully developed at forty-eight months after the start of the accident year. The IBNR reserve for each accident year is calculated by multiplying the reported losses for that accident year by the IBNR factor. The total IBNR reserve for the four accident years is $1,723,258. See the exhibit "Calculation of IBNR Reserve for X4 From Hypothetical Data Using the Percentage Method."

Calculation of IBNR Reserve for X4 From Hypothetical Data Using the Percentage Method

Historical Accident Year	Reported Losses ($)	Evaluation Point (Months of Development)	IBNR Factor	IBNR Reserve ($)
X1	4,725,679	48	0.00	0
X2	4,887,963	36	0.05	244,398
X3	4,878,845	24	0.10	487,885
X4	4,954,876	12	0.20	990,975
Total	$19,447,363			$1,723,258

[DA09067]

Loss Triangle Method

The third method for estimating IBNR reserves is the loss triangle method, which is also known as the loss development method, the chain link method, the chain ladder method, and the link ratio method. The loss triangle method uses historical loss data to calculate loss development factors with which to estimate IBNR reserves. This method is commonly used to determine IBNR reserves for liability insurance, particularly liability insurance that requires many years to fully develop. The loss triangle method is subject to wide variability in the first year or two of loss development and is more complex than the other reserving methods already presented. As with all loss reserving methods, this method will not produce reliable results unless the historical data and the actuarial assumptions are accurate.

A loss triangle is a display of historical loss data in the shape of a triangle. The data usually consist of the total reported losses for each historical year, although other data can be used, such as losses paid, number of claims paid, or average claim size. The nature of the estimates derived from a loss triangle depends on the data used in the triangle. The data in a reported losses triangle are used to project the development of total loss amounts for each historical year. IBNR loss reserves can then be derived based on this projected loss development. Because loss triangles analyze historical loss development patterns to forecast future loss development, a major assumption of the loss triangle method is that the historical pattern of development will continue.

The loss data used in a loss triangle may or may not include allocated loss adjustment expense (ALAE) information. If the loss data include ALAE, then the forecasted loss amounts will also include it. (In some cases, separate loss triangles are used to estimate ALAE.)

These are the four major steps for calculating IBNR reserves from a loss triangle:

1. Organize historical data in a loss triangle format
2. Calculate twelve-month loss development factors from the loss triangle
3. Calculate ultimate loss development factors from the twelve-month development factors
4. Use ultimate loss development factors to calculate the IBNR reserve

The first step in the loss triangle method is to organize historical data in a loss triangle format. A simplified loss triangle using the severity of reported losses is shown in the exhibit. This loss triangle is based on incurred losses not including ALAE, and it assumes that ultimate losses can be accurately estimated at seventy-two months after the start of an accident year. See the exhibit "Loss Triangle Based on Incurred Losses ($000)."

Loss Triangle Based on Incurred Losses ($000)

Accident Year	Months of Development (after beginning of accident year)					
	12	24	36	48	60	72 Ultimate
X1	10,000	10,200	10,300	10,350	10,375	10,375
X2	12,000	12,300	12,500	12,600	12,650	12,650
X3	14,000	14,500	14,750	14,850	14,900	
X4	16,000	16,600	16,900	17,050		
X5	18,000	18,800	19,200			
X6	20,000	21,000				
X7	22,000					

[DA09068]

Each row of data in the "Loss Triangle Based on Incurred Losses ($000)" exhibit shows historical estimates of the incurred loss amounts for the accident year shown at the left end of the row. For example, the first row shows data for accident year X1. On December 31, X1 (twelve months after the start of the X1 accident year), the primary insurer estimated its incurred losses for accident year X1 to be $10,000,000. On December 31, X2 (twenty-four months after the start of the X1 accident year), the estimate for X1 accident-year losses had increased to $10,200,000. By December 31, X6 (seventy-two months after the start of the X1 accident year), the estimate for X1 losses had reached $10,375,000. At that point, the primary insurer assumed that the incurred losses reserves for accident year X1 had reached their ultimate value.

The lowest diagonal of the table, running from $22,000,000 on the left to $12,650,000 on the right, shows the estimate for each year's losses as of December 31, X7, the latest year for which data are available. On December 31, X8, another diagonal of severity data should be added below the figures in the table.

The second step in the loss triangle method is to calculate twelve-month loss development factors from the loss triangle. The exhibit uses data in the "Loss Triangle Based on Incurred Losses ($000)" exhibit to calculate loss development factors based on changes in incurred losses over successive twelve-month periods. These factors are called twelve-month loss development factors (also known as age-to-age loss development factors and link ratios). For example, the first factor for X1 (1.020) shows the change in the company's estimates of X1 accident-year losses from December 31, X1, to December 31, X2. It was calculated by dividing the twenty-four month figure for X1 by the twelve-month figure for X1 ($10,200,000 ÷ $10,000,000 = 1.020). Each of the other figures in this exhibit's triangle was calculated in the same manner. The X7 year has no twelve-month loss development factor because two successive estimates are required to calculate a loss development factor, and only one estimate is available. See the exhibit "Calculating Twelve-Month Loss Development Factors."

Calculating Twelve-Month Loss Development Factors

Accident Year	Twelve-Month Loss Development Factors				
	12 to 24	24 to 36	36 to 48	48 to 60	60 to Ultimate
X1	1.020	1.010	1.005	1.002	1.000
X2	1.025	1.016	1.008	1.004	1.000
X3	1.036	1.017	1.007	1.003	
X4	1.038	1.018	1.009		
X5	1.044	1.021			
X6	1.050				
Average	1.036	1.016	1.007	1.003	1.000
5-Year Average	1.039	1.016	1.007	1.003	1.000
3-Year Average	1.044	1.019	1.008	1.003	1.000
Selected	1.044	1.019	1.008	1.003	1.000

[DA09069]

The lower section of the "Calculating Twelve-Month Loss Development Factors" exhibit shows the derivation of twelve-month loss development factors that are used to estimate ultimate loss amounts for each historical accident year. The row labeled "Average" shows the average of all of the twelve-month loss development factors above it. The next row shows the average of the twelve-month factors for the five most recent years above it.[3] The third row shows the average of the twelve-month loss development factors for the three most recent years.

The last row in the "Calculating Twelve-Month Loss Development Factors" exhibit, labeled "Selected," shows the twelve-month factors that an analyst may choose. Selecting twelve-month factors is a matter of judgment. In the exhibit, the averages show an increasing trend. That is, the three-year average is greater than the five-year average, and, in the first column, the five-year average is greater than the overall average. Therefore, an analyst would probably select the largest of the three averages, without modification. See the exhibit "Selecting Twelve-Month Loss Development Factors."

Selecting Twelve-Month Loss Development Factors

The selection process involves comparing the average factors for various periods, such as those used in the "Calculating Twelve-Month Loss Development Factors" exhibit. The time periods used reflect the types of claims being estimated. The following approach may be helpful in selecting a factor:

- If the three averages show an increasing trend, select the largest factor.
- If the three averages show a decreasing trend, select the smallest factor.
- If the three averages do not show a trend, select the factor intermediate in value.

A selected factor can be adjusted if, in the actuary's opinion, it is inconsistent with the loss data or other adjacent factors. For example, most actuaries would expect each twelve-month loss development factor to be smaller than the factor immediately preceding it because as losses age, loss development tends to slow down. For example, for X1, the twenty-four-to-thirty-six-month factor (1.010) is lower than the twelve-to-twenty-four-month factor (1.020).

[DA09070]

Ultimate loss development factor

A factor that is applied to the most recent estimate of incurred losses for a specific accident year to estimate the ultimate incurred loss for that year.

The third step in the loss triangle development method is to calculate **ultimate loss development factors** from the twelve-month loss development factors. The exhibit shows the calculation of ultimate loss development factors. Each selected factor from the "Calculating Twelve-Month Loss Development Factors" exhibit is multiplied by the other selected factors to its right to calculate an ultimate loss development factor. See the exhibit "Calculating Ultimate Loss Development Factors."

Calculating Ultimate Loss Development Factors

Time Period	Ultimate Loss Development Factor
60 Months to Ultimate	$1.000 = 1.000$
48 Months to Ultimate	$1.003 \times 1.000 = 1.003$
36 Months to Ultimate	$1.008 \times 1.003 \times 1.000 = 1.011$
24 Months to Ultimate	$1.019 \times 1.008 \times 1.003 \times 1.000 = 1.030$
12 Months to Ultimate	$1.044 \times 1.019 \times 1.008 \times 1.003 \times 1.000 = 1.076$

[DA09071]

The fourth step in the loss triangle method is to use ultimate loss development factors to calculate the IBNR reserve. Multiplying the ultimate loss development factor from the "Calculating Ultimate Loss Development Factors" exhibit by the latest evaluation of losses for each year ("Loss Triangle Based on Incurred Losses ($000)" exhibit) gives an estimate of ultimate losses for each accident year, as shown in column 5 of the exhibit. The IBNR reserve (column 6) is calculated by subtracting incurred and reported losses (column 2) from estimated ultimate losses (column 5). See the exhibit "Calculating IBNR Reserves Using Loss Development Factors."

Calculating IBNR Reserves Using Loss Development Factors

(1) Historical Accident Year	(2) Incurred and Reported Losses ($000)	(3) Months of Development	(4) Ultimate Loss Development Factor	(5) Estimated Ultimate Losses ($000)	(6) IBNR Reserve ($000)
X1	10,375	72	1.000	10,375	0
X2	12,650	72	1.000	12,650	0
X3	14,900	60	1.000	14,900	0
X4	17,050	48	1.003	17,101	51
X5	19,200	36	1.011	19,411	211
X6	21,000	24	1.030	21,630	630
X7	22,000	12	1.076	23,672	1,672
Total	$117,175			$119,739	$2,564

[DA09072]

The data in the "Loss Triangle Based on Incurred Losses ($000)" exhibit are consistent, making it easy for the analyst to arrive at reasonable loss development factors. Most loss triangles are less consistent and include anomalous data items.

Such anomalies may result from chance variations in loss frequency or severity, from changes in rules of law, or from delays in adjusting claims. They may also result from conscious decisions made by claim personnel to increase or decrease the level of case reserves, as well as from changes to the level of case reserves resulting from shifting responsibilities in the claims handling process.

Systematic increases in loss reserves over time indicate a consistent practice of carrying inadequate case reserves. These systematic increases create larger than normal loss development factors.

After a period of systematic increases in loss reserves, knowing whether the reserves are still inadequate, or whether they are now correct, is difficult. However, the typical assumption is that the reserves are still inadequate. The loss triangle itself does not indicate the adequacy of loss reserves. That determination requires a careful analysis of individual claims files or, in many cases, additional data on individual claims.

Loss Adjustment Expenses

Bulk reserves can be used for both ALAE and unallocated loss adjustment expense (ULAE).

Allocated Loss Adjustment Expense

Bulk reserves for ALAE can be estimated by applying a percentage factor to either earned premiums or incurred losses. The percentage factor is determined by analyzing the insurer's experience. For example, if experience shows that ALAE averages 25 percent of incurred losses, then 25 percent is applied to current incurred losses to estimate the reserve for ALAE.

One disadvantage of this method of estimating ALAE is that the calculation assumes no changes have occurred that affect the factor. If changes have occurred, the factor must be adjusted. Another disadvantage results from the manner in which losses are usually settled. Small losses, especially those settled without payment, are usually settled more quickly than large losses. Consequently, total loss reserves at any given time are likely to include a disproportionate number of large losses. Because large losses usually involve proportionately more ALAE than small losses, the percentage method may underestimate the ALAE reserve. Calculating ALAE using the loss triangle method may overcome this problem.

Unallocated Loss Adjustment Expense

By definition, ULAE cannot be attributed to specific claims. Consequently, the reserve for such expenses must be estimated on a bulk basis. The reserve for ULAE is usually estimated as a percentage of the sum of incurred losses and ALAE. The insurer determines the percentage based on experience.

Because ULAE consists of budgeted items, the total amount to be paid in a given year is easy to estimate at the beginning of the year. However, some of the ULAE paid in a given year is related to losses incurred in earlier years, particularly for long-tail liability insurance. Allocating current expenses to prior accident years is common, but such allocations may distort current accident year expense.

LOSS AND LOSS ADJUSTMENT EXPENSE ACCOUNTING

Several issues are related to loss and loss adjustment expense (LAE) accounting.

The largest expenses associated with insurance policies are claim payments (losses) and loss adjustment expense (LAE), while the largest liabilities on most insurers' balance sheets are loss reserves and LAE reserves.

Loss adjustment expenses include allocated loss adjustment expenses and unallocated loss adjustment expenses. Allocated loss adjustment expenses are those expenses, such as attorneys' fees and other legal costs, that are incurred in connection with and are assigned to specific claims. Unallocated loss adjustment expenses are all other claim adjustment expenses and include salaries, utilities, and rent apportioned to the claim adjustment function but not readily assignable to specific claims.

The definition of allocated and unallocated loss adjustment expenses for reserving purposes varies among insurers, and an individual insurer's practice for reserving may not always conform to its definition for statistical reporting or ratemaking purposes.[4]

These issues are related to loss and LAE accounting:

- Loss accounts
- Loss cycle
- Paid loss versus cash payment
- Recoverable amounts
- Accounting for discounted reserves
- Self-insurer issues[5]

Loss Accounts

There are two basic accounting transactions involving losses: payment of claims and changes (either increases or decreases) in claim reserves. (The terms "loss" and "claim" and the terms "reserve" and "liability" are used interchangeably in this discussion. Use of these terms varies by accounting framework and by jurisdiction, and sometimes by organization within a given accounting framework and/or jurisdiction.) These transactions affect the income statement through incurred losses. Incurred losses may be calculated using this formula:

Incurred losses = Paid losses + (Ending loss reserves – Beginning loss reserves)

Several loss reserve accounts may exist in an organization's ledger. All ledgers will generally have the categories of case reserve (the estimate of unpaid claims established by a claim adjuster or the claim system[6]) and incurred but not reported (IBNR) reserves, as several jurisdictions require that these amounts be disclosed separately in annual financial reports. These other accounts may also be established:

- Bulk reserve—This reserve represents the estimated deficiency in the aggregate of case reserves for known claims. If forced to assign this to either case reserves or IBNR reserves, some will assign it to case reserves, as it represents reserves for claims that have already been reported. Others will assign it to IBNR, as it represents an aggregate calculation above claim adjuster estimates not reliably assignable to an individual claim.

- Additional case reserve—This represents an additional reserve for an individual claim, above the level established by the claim adjuster. This reserve is most common for claims under assumed reinsurance contracts, where the case reserve comes directly from the ceding company, as it allows the assuming company to record a different estimate for the value of a claim than that recorded by the ceding company.

Organizations may or may not also set up loss reserve accounts for reopened claims, anticipated subrogation or salvage recoveries, deductible recoveries (where the full loss is paid by the insurer, who then bills the insured for the deductible), expected legal defense costs, and similar items.

Reserve amounts may be positive or negative. For example, bulk reserves could be negative if the assumption is that case reserves will be redundant in the aggregate. Case reserves for a claim could be negative if the assumption is that amounts paid-to-date on a claim are greater than the ultimate value and that some future recovery of paid amounts is expected. Some insurers' claim systems may disallow negative case reserves, in which case the possibility of redundant or excessive case reserves would need to be addressed through other reserves, such as bulk reserves or subrogation and salvage reserves.

Loss Cycle

Incurred losses reported in financial statements are typically broken into two parts:

- The initial estimate of incurred losses for the most recent exposure period (generally the most recent accident year)
- The changes in the estimate of incurred losses for prior periods (usually prior accident years)

Two general approaches are used to determine the initial recognition of losses for the current accident year: those based on actual claim activity and those based on accrual of estimated incurred losses based on the level of earned exposure. The life cycle of incurred claims for each of these approaches can be tracked.

Actual Claim Activity

Under the actual claim activity approach, the incurred losses for the most recent exposure period are initially established based on the actual claim activity, with possible additional loss reserves established to allow for IBNR claims or any expected deficiency/redundancy in the case reserves established by the claim adjuster. For subsequent valuations of the same group of claims, changes in claim adjuster estimates directly affect incurred losses. The aggregate reserves, such as bulk and IBNR reserves, are run off over time based on studies of historical data or other actuarial studies. See the exhibit "Example—Where Reserving Is Based at Inception on Actual Claim Activity."

Example—Where Reserving Is Based at Inception on Actual Claim Activity

Accident Month	Accounting Month	Reported Claims	Paid	Case Reserves	IBNR	Ending Reserves	Beginning Reserves	Incurred Losses
a	b	c	d	e	f	g	h	i
						$(g)=(e)+(f)$		$(i)=(d)+(g)-(h)$
Jan. XX	Jan. XX	3	15	15	30	45	0	60
Jan. XX	Feb. XX	2	25	10	20	30	45	10
Jan. XX	Mar. XX	0	10	0	10	10	30	-10
Jan. XX	Apr. XX	1	5	5		5	10	0
Jan. XX	May XX		5	0		0	5	0
			60					60

[DA06367]

The exhibit tracks the accounting entries resulting from claims for accident month January 20XX for a hypothetical company and line of business, from initial valuation to the final payment for the accident month.

To simplify the example, these assumptions are made:

- All claims are reported within four months of the loss event.
- Earned premium for the month is $100.
- Each claim is worth $10, one-half paid in the month of reporting, and one-half paid in the subsequent month.
- Case reserves are established at $10 once the claim is reported.
- The initial IBNR is set based on thirty percent of earned premium, run off evenly over the next three months.
- No bulk reserve is necessary (beyond that which may be implicit in the IBNR calculation).

This example displays the loss cycle for a particular accident month. The insurer's financial reports for a particular accounting month will reflect numerous accident months with multiple transactions of loss payments and changes in reserves during that month.

The establishment of the initial reserves for an exposure period based on actual activity is commonly used when most of the claims are reported relatively quickly and settled quickly, such as for certain property lines in many jurisdictions. This approach is not possible if claims are reported slowly and/or where the initial claim adjuster estimates are not sufficiently reliable indicators of ultimate payout.

Accrual of Estimated Incurred Losses Based on the Level of Earned Exposure

The initial incurred loss estimate is commonly established based on an *a priori* estimate of loss exposure for the period for product lines with slower reporting and/or payment patterns or when the initial case reserves are less reliable at initial valuation. An initial estimate of incurred losses based on an expected loss ratio times earned premium is an example of this approach. See the exhibit "Example—June 20XX Reserve Setting."

Example—June 20XX Reserve Setting

Step 1—Determine Incurred Losses

AY 20XX

June 20XX earned premium	$1,000	a
Expected loss ratio	60%	b
Incurred losses	$600	c

All prior years

Change in prior estimate of ultimate incurred losses	500	d

Step 2—Determine IBNR Reserves

		AY 20XX	All Prior	Total		Source
	May 31, 20XX case reserves	$500	$4,800	$5,300	e	ledger
	May 31, 20XX IBNR	900	5,300	6,200	f	ledger
	May 31, 20XX total reserves	1,400	10,100	11,500	g	(e) + (f)
−	Paid losses in June 20XX	100	400	500	h	ledger
+	Incurred losses in June 20XX	600	500	1,100	i	(c) + (d)
	June 30, 20XX total reserves	$1,900	$10,200	$12,100	j	(g)−(h)+(i)
	June 30, 20XX case reserves	700	4,750	5,450	k	ledger
	June 30, 20XX IBNR reserves	1,200	5,450	6,650	l	(j) − (k)

[DA06368]

To simplify the example, these assumptions are made:

- Claim activity is tracked and reserves are established by accident year.
- Earned premium for the 20XX calendar year is $1,000 per month.
- Based on an analysis of pricing and loss trends and expected underwriting, management expects a 60 percent loss ratio for the 20XX accident year.

- Only two loss reserve accounts are maintained: case reserves and IBNR reserves.
- These two reserve accounts are further split into two parts: the current accounting year (which is 20XX in this example) and all prior years.

In this example, management determines the incurred losses for the current accident year based on earned premium for the period multiplied by the selected loss ratio, and then performs regular (periodic) actuarial loss reserve reviews (such as every quarter or every year) to determine whether prior accident year estimates should be changed. It is not unusual for an insurer to schedule these periodic reviews such that the prior accident year claim liabilities from some product lines are reviewed more frequently than others—for example, lines with the slowest development patterns may be reviewed only annually, while those with faster development may be reviewed quarterly or even monthly.

An insurer can use one of the approaches for some of its lines and the other approach for its other lines. Both approaches may be used on the same line by basing the reserves early in an accident year on a loss ratio times earned premium and then changing the approach to reserve based on actual claims experience once the available claims data becomes more credible. An insurer may also choose to use one method for some loss types and the other method for other loss types for the same product line (for example, liability and physical damage for private passenger automobile insurance). The insurer can generally choose its approach unless the applicable accounting rules and/or insurance laws and regulations dictate a particular reserve estimation method.

Paid Loss Versus Cash Payment

The accounting examples provided include entries for paid losses. Non-accountants may believe that paid losses is equivalent to cash paid to claimants. In most cases, it is, but there may be lags and estimates involved.

When a claim adjuster writes a check to a claimant, a simultaneous paid loss transaction may not be recorded in the accounting system. For example, if an adjuster is writing checks to policyholders in the middle of a catastrophe zone, the insurer may not be able to instantly record the payment in the claim accounting ledger. Instead, the necessary detail to record the payment in an accounting ledger may not be available for days.

When a payment is made but the corresponding entry (such as "paid losses") has not yet been made, the payment is registered to a suspense account. Growth in the claim suspense account would normally signify some backlog in clearing records in the claim system, or an influx of claim activity that has yet to be recorded as paid losses because of the need to incorporate additional details (such as including all the requisite claim coding fields).

Booking lags can also generate differences between what is recorded in paid losses and true cash transactions. For example, a company that closes one of its subsidiary ledgers prior to the actual calendar year closing date (such as closing a claim ledger on November 30 for December 31 reporting) may be required by their accounting rules to estimate the paid amounts that occurred between the subsidiary ledger closing and the accounting "as of" date. These estimated paid amounts would be adjusted to actual amounts once the actual values are known.

Recoverable Amounts

Many insurance operations have various types of recoverables or cash offsets to paid claims. These recoverables can vary by jurisdiction and product. These are some common types of recoverables or offsets:

- Salvage and subrogation
- Ceded reinsurance
- Deductibles

Salvage represents any amount that the insurer is able to collect from the sale of assets the insurer takes over ownership of as a result of the claim payment (such as when an insurer sells the remains of a wrecked automobile as scrap metal).

Subrogation refers to an insurer's right to recover the amount of claim payment from a third party responsible for the injury or damage. Ceded reinsurance represents a recoverable based on the insurer's ceded reinsurance contracts.

Recoverables associated with deductibles arise when the insurer pays the entire claim and then seeks reimbursement from the insured for the amount of deductible. There are no such recoverables for deductibles when the insurer pays only the portion of the claim above the deductible.

These recoverables are generally recorded as negative paid losses, but the timing of the negative paid entry may not match the actual cash transaction. For example, items that require billing a third party for the recoverable amount may be recorded as "negative paid" when the bill is sent. See the exhibit "Example—Ceded Reinsurance."

Several possible approaches may be used for an accounting framework if the billed amounts are subsequently determined to be unrecoverable. The accounting may require a reversal of the original recoverable entries (such as is required in United States statutory reporting for ceded reinsurance). The accounting may also require a write-off of the recoverable balance in a different income statement account (such as "other income," as currently occurs for U.S. statutory reporting as of 2007 for billed deductible recoverable amounts).

Example—Ceded Reinsurance

Assume paid direct losses in May 20XX of $100, subject to a 50 percent cession. Assume the reinsurance billing was lagged one month (June 20XX), with collection lagged an additional month (July 20XX). (Note that this ignores any loss reserve or underwriting income statement entries that may result.)

May 20XX (selected) accounting entries
Paid losses $ 100

June 20XX (selected) accounting entries/balances
Paid losses   −$ 50
Reinsurance recoverable (asset) $ 50

July 20XX (selected) accounting entries/balances
Reinsurance recoverable (asset) $ 0
Cash $ 50

[DA06369]

Accounting for Discounted Reserves

Designing an accounting framework using discounted loss reserves creates its own issues in that the ultimate paid losses will be recorded at nominal value, which is more than the recorded discounted loss reserves. The accounting framework must therefore determine how to treat the increase in the reserve resulting from the amortization of the discount.

There are several possible approaches for handling discounting in an accounting framework. The accounting framework will generally specify which balance sheet and income statement discounting approaches will apply to that framework, or whether certain options exist for the treatment of discounting under that framework.

For balance sheet purposes, the amount of the discount could be treated as an asset with the liability reported on an undiscounted basis. Alternatively, the liability could be established on a discounted basis directly. Other options may exist, such as including the discount as a contra-liability in a separate liability account.

The establishment of any present value estimates will require the reporting of the unwinding of discount over time, somewhere in the income statement. The current approach used in many jurisdictions is to record the increase resulting from the discount amortization as incurred losses. This may appear to strengthen reserves in certain reports unless accompanied by adequate disclosure.

An alternative approach (not yet widely used for insurance loss accounting) is to record the income statement effect of increasing loss reserves resulting from discount amortization as interest expense. When interest expense is reported together with interest income, incurred losses would remain at the initial discounted value, unless incurred loss estimates change. Additionally, investment income would be less in this accounting framework than in many current insurance accounting frameworks.

Self-Insurer Issues

Current insurance accounting standards do not cover liability for events that are self-insured. Instead, liability for these events may fall under more generic accounting requirements that apply to all businesses. For example, liability for many of these events in the U.S. would be covered by Financial Accounting Standard (FAS) 5 "Accounting for Contingencies," while the applicable accounting rule for those following International Accounting Standards Board (IASB) standards is International Accounting Standard (IAS) 37 "Provisions, Contingent Liabilities and Contingent Assets." FAS 5 generally requires amounts to be reliably estimable before they are booked, and a self-insurer may or may not have sufficient volume to allow for reliable estimation of its aggregate self-insured liabilities. Additionally, reported claims may be estimated reliably enough to meet the accounting recognition requirements, even when IBNR claims cannot be estimated reliably. Recent changes in IAS 37 will result in a revised approach.

When the self-insured liabilities are related to employees, such as workers compensation or self-insured employee health insurance, special accounting rules designed for employee benefits may apply. This is currently the case under FASB and IASB rules.

SUMMARY

Insurers establish loss reserves to reflect amounts that will be needed in the future to pay claims that have occurred but are not yet closed. Inadequate loss reserves can lead to overstating or understating an insurer's profitability.

Case reserves are reserves established for the settlement of an individual claim. They can be established for three categories of loss reserves: reported losses–payment certain, reported losses–payment uncertain, and allocated loss adjustment expenses. The three general methods of establishing case loss reserves when the amount of payment is uncertain are the judgment method; the average, or factor, method; and the tabular method.

Bulk reserves are reserves established for settling an entire group of claims. They can be established for three categories of loss reserves: reported losses–payment uncertain; IBNR reserves; and loss adjustment expenses, both allocated and unallocated. The three basic methods of establishing IBNR reserves are the loss ratio method, the percentage method, and the loss triangle method.

These issues are related to loss and loss adjustment expense (LAE) accounting:

- Loss accounts
- Loss cycle
- Paid loss versus cash payment
- Recoverable amounts
- Accounting for discounted reserves
- Self-insurer issues

ASSIGNMENT NOTES

1. National Association of Insurance Commissioners, Accounting Practices and Procedures Manual, vol. III, Statutory Issue Paper no. 55 (Washington, D.C.: National Association of Insurance Commissioners, 2009), p. IP-55-2.

2. (1) The remarriage table is used only if the provisions of the insurance policy state that benefits are terminated by remarriage.

3. Because of the abbreviated nature of this exhibit, the average of all years and the average for five years are the same except for the first column. This would not usually be the case in practice.

4. "Casualty Actuarial Society, Statement of Principles Regarding Property and Casualty Loss and Loss Adjustment Expense Liabilities," www.casact.org/library/astin/vol10no3/305.pdf (accessed September 17, 2010).

5. Material is adapted with permission from the Casualty Actuarial Society Study Note, "Basic Insurance Accounting—Selected Topics" by Ralph Blanchard.

6. Note that some claim departments define the case reserve as their estimate of the ultimate value for the claim, including amounts paid-to-date. This can occur even when the term is used to represent unpaid amounts only among the actuaries in the same company.

6

Insurer Asset Valuation and Management

Educational Objectives

After learning the content of this assignment, you should be able to:

▷ Explain how bond and stock investments are valued and reported on both GAAP and statutory financial statements.

▷ Explain how private placements, commercial mortgage-backed securities (CMBS), residential mortgage-backed securities (RMBS), and originated mortgages are valued and reported on both GAAP and statutory financial statements.

▷ Explain how deferred tax assets, guaranty funds receivable, and fixed assets are valued and reported on both GAAP and statutory financial statements.

▷ For property-casualty and life/annuity companies, explain the following:

• Asset portfolio management

• Asset concentrations

• Asset-liability matching

▷ Explain how states regulate insurer assets.

Insurer Asset Valuation and Management

FINANCIAL REPORTING OF BONDS AND STOCKS

The majority of insurer assets consist of bond and stock investments. Insurers must follow accounting rules for valuing and reporting bonds and stocks under both generally accepted accounting principles (GAAP) and statutory accounting principles (SAP). The valuation of these securities has a significant effect on insurers' reported earnings and capital.

GAAP provide guidance for the valuation and reporting of bonds and stocks. This guidance depends primarily on the length of time the investor intends to hold the bond or stock. SAP employ similar valuation concepts to those of GAAP, but SAP differ in the treatment of bonds. Under SAP, the reported value of bonds also depends on their credit rating and whether they are held by a property-casualty insurer or a life insurer.

GAAP Reporting

Under GAAP, the Financial Accounting Standard Board's (FASB's) Accounting Standards Codification (ASC) Topic 320 provides guidance on accounting and reporting for assets held in an investment portfolio. At the core of FASB ASC 320 is fair value accounting—the concept that any asset or liability that will ultimately settle for cash should be held at fair value. FASB ASC 320 outlines the holding-period classifications for assets, valuation on the balance sheet, and the treatment of realized capital gains or losses and **unrealized capital gains** or losses.

Holding-Period Classifications

An organization investing in securities must classify them for GAAP purposes as "held-to-maturity securities," "available-for-sale securities," or "trading securities." The held-to-maturity classification applies only to debt securities.

Classifying a debt investment (bond) as a held-to-maturity security means the investing organization must intend, and have the ability, to hold the debt security to its maturity date. Under GAAP, held-to-maturity debt securities are valued at **amortized cost**.

Trading securities are equity (stocks) and debt (bonds) investments that an organization holds for a short period and intends to sell in the near future.

Unrealized capital gain

The profit not yet earned on a held asset when it exceeds its original purchase price but has not been sold.

Amortized cost

An accounting recognition of the difference between a bond's purchase price and face value from purchase date to maturity.

Securities brokerage firms and banks that engage in the business of trading commonly classify their holdings as trading securities. Insurers generally do not use this classification. Under GAAP, trading securities are reported at fair value.

Available-for-sale securities are equity (stocks) and debt (bonds) investments that management does not intend to sell in the near future. For stocks, this classification applies if the investments are not classified as trading securities. (The held-to-maturity classification is not available for stocks because they never mature.) For bonds, this category applies if the investments are not positioned for near-term sale but the organization does not intend to hold them to maturity. Under GAAP, available-for-sale securities are reported at fair value.

Different insurers have different rationales and motivations for classifying their debt securities as held-to-maturity or available-for-sale. An insurer may, for example, designate its bonds as available-for-sale, rather than held-to-maturity, to support its investment strategy of selling bonds in response to changes in interest rates.

Realized Gains and Losses

Gains and losses are realized at the time of the sale of an investment. If an investment is sold for more than its cost/amortized cost, a profit, or gain, is realized. If an investment is sold for less than its cost/amortized cost, a loss is realized. Under GAAP, realized gains or losses on available-for-sale securities and held-to-maturity securities (if any are sold prior to maturity) are included in earnings (net income).

Unrealized Gains and Losses

Unrealized gains or losses occur because of fluctuations in the market price of an investment after acquisition but before its sale or maturity. If an investment's current market value is more than its cost/amortized cost, the investor has an unrealized gain. If market conditions change and the same investment's market value falls below its cost/amortized cost, the investor has an unrealized loss. As such, the unrealized gains or losses on an investment can change over time.

The valuation of a bond or stock and the recognition of unrealized gains or losses on the investor's financial statements depend on the bond or stock's holding-period classification. See the exhibit "Bonds and Stocks—GAAP Valuation and Treatment of Unrealized Gains and Losses."

Many insurers classify their bond investments as available-for-sale rather than held-to-maturity. Accordingly, their bond investments are reported at fair value rather than amortized cost, with unrealized gains and losses reported in a separate component (other comprehensive income) of shareholders' equity.

Bonds and Stocks—GAAP Valuation and Treatment of Unrealized Gains and Losses

Investment Category	Classification	Carrying Value	Unrealized Gains and Losses
Bonds	Held-to-maturity	Amortized cost	• Excluded from earnings (net income) and shareholders' equity • Disclosed in the notes to financial statements
Bonds and stocks	Available-for-sale	Fair value	• Excluded from earnings (net income) • Reported in a separate component of shareholders' equity (other comprehensive income)
Bonds and stocks	Trading	Fair value	• Included in earnings (net income)

[DA06490]

Impairment of Financial Assets

An **impairment** in one or more of an organization's invested assets can significantly reduce its shareholders' equity (net worth). In general, an invested asset is considered impaired when its fair value is less than its cost/amortized cost. For accounting purposes, impairment is associated with an "other-than-temporary" (permanent) state in which various factors, such as deterioration of the issuer's creditworthiness or its failure to pay interest or dividends, indicate that the cost/amortized cost of the invested asset, as recorded on the balance sheet, may not be recoverable. An accounting impairment results in a reduction of an asset's cost basis.

Impairment policy is a set of principles-based rules that are consistently applied to the organization's portfolio of investments to identify specific positions that should be marked for impairment review. Best practices dictate that the policy should contain both severity and duration thresholds for a position's unrealized losses to trigger an impairment review. Common thresholds are a severity of 95 percent of cost/amortized cost (fair value is at least 5 percent less than cost/amortized cost) and a reduction in value that has persisted for twelve months. An asset that is identified through these impairment indicators undergoes a formal assessment.

Impairment

In accounting, the reduction in the cost basis of a financial asset by an amount that is deemed to be unrecoverable.

If an invested asset, carried at cost/amortized cost, is determined to have an other-than-temporary impairment (OTTI), its balance sheet value is reduced by the amount of the impairment. FASB ASC 320 provides that a security with an OTTI should use fair value as the new, lower cost basis, and the difference between the previous cost and fair value should be accounted for as a realized loss and reflected in earnings (net income). This concept also applies to securities for which changes in fair value are not normally recognized in earnings, such as bonds or stocks classified as available-for-sale. See the exhibit "Other-Than-Temporary Impairment (OTTI)."

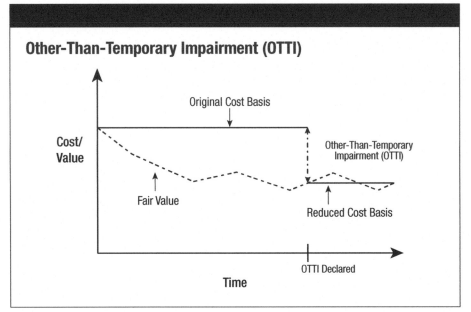

Other-Than-Temporary Impairment (OTTI)

[DA06494]

Statutory Financial Reporting

Property-casualty insurers and life insurers file statutory annual statements with the National Association of Insurance Commissioners (NAIC). The annual statement instructions and statutory Statements of Standard Accounting Practice (SSAP) dictate how and where the valuations are reported. The statutory annual statement includes several prescribed schedules that incorporate significant details on each individual security. This level of detail is not required in GAAP statements.

In the NAIC Annual Statement, stocks and other equity-like securities are generally carried at fair value (market value), similar to the way they are valued under GAAP. Bonds, preferred stocks, and other credit-related investments are valued at either amortized cost or at the lower of amortized cost or fair value (market value), depending on the credit quality of the issuer. Credit-rating categories range from 1 (highest quality) to 6 (lowest quality). These ratings are assigned by either the NAIC Securities Valuation Office or one of the designated public rating agencies. NAIC-1 and NAIC-2 ratings are assigned to investment-grade securities, while NAIC-3 through NAIC-6 are used for speculative-grade securities.

Property-Casualty Insurers

Property-casualty insurers report equities at fair value. Bonds rated NAIC-1 (low default risk) and NAIC-2 are reported at amortized cost, while those rated NAIC-3 through NAIC-6 (in or near default) are reported at the lower of amortized cost or fair value. The change in unrealized capital gains and losses on invested assets reported at fair value is shown as a direct adjustment to the Capital and Surplus Account, so it is not recorded as an expense for the purpose of calculating net income.

SAP for property-casualty insurers require that asset impairment be recognized under certain conditions. The cost/amortized-cost basis for invested assets determined to be OTTI is reduced, and the reduction in value flows through the statement of income as a realized capital loss.

Life Insurers

Generally, life insurers use amortized cost for bonds with credit ratings between NAIC-1 and NAIC-5 and the lower of amortized cost or fair value for bonds rated NAIC-6. The difference in accounting treatment from that for property-casualty insurers is based on an assumption that life insurers have a greater tendency to hold securities until maturity because they have less need for liquidity. Similar to property-casualty insurers, life insurers use fair value to record the value of equity securities.

The recognition of realized and unrealized capital gains and losses differs for life insurers compared with property-casualty insurers because of two special reserve accounts required by SSAP No. 7—Asset Valuation Reserve and Interest Maintenance Reserve. Realized and unrealized capital gains and losses that are credit-related go through an asset valuation reserve (AVR). The AVR helps protect policyholders' surplus by absorbing fluctuations in asset values. Realized capital gains and losses that stem from changes in market interest rates go through an interest maintenance reserve (IMR), which spreads their recognition over time. In effect, the AVR and IMR are allocated surplus to help offset sharp fluctuations in the values of invested assets.

The AVR is determined by a complex formula, the details of which are reported in the annual statement. Further additions are made based on historical risk parameters applied to statement values. This aggregate value is then adjusted higher or lower so that it falls within a specified range. The end result is that capital gains and losses are subject to caps and floors as they are recorded through the AVR. The overall change in the AVR, which can be positive or negative, is then applied directly to surplus and is therefore not recorded as a gain or loss for the purpose of calculating net income.

Realized capital gains and losses that flow through the IMR are amortized into investment income over the remaining life of the underlying investments. Therefore, realized capital gains and losses from changes in market interest rates are not immediately recognized as an investment gain or loss; instead, they are recognized over the remaining life of the sold assets. The IMR reduces incentives for life insurers to manipulate earnings by selling off bonds that have had material gains because of reductions in market interest rates while retaining bonds that have had material losses because of increases in market interest rates.

The AVR/IMR adjustment has no counterpart in United States GAAP or SAP reporting by property-casualty insurers. Values reported in the AVR/IMR are net of any associated capital gains taxes. See the exhibit "Bonds and Stocks—Statutory Accounting Principles (SAP) Valuation and Treatment of Capital Gains and Losses."

Bonds and Stocks—Statutory Accounting Principles (SAP) Valuation and Treatment of Capital Gains and Losses

Asset Class	Credit rating	Property-Casualty	Life
Bonds	1	Amortized cost.	Amortized cost.
	2	Amortized cost.	Amortized cost.
	3	Lower of amortized cost or fair value.	Amortized cost.
	4	Lower of amortized cost or fair value.	Amortized cost.
	5	Lower of amortized cost or fair value.	Amortized cost.
	6	Lower of amortized cost or fair value.	Lower of amortized cost or fair value.
Stocks	n/a	Fair value.	Fair value.
Capital gains/ losses treatment		Realized capital gains/losses are added to investment income; changes in unrealized capital gains/losses are charged directly to surplus.	Asset valuation reserve (AVR)—credit-related changes to the value of invested assets are added to/subtracted from the asset valuation reserve; changes to AVR are charged directly to surplus; caps and floors are applied, which helps spread changes over time. Interest maintenance reserve (IMR)—interest-rate-related realized capital gains/losses are added to/subtracted from the IMR; IMR is amortized into investment income; unrealized gains/losses that are interest-rate related (do not flow through the IMR) are charged directly to surplus.

[DA11139]

FINANCIAL REPORTING OF PRIVATE PLACEMENTS, CMBS, RMBS, AND ORIGINATED MORTGAGES

A significant proportion of the invested assets of insurance companies are in fixed-maturity investments that require special consideration when assessing their financial value.

Bonds are the largest asset class for both life insurers and property-casualty insurers, but other fixed-maturity securities such as mortgages make up a significant portion of an insurer's investment portfolio. Additionally, a bond portfolio includes several important subgroupings of specialty types of fixed-maturity debt securities that require special valuation techniques. These are some of the specialty types that are important to the insurance industry:

- Private placements
- Commercial mortgage-backed securities (CMBS)
- Residential mortgage-backed securities (RMBS)
- Originated mortgages

Although both life insurers and property-casualty insurers participate in each of these markets, the life insurance industry has a relatively higher participation rate in these specialty areas because its greater underwriting stability lowers the need for liquidity. The valuation of these securities is similar under both statutory accounting principles and generally accepted accounting principles (GAAP), with the major difference being that statutory accounting tends to more readily allow amortized cost valuation.

Private Placements

Private placements include bonds and other fixed-maturity securities that are exempt from registration with the United States Securities and Exchange Commission. The registration exemption is based on the assumption that both issuers and purchasers of such securities are equally sophisticated and knowledgeable and can negotiate as equals. Because the terms are negotiated directly between the issuer and purchaser, the loan terms and cash flows can be tailored to fit the exact needs of both parties.

Private placements can benefit both parties to the loan. The advantage to the issuer is that less regulatory red tape is involved with placing the securities relative to a public offering. The process takes less time, and fewer administrative burdens are associated with issuance and service of the bonds. The main disadvantage to the issuer is the higher yield that must be paid to the purchaser. Private placement yields are typically 0.25 percent to 0.50 percent higher than comparable publicly traded bonds to compensate the purchaser for the reduced liquidity of the securities. Restrictions applying to the resale of these securities require that investors have a degree of sophistication in evaluating the risks associated with the investment. However, life insurers tend to hold these securities to maturity, and therefore the reduced liquidity is less of an issue.

In addition to benefitting from higher yields, the purchaser also benefits from the ability to tailor the terms of the loan to its own special requirements. The purchaser can add restrictive covenants that protect it from increased risk, such as restricting the issuer's ability to take on additional debt or the maintenance of minimum ratio values. Violation of the covenants may trigger a default or require additional compensation to the purchaser from the issuer. These protective covenants reduce the credit risk to the purchaser. Another advantage is that the purchaser can also negotiate the structure of the cash flows to meet its asset-liability matching strategy.

In the statutory financial statement filed by insurers, private placement fixed-maturity securities are assigned to one of the six National Association of Insurance Commissioners (NAIC) credit rating categories (NAIC-1 [highest quality] through NAIC-6 [lowest quality]) by either the Securities Valuation Office or one of the designated public rating agencies. The NAIC category determines the statement value. Generally, life insurers use amortized cost for NAIC-1 through NAIC-5 and market value for NAIC-6. Property-casualty insurers, however, use market value for all speculative-grade debt instruments (NAIC-3 through NAIC-6).

For private placement bonds that are carried at amortized cost, valuation and reporting are the same as for publicly traded bonds. For private placement bonds that must be carried at market value, the insurer must estimate a market value by using broker estimates or value comparisons with similar publicly traded securities, or by employing available financial information on interest rates and default rates to produce a present value estimate.

Under GAAP, fixed-maturity securities classified as "held to maturity" are reported at amortized cost, while those classified as "available for sale" or "trading securities" are reported at fair value. A private placement bond that was originally classified as "held to maturity" may be subsequently categorized as "available for sale" if the issuer's financial condition deteriorates.

At the end of 2012, life insurers held more than $700 billion of private placement bonds, with more than 90 percent of those bonds rated as investment grade. The higher liquidity needs of the property-casualty insurance business lead to relatively lower participation in the private placement market and greater participation in the publicly traded bond market.

Mortgage-Backed Securities

Mortgage-backed securities are reported as bonds in Schedule D of the statutory financial statement. This class of bonds has different risk characteristics than traditional bonds, which have very predictable cash flows and investment returns. The cash flows from mortgage-backed securities come from the underlying pool of mortgages. The ultimate maturity is known, but the timing of the cash flows, which include both the principal and interest payments on the underlying mortgages, is affected by default rates and prepayment rates in the pool.

Schedule D has separate categories for RMBS and CMBS. The majority of the RMBS investments are U.S. government agency debt issued by the Federal National Mortgage Association, the Federal Home Loan Mortgage Corporation, or the Government National Mortgage Association. Although these securities are rated NAIC-1 and carried at amortized value, the amortization of the discount or premium from the purchase of these securities must

Mortgage-backed security
A financial instrument collateralized by a pool of mortgages.

be adjusted for the estimated timing and amount of prepayments and default-related costs of the underlying mortgage loans. The CMBS investments typically pool commercial mortgage loans that entail significant prepayment penalties and therefore involve less prepayment risk, but the credit risk may be significantly higher.

Like other bonds, investment-grade CMBS and RMBS are carried at amortized cost. Life insurers use amortized cost for NAIC-3, NAIC-4, and NAIC-5 speculative-grade bonds, but property-casualty insurers report those at the lower of market value or amortized cost. All NAIC-6 bonds are carried at estimated market value.

In 2009, the NAIC adopted *Statement of Statutory Accounting Principles No. 43—Revised, Loan-Backed and Structured Securities* to address market disruptions in the asset-backed securities market during the financial crisis in the late 2000s. The revised rating methodology is used to evaluate individual asset-backed securities and to establish adjusted carrying values that are based on published formulas.

For GAAP purposes, the valuation of mortgage-backed securities depends on their classification. Securities that are available for sale or trading are carried at fair value, while those that are held to maturity can be valued at amortized cost. See the exhibit "U.S. Insurance Industry Mortgage-Backed Securities Investment in 2012."

Originated Mortgages

Originated mortgages are direct loans to borrowers, similar to private placement bonds but secured by real estate. Mortgages make up nearly 10 percent of total invested assets for the life insurance industry but are much less prevalent in the property-casualty industry. The proportion of directly owned mortgages to total assets has declined over the years because insurers can achieve similar results by investing in mortgage-backed securities, which are treated as bonds.

Mortgages are normally reported at their outstanding principal balance, net of unamortized premium or discount and book value adjustments. Other-than-temporary-impairment (OTTI) adjustments are reported when it becomes probable that principal and/or interest payments specified in the loan contract will not be met. OTTI adjustments reduce the statement value of mortgage loans to the fair value of the collateral net of anticipated transaction costs to sell the property.

Schedule B of the statutory statement reports details of mortgages owned, acquired, or disposed of during the year. The schedule includes loan-specific information on location, data related to latest appraisal, statement carrying value, interest rate, date of acquisition, and realized and unrealized changes in book value from amortizations and impairments.

U.S. Insurance Industry Mortgage-Backed Securities Investment in 2012

This table shows the aggregate investment of the insurance industry in mortgage-backed securities as of the end of 2012. Life insurance companies own more than 70 percent of the total.

	Life Insurers (in $ millions)	Property- Casualty Insurers (in $ millions)	Other Insurers (in $ millions)	Industry Total (in $ millions)
Agency-Backed Residential Mortgage-Backed Securities	213,288	91,832	25,670	330,790
Private-Label Residential Mortgage-Backed Securities	96,744	17,705	2,828	117,277
Subtotal: Residential Mortgage-Backed Securities	310,032	109,537	28,498	448,067
Agency-Backed Commercial Mortgage-Backed Securities	19,287	6,624	2,060	27,971
Private-Label Commercial Mortgage-Backed Securities	131,566	26,811	6,247	164,624
Subtotal: Commercial Mortgage-Backed Securities	150,853	33,435	8,307	192,595
Total Mortgage-Backed Securities	460,885	142,972	36,805	640,662

Adapted from National Association of Insurance Commissioners Capital Markets Special Report "Update on Insurance Industry Investments Portfolio Asset Mix," September 2013, www.naic.org/capital_markets_archive/130924.htm (accessed February 26, 2014). [DA11132]

Apply Your Knowledge

Which one of the following valuation bases is typically used for mortgage loans that are not in default?

a. Amortized cost

b. Fair value

c. Outstanding principal balance

d. OTTI

Feedback: c. Mortgages are typically valued at the outstanding principal balance.

OTHER ASSETS

Generally accepted accounting principles (GAAP) reflect going-concern valuations; statutory accounting principles (SAP) reflect breakup values. Therefore, valuations in both income statements and balance sheets differ depending on which accounting standard is used.

Although GAAP and SAP are consistent for the most part, they do have material differences. GAAP accounting, which reports a company's financial position as a going concern over time, provides information to investors and the general public. In contrast, SAP accounting reports a company's financial position based on its breakup value. SAP are meant for regulators. GAAP match expenses and revenues to the time they occur. Reflecting a more conservative approach, SAP recognize expenses earlier than GAAP do. These different accounting philosophies lead to differences in reporting **deferred tax assets and liabilities**, guaranty fund receivables, and fixed assets.

Deferred tax assets and liabilities

Accounts that recognize expected future tax benefits or obligations that arise from temporary differences between valuations on the balance sheet being reported and those on the tax balance sheet.

Deferred Tax Assets

Both GAAP and SAP require insurers to recognize current taxes as well as deferred tax assets and liabilities. Current income tax assets and liabilities are tax amounts payable or recoverable in the current tax year as well as any current-year adjustments to taxes from prior years. Deferred-income tax assets and liabilities are recorded for expected future tax obligations or benefits that arise from differences between GAAP and taxable income. GAAP income tax guidance is found in Financial Accounting Standards Board (FASB) Statement No. 109, Accounting for Income Taxes, while SAP income tax guidance is found in Statement of SAP (SSAP) No. 101, Income Taxes.

Deferred tax assets and liabilities are identified by comparing the GAAP or SAP balance sheet values to the tax balance sheet. Temporary differences between the balance sheet valuations create the deferred tax assets and liabilities. Deferred income taxes are the product of current tax rates multiplied by the temporary valuation difference. A deferred tax asset is a tax deduction that has not been realized. A deferred tax liability is an additional tax that is not yet due. See the exhibit "Deferred Tax Assets and Liabilities."

Deferred tax assets may or may not be realized, so a valuation allowance is recorded if it is more likely than not that any portion of the deferred tax assets will not be realized. Judgment is required to determine the amount of any valuation allowance based on the likelihood that the deferred tax assets will be realized. These considerations are included in the evaluation process:

• The types of assets and liabilities that gave rise to the deferral

• The timing of the recognition into current taxes

• Tax carryforward and carryback provisions and the timing of future company tax offsets

• Classification of the taxes as ordinary income or capital gains and losses

Deferred Tax Assets and Liabilities

Bond X cost $102,000 when purchased. The statutory accounting principles (SAP) statement carries the bond at its amortized cost, and the generally accepted accounting principles (GAAP) statement carries the bond at fair market value, which has increased since the time the bond was purchased. The temporary differences between the tax basis and the statement value create a deferred tax event. If the future tax event is positive, it is a deferred tax liability. If the future tax event is negative, it is a deferred tax asset.

Bond X

Original Cost	$102,000
Amortized Cost	$101,000
Fair Market Value	$103,000

	GAAP Statement	SAP Statement
Balance Sheet Value	$103,000	$101,000
Tax Statement Value	$102,000	$102,000
Temporary Difference	$1,000	($1,000)
Tax Rate	35%	35%
Deferred Tax Result	$350	($350)
Deferred Tax Asset		$350
Deferred Tax Liability	$350	

[DA11115]

Although current taxes are the same under both GAAP and SAP, timing differences lead to temporary divergences between GAAP and SAP deferred tax valuations. These are some examples of the differences in deferred taxes between GAAP and SAP:

- Insurers report bonds at fair value for GAAP and at amortized value for SAP. When a bond is eventually sold, the difference between the sale price and the tax basis becomes a current tax obligation and is recognized in both GAAP and SAP. However, while the bond remains in inventory, the differences in carrying values between GAAP and SAP lead to temporary differences in the deferred tax effects. Additionally, SAP values certain bonds of life insurers differently than the same bonds of property-casualty insurers, creating differences in the SAP-based deferred taxes for the two types of insurers.

- Nonadmitted assets are included in GAAP statements but omitted from SAP statements. For example, sale of office furniture, a nonadmitted asset, at higher than book value would result in future tax obligations, which would then be recognized under GAAP but not under SAP.

- Acquisition costs, such as agents' commissions, are recognized immediately in SAP but are amortized over the policy period under GAAP. The policy acquisition costs for life insurance tend to be higher for many of the long-term life insurance products, so the impact of the timing differences is often greater for life insurers than for property-casualty insurers.

- GAAP require recognition of both state and federal deferred tax assets and liabilities. SAP restrict recognition to federal tax items only and prohibit recognition of deferred state tax assets and liabilities.

- Changes in deferred taxes flow through the GAAP income statement, while under SAP, they are applied directly to surplus.

Apply Your Knowledge

The tax rate used to establish deferred tax assets and deferred tax liabilities is:

a.   The long-term capital gains tax rate.

b.   The tax rate anticipated to be in effect when the taxes become current.

c.   The current tax rate.

d.   The lower of the company's average tax rate or 10 percent.

Feedback: c. Deferred taxes are based on current tax rates.

Guaranty Funds Receivable

Guaranty fund

A state-established fund that provides a system for the payment of some of the unpaid claims of insolvent insurers licensed in that state, generally funded by assessments collected from all insurers licensed in the state.

Each state operates **guaranty funds** for both property-casualty insurance and life and health insurance and annuities. Licensed insurers record a liability for their best estimate of the amount of the future obligation when an insurer becomes insolvent, and the guaranty fund assumes responsibility for the obligations. Most states allow insurers to recover assessments paid to the guaranty fund through premium tax offsets or through surcharges applied to future policyholder premiums.

Timing is mismatched between when obligations to the guaranty fund are incurred and when funds are actually recovered from the tax offsets or the premium surcharges. This timing mismatch is recorded as a guaranty fund receivable. The amount of the receivable is established based on the probability that the insurer can recover those amounts in the future.

GAAP reporting standards for guaranty fund receivables are found in FASB Accounting Standards Codification (ASC) 405-30. SAP reporting standards are contained in SSAP 35R, Guaranty Fund and Other Assessments. SAP accounting for guaranty fund assessments is generally consistent with GAAP accounting. These are the main differences:

- GAAP accounting allows recognition of the time value of money in measuring anticipated recoveries, but SAP accounting specifically prohibits it.
- GAAP accounting allows a valuation allowance for doubtful recoveries, while SAP accounting requires that unrecoverable amounts are written down and recognized in current income.

Fixed Assets

Fixed assets are long-term assets held by a firm to support its business operations. These assets include both real property and personal property. Real property includes land and structures permanently attached to land, such as an insurer's home office building. Everything that is not real property is considered personal property and includes office equipment, automobiles, and furniture.

Fixed assets are relatively illiquid, so they cannot be readily converted into cash to meet obligations. For that reason, certain tangible fixed assets such as office furniture are classified as nonadmitted for SAP purposes, although they are included in GAAP-based statements.

Fixed assets are normally reported at original cost, less accumulated depreciation and net of encumbrances such as mortgages. The carrying value of fixed assets may be adjusted to recognize permanent impairments that reduce the value of the asset below its amortized value. The adjustments to the historical cost basis are recorded as contra assets on the asset page rather than as liabilities to make matching the value reduction to the specific asset easier.

The main difference between GAAP and SAP reporting and tax accounting is the manner in which depreciation is calculated: with reporting, both allow a number of different depreciation methods. In contrast, tax accounting specifies a tax-based depreciation system. Tax-based depreciation typically amortizes the value of assets over a shorter period, which speeds up the receipt of current tax benefits.

INSURER ASSET MANAGEMENT

Insurers use the same types of asset management techniques that other financial firms, such as banks and mutual funds, routinely employ.

Asset management is an integral part of insurers' operations. The earnings generated by insurers' investment portfolios supplement the premiums paid by policyholders to pay claims. To ensure that the investment earnings are adequate, insurers must manage those assets wisely. In addition to following traditional portfolio management practices, insurers are subject to regulatory restrictions that limit the type of assets and the concentration of risk. Insurers generally match the investment inflows to the expected benefit outflows in order to minimize risk.

Asset Portfolio Management

Asset portfolio management encompasses all the activities involved in selecting the mix of assets to be included in an asset portfolio, monitoring and managing the resulting cash flows, measuring and monitoring the various risks associated with the portfolio, and matching the asset cash flows to payment obligations. Bond portfolio management is particularly important for insurers because investments in bonds typically account for 55 percent to 60 percent of the industry's admitted assets. See the exhibit "2012 Insurance Industry Asset Portfolio Mix."

Unlike equity investments in common or preferred stocks, bonds have a fixed maturity date—a specified time when the issuer must repay the principal (face) amount of the bond. Although the payment of cash dividends on stocks is at the discretion of a company's board of directors, interest payments on debt are a contractual obligation that must be met according to a predetermined schedule. These two characteristics of debt securities—a fixed maturity date and a fixed interest-payment schedule—are particularly valuable to insurers, which must ensure that adequate funds are available when needed to pay their obligations to policyholders.

The most important objective of portfolio management in general, and bond portfolio management in particular, is to structure a portfolio so that the amount and timing of investment cash inflows correspond to the firm's expected cash outflows. For property-casualty insurers, the amount and timing of expected cash outflows are largely determined by the composition of the underwriting portfolio. Property losses tend to be settled quickly, with most loss payments being made within two years. Consequently, relatively short-term investments are needed to ensure that adequate funds are available to pay losses when due. In contrast, some liability losses may be outstanding for many years before they are fully settled. This extended payment period suggests that at least a portion of the insurer's assets should be invested in longer-term investments that have the potential to generate higher returns. Life insurers' obligations tend to be longer term, and there is less need for liquidity in the portfolio. Therefore, life insurers' assets tend to have longer durations than property-casualty insurers'.

Investing in bonds exposes investors to some additional sources of risk. One source of risk is credit risk, the uncertainty about an issuer's ability to make the required principal and interest payments as they become due. Obligations backed by the United States government are considered to have no default risk and are commonly referred to as "risk free," but that refers only to credit risk. In contrast, all debt issued by states, municipalities, foreign governments, or corporations has an element of default risk. The amount of default risk varies from one issuer to the next. National Association of Insurance Commissioners (NAIC) credit ratings, ranging from NAIC-1 (low default risk) to NAIC-6 (in or near default), are used to classify the level of credit risk. Private bond-rating agencies also issue credit ratings. Investors require a risk premium in the form of higher interest rates to hold riskier securities. The

2012 Insurance Industry Asset Portfolio Mix

Invested assets for the life insurance industry (general accounts only) and the property-casualty insurance industry at the end of 2012 show that the bulk of the invested assets are bonds. Life insurer portfolios tend to include assets with higher levels of risk because of the greater stability in the liability portfolio. Dollar amounts are in millions.

	Life (General Accounts)	% of Total	Property-Casualty	% of Total
Corporate Bonds	1,506,762	43.2%	292,781	18.5%
Municipal Bonds	149,453	4.3%	346,059	21.9%
U.S. Government Bonds	143,240	4.1%	84,823	5.4%
Agency-Backed Residential Mortgage-Backed Securities	213,288	6.1%	91,832	5.8%
Agency-Backed Commercial Mortgage-Backed Securities	19,287	0.6%	6,624	0.4%
Private-Label Residential Mortgage-Backed Securities	96,744	2.8%	17,705	1.1%
Private-Label Commercial Mortgage-Backed Securities	131,566	3.8%	26,811	1.7%
Foreign Governments	78,265	2.2%	27,351	1.7%
Hybrid Securities	29,259	0.8%	2,077	0.1%
Asset-Backed Securities and Other Structured Securities	179,796	5.2%	38,580	2.4%
Subtotal - Bonds	**2,547,660**	**73.1%**	**934,643**	**59.0%**
Preferred Stock	7,841	0.2%	12,144	0.8%
Common Stock	143,832	4.1%	406,566	25.7%
Mortgages, First Liens	335,611	9.6%	5,686	0.4%
Real Estate	21,430	0.6%	10,455	0.7%
Cash & Short-Term Investments	106,678	3.1%	85,075	5.4%
Contact Loans	127,569	3.7%	1,952	0.1%
Schedule BA Assets	139,088	4.0%	115,841	7.3%
Other Receivables	1,828	0.1%	7,723	0.5%
Derivatives	41,580	1.2%	592	0.0%
Securities Lending (Reinvested Collateral)	10,829	0.3%	2,852	0.2%
Total Invested Assets	**3,483,946**	**100.0%**	**1,583,529**	**100.0%**

NAIC Capital Markets Report—Update on Insurance Industry Investments Portfolio Asset Mix, September 2013, www.naic.org/capital_markets_archive/130924.htm (accessed February 1, 2014). [DA11140]

higher the risk of default, the higher the risk premium. As this risk is specific to an individual debtor, it can be minimized by diversifying the bond portfolio over a large number of issuers.

Another source of risk to the fixed-income portfolio is **interest rate risk**. Bonds are issued at a fixed interest rate for the life of the bond. If market rates go up, the value of a bond goes down to reflect the lost earnings that

Interest rate risk

The risk that a security's future value will decline because of changes in interest rates.

opportunity holders have in the lower interest rate. Interest rate risk cannot be eliminated through diversification because changes in the levels of interest rates affect the prices of all debt securities. Although U.S. government obligations have no credit risk, they are exposed to interest rate risk just like other fixed-income securities. Increases in the general level of interest rates create unrealized capital losses in the bond portfolio.

Apply Your Knowledge

An insurer's most important objective of managing its investment portfolio is to ensure that

a. The portfolio contains U.S. Treasury securities.
b. The inflows from the asset portfolio are matched to the expected outflows from its liabilities.
c. The interest rate risk is maintained at a high level.
d. The duration of the investment portfolio is maintained at zero.

Feedback: b. The inflows from the investment should match the expected outflows to policyholders and claimants.

Reinvestment risk

The risk that the rate at which periodic interest payments can be reinvested over the life of the investment will be unfavorable.

Investments are also subject to **reinvestment risk**. Investment income is used to pay operating expenses, and any excess funds are then reinvested. The insurer may not be able to reinvest the funds at the same favorable interest rate. Some types of bonds, such as mortgage-backed securities, are pass-through investments, which means that proceeds from the underlying bundle of securities are passed through to the investor. An insurer with large holdings of residential mortgage-backed securities is exposed to prepayment risk. If mortgage rates drop significantly, borrowers prepay their mortgages at a higher rate than was anticipated when the insurer purchased the bond, and the insurer does not realize the expected income from the investment. The insurer must now reinvest those funds at the lower prevailing interest rates.

Asset-Liability Matching

Portfolio immunization (asset-liability matching)

The process of matching investment duration and liability duration.

Portfolio immunization (asset-liability matching) seeks to reduce an insurer's exposure to both interest rate risk and reinvestment risk by matching the duration of the assets to the duration of the liabilities they support. Duration refers to the average maturity of the assets or liabilities. Income from the investment portfolio is matched to the anticipated outflows from the insurers' obligations to claimants. This minimizes the risk that an insurer will have to sell investments at a loss to raise cash. Although the price of a fixed-income security rises and falls with changes in market interest rates, the resulting price changes are unrealized gains and losses. If the insurer never sells the security and allows it to mature, those interest-rate-related gains and losses never materialize.

To illustrate the effects of asset-liability matching on interest rate risk, suppose that an insurer sells a product and expects to have to pay a $1 million benefit on that product exactly one year from now. A simple and conservative approach would be to cash-match the cash flows from the investment to the cash flows to the liability by purchasing a bond with a face amount of $1 million that will mature exactly one year from now. For simplicity, assume that the bond is a zero-coupon bond that pays no interest during the year. If the current market interest rate for a one-year bond is 5 percent, the insurer will pay $952,381 today and receive $1 million one year from now when the bond matures. The portfolio is immunized from changes in interest rates because the assets are exactly matched to the liabilities.

The effect of interest rate risk can be seen by looking at the possibility of funding the same $1 million liability with a longer-duration bond. Interest rates are typically higher for longer-duration bonds. Assume that the market interest rate on a two-year zero-coupon bond is 6 percent. If the insurer buys a bond that matures in two years with a face value of $1,070,095, the cost of that bond will also be $952,381 today. One year from now, assuming that interest rates have not changed, the insurer will own a bond with a maturity of one year. The market interest rate for a one-year bond, assuming no change in market interest rates, will be 5 percent, so the value of the bond one year from now will be $1,019,138 ($1,070,095 ÷ 1.05). The insurer could then sell the bond and use $1,000,000 of the proceeds to pay its policyholder obligations. The insurer would also earn an additional $19,138 to increase its profit.

However, if interest rates change in the next year, the insurer retains the risk that the price of its bond will not be sufficient to pay its obligation one year from now. For example, if the market interest rate of a one-year bond increased during the year to 8 percent instead of staying steady at 5 percent, the insurer would receive only $990,829 ($1,070,095 ÷ 1.08) when it sells the bond one year from now. The shortfall between the $1 million obligation and the realized asset value of $990,829 would have to be made up from surplus. By exactly matching the maturity of its bond investment to the anticipated policyholder cash outflow, the insurer immunizes itself against interest rate risk.

Asset-liability matching is difficult to achieve in practice. Insurers estimate their expected cash outflows over time and then attempt to invest so that the asset inflows are duration-matched to these outflows. There is a tradeoff between bond duration and yield. Longer-duration bonds pay higher market interest rates, but funds are locked into those interest rates for longer periods. In a rising-interest-rate environment, that means that insurers are locking in lower rates. The insurers are also increasing their exposure to interest rate risk.

For property-casualty insurers, this exposure is less of a problem because their products are constantly being repriced at renewal. Life insurance products, such as cash-value life insurance or fixed annuities, on the other hand, are multidecade products. Life insurers must build investment-yield assumptions into the pricing for those products today, and once sold, the price is guaranteed for the life of the agreement.

Another consideration for life insurance products is that insurers often guarantee minimum interest rate yields as part of the cash-value buildup. Yields in the U.S. bond market have been declining since the 1980s and reached unprecedented lows as the country attempted to work its way out of the 2007–09 recession. Yields on thirty-year U.S. Treasury securities dropped below 2.5 percent in July 2012. Guaranteed minimum investment yields of 4 percent to 6 percent were not uncommon in the 1980s. For life insurers with large portfolios of seasoned life insurance policies, the spread between the minimum returns those insurers are paying to policyowners and the yields they are earning on investments has been compressed.

These historically low rates are attributable in part to efforts by the U.S. Federal Reserve to stimulate the economy. When those efforts end and the world economy fully recovers, the rates on these securities will climb. This creates a dilemma for life insurers:

Disintermediation

Withdrawal of deposits from depository institutions to be reinvested elsewhere, such as in money market mutual funds.

Yield curve

A graphical representation of the relationship between yields at different maturities.

- If they invest in long-term securities that match their long-term liabilities, they are locking in low yields that can reduce their potential earnings for decades. If interest rates materially increase over the next decade, they may face **disintermediation** risk as policyowners either surrender their policies or borrow the cash value out of the policy so that they can invest in higher-yielding alternatives. These life insurers also face high interest rate risk if they purchase long-term bonds at historically low interest rate levels because long-maturity, low-coupon bonds are much more sensitive to interest rate risk than shorter-maturity bonds.

- If they invest in short-term securities, they earn less investment income. The normal shape of the **yield curve** is upward sloping, which means that short-term interest rates tend to be lower than long-term interest rates. Insurers can invest in short-term bonds and then roll them over into longer-maturity securities once interest rates do increase, but in the interim, they earn a lower rate of return. They also face the risk that changes in the shape of the yield curve exacerbate the investment-earnings problem over time. The steeper the yield curve, the more attractive the fixed-annuity products offered by life insurers because they can build in to the product yields that are significantly higher than short-term yields. A steep yield curve helps increase current sales and also reduces disintermediation risk because life insurance policyowners have fewer attractive alternative investments. A flatter yield curve would increase disintermediation as life insurance customers flee to other investment products.

To some extent, insurers can mitigate exposure to interest rate risk by diversification in both the asset and liability portfolios. Property-casualty insurers can mix shorter-duration products, such as property insurance, with longer-duration products, like general liability, through direct writing or reinsurance. Property-casualty insurers, for the most part, sell products that reprice quickly, so pricing mistakes can be addressed rapidly. Life insurers can reduce their exposure as well. Variable life insurance and variable annuities shift most, if not all, of the investment risk back to the policyowner. The relative stability and predictability of life insurers' obligations also provide insurers with additional time to fix pricing mistakes, as well as allow them to invest in longer-term and riskier assets because they are faced with less volatility in their liabilities.

Asset Concentrations

Insurers manage asset-concentration risk by investing in a diverse portfolio of assets and limiting the concentration of invested assets by both type and issuers of investments. A well-diversified investment portfolio simultaneously maximizes returns while minimizing risk. Different types of assets have different levels of sensitivity to changes in the economic environment. The returns on common stock are typically higher than the returns on fixed-income securities, but the risk is higher as well. Stocks have more risk because stock prices are also more sensitive to the business cycle than bond prices and because bondholders have a priority claim on the assets of a financially impaired company.

Even within an asset class, insurers have to manage the level of concentrations. For example, bonds with longer maturities have more interest rate risk than bonds with shorter maturities. The tradeoff is that bonds with longer maturities also earn higher rates of interest than bonds with shorter maturities. Life insurers have less liquidity risk than property-casualty insurers, so they tend to hold longer-maturity fixed-income instruments, but an excessive concentration in long-term securities should be avoided.

Insurers also limit their asset concentration by issuer and by industry. A portfolio of corporate bonds issued by only a handful of companies would be extremely risky because even AAA-rated bonds experience defaults. A concentration in a particular industry, such as banking or auto manufacturing, would leave an insurer exposed to risk if the entire industry were to become troubled. In the early 2010s, sovereign debt instruments issued by several European countries, including Italy, Spain, and Greece, were jointly affected by economic problems in the European Union. During the U.S. recession of 2007 to 2009, much of the mortgage-backed bond market went from AAA-rated, low-risk investments to junk-bond status.

Insurance regulators place restrictions on the type and amount of certain assets that insurers can own, although the restrictions have eased over time. However, insurers are subject to regulatory capital standards that apply additional capital charges to assets concentrated in one issuer. The reasoning is that, although there is some level of diversification in owning different asset classes, natural diversification would disappear if a particular issuer were to become financially unstable. In that case, the value of all of its securities—bonds, stocks, mortgages, or derivatives—would decrease because all of those obligations rely on the solvency of the same issuer.

STATE REGULATION OF INSURER ASSETS

All states regulate insurer investments. This regulation helps ensure insurer solvency and liquidity so that, ultimately, all covered claims can be paid.

State regulation effectively mandates that insurers hold investment portfolios that are prudent (some would even say quite conservative) and well diversified. In keeping with their conservative and consistent approach to protecting insurer solvency, regulators are the primary source of constraints imposed on insurer investment practices. These constraints take two main forms: asset restrictions and investment limitations. Insurers are permitted to show only certain assets on their balance sheets and are limited in the types of investments they can hold. To achieve diversification in insurer investment portfolios, regulators also restrict how much an insurer can hold in any single investment. To ensure uniform valuation and treatment of securities, insurance regulators rely on the services of the National Association of Insurance Commissioners' (NAIC's) Securities Valuation Office (SVO).

Securities Valuation Office

Although the states are individually responsible for regulating the insurers licensed in their jurisdictions, they also operate collectively through the NAIC, a regulatory support organization whose membership includes each of the states' chief insurance regulators. Through these collective efforts, state regulators are able to implement consistent national regulatory policies in certain areas, including regulations dealing with insurer investments.

Asset valuation and reporting is critical to maintaining solvency standards. The NAIC Valuation of Securities Task Force (VOSTF) is charged with maintaining uniform valuation of securities, assessing credit quality of those securities, establishing uniform classification and reporting of securities, and establishing consistent investment securities policies for the NAIC membership. The SVO is one of the NAIC staff-support offices that performs the day-to-day actions in support of the VOSTF mission. In operation for more than seven decades, the SVO was reorganized in 2011 as a division of the NAIC Capital Markets and Investment Analysis Office.

SVO professional investment analysts—who are employees of the NAIC, not state regulators— work to support the mission of the regulatory members of the VOSTF. The SVO's duties and responsibilities are spelled out in the *Purposes and Procedures Manual of the NAIC Securities Valuation Office*, which is updated twice a year.

These are some of the SVO's routine day-to-day activities:

- The SVO maintains the database of insurance industry investment securities to ensure uniform treatment of these assets across jurisdictions and across insurers. Insurers are required to file detailed information on illiquid securities with the SVO, but publicly traded stocks and bonds may be exempted from the filing requirements if they are already subject to public scrutiny through the various investment rating agencies.

- The SVO performs credit analysis of certain illiquid securities that are normally reported in Schedule D of the NAIC Annual Statement, such as privately placed bonds that have not been rated by one or more of the Acceptable Rating Organizations (AROs) such as Standard & Poor's and Moody's. The SVO assigns ratings to such securities ranging from NAIC-1 (highest credit quality) to NAIC-6 (in or near default) and, in some instances, also assigns a valuation to the security for statutory reporting purposes. Publicly traded securities that have already been credit-rated by one of the AROs are assigned NAIC credit quality designations based on the credit ratings assigned by the AROs. Common stocks that are publicly traded on the major exchanges are likewise exempt from the requirement for an SVO analysis and evaluation; the valuation of those securities is based on market values.

- Certain Schedule BA assets, which are investment assets that do not fit conveniently into one of the traditional classifications like real estate (Schedule A), mortgages (Schedule B), or bonds (Schedule D), are normally treated in financial statements as if they were rated NAIC-6. However, insurers can file these securities with the SVO to attain a more favorable rating and classification. This is especially important to life insurers because the regulatory capital requirements and the asset valuation reserve requirements are affected by the credit quality rating. Schedule BA assets that are classified as having the characteristics of bonds or the characteristics of preferred stock and that receive a higher NAIC credit quality designation receive more favorable treatment from the risk-based capital formula and the asset valuation reserve rules.

- SVO investment analysts evaluate new financial products to identify the investment risks those securities pose to insurer solvency. The Regulatory Treatment Analysis Service allows insurers to establish the anticipated statutory accounting valuation and classification of securities before they commit to purchasing them. Insurers are still required to file those securities with the SVO when they purchase them, but this service allows an insurer to better plan its investment portfolio by taking some of the uncertainty out of the regulatory process. Any interested party, including a brokerage that is attempting to market the securities to insurance company clients, can use this service for a fee.

- The SVO provides the VOSTF with analysis of trends in capital markets, industry analysis, and other financial reports on request. The NAIC's New York office is located in the financial district of New York City, which gives the professional staff direct access to current information about the world's capital markets. The NAIC Capital Markets Bureau also monitors developments in the capital markets, evaluates the potential impact on United States insurance companies, disseminates regulators-only reports as well as open-access public reports, and assists state insurance examiners with on-site financial examinations when requested.

Asset Restrictions

While insurers can invest in a wide variety of assets, only certain assets are permitted to be included on an insurer's balance sheet. Any other investment by an insurer must be assigned zero value on the insurer's balance sheet, a more-than-sufficient incentive to avoid large investments in nonadmitted assets.

Generally, permitted investments for insurers include money market instruments; high-quality investments that mature in less than one year, such as U.S. Treasury bills and commercial paper; bonds of investment grade or better (issued by the U.S. Treasury, state governments, certain municipalities, or credit-worthy private corporations); common stock; preferred stock; real estate loans (mortgages); and real estate.

In many states, insurers must invest an amount equal to their required capital (or required capital plus certain other reserves) in an even narrower list of permitted investments.

Investment Restrictions

An insurer's investment strategy can be stated as seeking to earn the highest possible return for a given level of risk or, alternatively, to minimize the risk associated with earning a given expected return. Compared with undiversified portfolios (or insufficiently diversified portfolios), properly diversified portfolios can be expected to produce consistently higher returns for a given level of risk or lower risk for a given level of return. The mechanics of designing a properly diversified portfolio are beyond the scope of this discussion, but such a portfolio requires dozens of different investments.

The primary goals of state regulation of insurer investments are to ensure liquidity and to ensure solvency for the sake of policyholders. Three investment restrictions help ensure that insurers have well-diversified portfolios that support the goals of liquidity and solvency:

- Insurers can invest only up to a certain percentage of their assets in many of the permitted investments. For example, an insurer might be allowed to invest only up to 20 percent of its assets in common stocks. Any investment in common stock beyond such a restriction would result in the assets being nonadmitted.

- Insurers are typically restricted in how much of their assets can be invested in any single investment. For example, an insurer might be allowed to invest no more than 5 percent of its assets in a single investment, such as the AAA-rated bonds of XYZ Corporation. No matter how high the quality of XYZ's bonds might be, an insurer cannot invest more than 5 percent of its assets in such a single investment.

- Insurers are restricted in the percentage of another company's securities they can own. For example, insurers cannot own more than 5 percent of the common stock of any particular company (other than subsidiaries and

affiliates). This last restriction ensures that insurers remain passive financial investors in companies in other industries and do not become active
managers or owners.

The overall effect of the investment restrictions on insurers is to encourage
predominant investment in high-quality bonds. Investment in bonds helps
insurers meet their cash needs to satisfy claims.

Apply Your Knowledge

A typical investment restriction on an insurer's asset holdings might require
that insurer to

a.   Invest only in AAA-rated securities.

b.   Take an active role in managing the companies in which it invests.

c.   Nonadmit any common stock holdings in excess of 20 percent of its
     portfolio.

d.   Divest any bond holdings rated NAIC-6.

Feedback: c. Investment restrictions generally limit the admissibility of certain
asset classes, such as common stock.

SUMMARY

Insurers' GAAP valuation of bonds and stocks and reporting of capital gains
and losses are based on the holding-period classification of the security. For
securities whose changes in fair value are not included on the balance sheet
and in earnings (net income), an impairment in value must be recognized
under certain circumstances. Insurers' statutory valuation and reporting of
bonds (and other credit-related investments) are based on the investment's
credit rating, with differences in valuation by individual credit rating depending on whether the investment is made by a property-casualty insurer or a life
insurer. For reporting of capital gains/losses, life insurers employ an IMR and
an AVR, which help protect their surpluses from sharp fluctuations in asset
values.

The insurance industry plays a large role in providing liquidity to capital markets. Life insurers in particular are active in the market for privately placed
bonds and for asset-backed securities such as residential mortgage-backed
securities and commercial mortgage-backed securities. The carrying value of
these bonds is typically amortized value. Insurers also originate mortgages for
both residential and commercial borrowers, which are carried at the value of
the unpaid principal.

Deferred tax assets and liabilities reflect differences in the timing of tax obligations. These differences are estimated by comparing a GAAP- or SAP-basis

balance sheet with a tax-basis balance sheet. Insurers incur financial obligations to pay for the costs of insolvencies but are allowed to recover the costs over time. Differences in the timing of the recoveries lead to differences in the GAAP and SAP balance sheets. Although the valuation of fixed assets is, for the most, part consistent between GAAP and SAP, the statutory practice of nonadmitting certain illiquid assets creates valuation differences.

Insurers use standard portfolio management techniques such as diversification and asset-liability matching to limit their risk while at the same time maximizing their investment returns. In addition to regulatory restrictions that limit the type of assets and the concentration of risk, insurers limit their concentration of assets by type of investment, industry, and risk profile.

Investment quality is a cornerstone of insurer financial regulation. States rely on the NAIC's SVO to maintain a database of invested assets to ensure uniform regulatory treatment of insurer investment portfolios. The SVO also performs credit evaluations, analyzes capital markets, and determines statutory statement values for certain illiquid invested assets that are not widely traded in financial markets. The rating and classification of securities is an important issue because insurers are subject to regulatory restrictions on the types of assets that they own as well as on the mix of assets in their investment portfolios.

Direct Your Learning ▶▶

7

Reinsurance Accounting and Insurer Taxation

Educational Objectives

After learning the content of this assignment, you should be able to:

▷ Describe reinsurance and its principal functions.

▷ Describe treaty reinsurance and facultative reinsurance.

▷ Describe the types of pro rata reinsurance and excess of loss reinsurance and their uses.

▷ Explain the accounting and financial reporting considerations, including how values in insurers' financial reports are influenced by lags in the reporting of reinsurance transactions and bordereau reporting, for these types of reinsurance:

- Assumed reinsurance

- Ceded reinsurance

- Commutations

- Prospective versus retrospective reinsurance

▷ Explain the following with regard to property-casualty insurer taxation:

- Requirements for a company to be taxed as an insurer

- Tax treatment of future liabilities

- Types of state taxes

Reinsurance Accounting and Insurer Taxation

7

REINSURANCE AND ITS FUNCTIONS

A single insurer that sells a $100 million commercial property policy and a $100 million commercial umbrella liability policy to the owners of a high-rise office building may appear to be jeopardizing its financial stability. Insurers who provide billions of dollars of property insurance in wind-prone Florida and earthquake-prone California may seem similarly imperiled. However, such transactions are possible when the insurers use reinsurance as a tool to expand their capacity.

No insurer intentionally places itself in a situation in which a catastrophic event could destroy its net worth. Additionally, insurance regulators attempt to prevent insurers from being left in such a position. Reinsurance is one way insurers protect themselves from the financial consequences of insuring others. This section introduces basic reinsurance terms and concepts, including the principal functions of reinsurance.

Basic Terms and Concepts

Reinsurance, commonly referred to as "insurance for insurers," is the transfer from one insurer (the **primary insurer**) to another (the **reinsurer**) of some or all of the financial consequences of certain loss exposures covered by the primary insurer's policies. The loss exposures transferred, or ceded, by the primary insurer could be associated with a single subject of insurance (such as a building), a single policy, or a group of policies.

An insurer that transfers liability for loss exposures by ceding them to a reinsurer can be referred to as the reinsured, the ceding company, the cedent, the direct insurer, or the primary insurer. Although all these terms are acceptable, "primary insurer" will be used to denote the party that cedes loss exposures to a reinsurer.

Reinsurance is transacted through a **reinsurance agreement**, which specifies the terms under which the reinsurance is provided. For example, it may state that the reinsurer must pay a percentage of all the primary insurer's losses for loss exposures subject to the agreement, or must reimburse the primary insurer for losses that exceed a specified amount. Additionally, the reinsurance agreement identifies the policy, group of policies, or other categories of insurance that are included in the reinsurance agreement.

Reinsurance

The transfer of insurance risk from one insurer to another through a contractual agreement under which one insurer (the reinsurer) agrees, in return for a reinsurance premium, to indemnify another insurer (the primary insurer) for some or all of the financial consequences of certain loss exposures covered by the primary's insurance policies.

Primary insurer

In reinsurance, the insurer that transfers or cedes all or part of the insurance risk it has assumed to another insurer in a contractual arrangement.

Reinsurer

The insurer that assumes some or all of the potential costs of insured loss exposures of the primary insurer in a reinsurance contractual agreement.

Reinsurance agreement

Contract between the primary insurer and reinsurer that stipulates the form of reinsurance and the type of accounts to be reinsured.

Insurance risk

Uncertainty about the adequacy of insurance premiums to pay losses.

Retention

The amount retained by the primary insurer in the reinsurance transaction.

The reinsurer typically does not assume all of the primary insurer's **insurance risk**. The reinsurance agreement usually requires the primary insurer to retain part of its original liability. This **retention** can be expressed as a percentage of the original amount of insurance or as a dollar amount of loss. The reinsurance agreement does not alter the terms of the underlying (original) insurance policies or the primary insurer's obligations to honor them. See the exhibit "Risk."

Risk

Although "risk" is often defined as uncertainty about the occurrence of a loss, risk has several other meanings that are useful in understanding reinsurance practices. In reinsurance, the term risk often refers to the subject of insurance, such as a building, a policy, a group of policies, or a class of business. Reinsurance practitioners use the term risk in this way and include it in common reinsurance clauses.

[DA05756]

Reinsurance premium

The consideration paid by the primary insurer to the reinsurer for assuming some or all of the primary insurer's insurance risk.

Ceding commission

An amount paid by the reinsurer to the primary insurer to cover part or all of the primary insurer's policy acquisition expenses.

Retrocession

A reinsurance agreement whereby one reinsurer (the retrocedent) transfers all or part of the reinsurance risk it has assumed or will assume to another reinsurer (the retrocessionaire).

Retrocedent

The reinsurer that transfers or cedes all or part of the insurance risk it has assumed to another reinsurer.

Retrocessionaire

The reinsurer that assumes all or part of the reinsurance risk accepted by another reinsurer.

The primary insurer pays a **reinsurance premium** for the protection provided, just as any insured pays a premium for insurance coverage, but, because the primary insurer incurs the expenses of issuing the underlying policy, the reinsurer might pay a **ceding commission** to the primary insurer. These expenses consist primarily of commissions paid to producers, premium taxes, and underwriting expenses (such as policy processing and servicing costs, and risk control reports).

Reinsurers may transfer part of the liability they have accepted in reinsurance agreements to other reinsurers. Such an agreement is called a **retrocession**. Under a retrocession, one reinsurer, the **retrocedent**, transfers all or part of the reinsurance risk that it has assumed or will assume to another reinsurer, the **retrocessionaire**. Retrocession is very similar to reinsurance except for the parties involved in the agreement. The discussions of reinsurance in the context of a primary insurer-reinsurer relationship also apply to retrocessions.[1]

Reinsurance Functions

Reinsurance helps an insurer achieve several practical business goals, such as insuring large exposures, protecting policyholders' surplus from adverse loss experience, and financing the insurer's growth. The reinsurance that an insurer obtains depends mainly on the constraints or problems the insurer must address to reach its goals. Although several of its uses overlap, reinsurance is a valuable tool that can perform six principal functions for primary insurers:

- Increase large-line capacity
- Provide catastrophe protection
- Stabilize loss experience

- Provide surplus relief
- Facilitate withdrawal from a market segment
- Provide underwriting guidance

Depending on its goals, a primary insurer may use several different reinsurance agreements for these principal functions.

Increase Large-Line Capacity

The first function of reinsurance is to increase **large-line capacity**, which allows a primary insurer to assume more significant risks than its financial condition and regulations would otherwise permit. For example, an application for $100 million of property insurance on a single commercial warehouse could exceed the maximum amount of insurance that an underwriter is willing to accept on a single account. This maximum amount, or **line**, is subject to these influences:

- The maximum amount of insurance or limit of liability allowed by insurance regulations. Insurance regulations prohibit an insurer from retaining (after reinsurance, usually stated as net of reinsurance) more than 10 percent of its policyholders' surplus (net worth) on any one loss exposure.
- The size of a potential loss or losses that can safely be retained without impairing the insurer's earnings or policyholders' surplus.
- The specific characteristics of a particular loss exposure. For example, the line may vary depending on property attributes such as construction, occupancy, loss prevention features, and loss reduction features.
- The amount, types, and cost of available reinsurance.

Reinsurers provide primary insurers with large-line capacity by accepting liability for loss exposures that the primary insurer is unwilling or unable to retain. This function of reinsurance allows insurers with limited large-line capacity to participate more fully in the insurance marketplace. For example, a primary insurer may want to compete for homeowners policies in markets in which the value of the homes exceeds the amount the primary insurer can safely retain. Reinsurance allows the primary insurer to increase its market share while limiting the financial consequences of potential losses.

Provide Catastrophe Protection

Without reinsurance, catastrophes could greatly reduce insurer earnings or even threaten insurer solvency when a large number of its insured loss exposures are concentrated in an area that experiences a catastrophe. Potential catastrophic perils include fire, windstorm (hurricane, tornado, and other wind damage), and earthquakes. Additionally, significant property and liability losses can be caused by man-made catastrophes, such as industrial explosions, airplane crashes, or product recalls.

Large-line capacity
An insurer's ability to provide larger amounts of insurance for property loss exposures, or higher limits of liability for liability loss exposures, than it is otherwise willing to provide.

Line
The maximum amount of insurance or limit of liability that an insurer will accept on a single loss exposure.

The second function of reinsurance is to protect against the financial consequences of a single catastrophic event that causes multiple losses in a concentrated area. For example, an insurer might purchase reinsurance that provides up to $50 million of coverage per hurricane when the total amount of loss from a single hurricane exceeds the amount the insurer can safely retain.

Stabilize Loss Experience

An insurer, like most other businesses, must have a steady flow of profits to attract capital investment and support growth. However, demographic, economic, social, and natural forces cause an insurer's loss experience to fluctuate widely, which creates variability in its financial results. Volatile loss experience can affect the stock value of a publicly traded insurer;[2] alter an insurer's financial rating by independent rating agencies; cause abrupt changes in the approaches taken in managing the underwriting, claim, and marketing departments; or undermine the confidence of the sales force (especially independent brokers and agents who can place their customers with other insurers). In extreme cases, volatile loss experience can lead to insolvency.

Reinsurance can smooth the resulting peaks and valleys in an insurer's loss experience curve. In addition to aiding financial planning and supporting growth, this function of reinsurance encourages capital investment because investors are more likely to invest in companies whose financial results are stable.

Reinsurance can be arranged to stabilize the loss experience of a line of insurance (for example, commercial auto), a class of business (for example, truckers), or a primary insurer's entire book of business. In addition, a primary insurer can stabilize loss experience by obtaining reinsurance to accomplish any, or all, of these purposes:

• Limit its liability for a single loss exposure
• Limit its liability for several loss exposures affected by a common event
• Limit its liability for loss exposures that aggregate claims over time

The exhibit illustrates how reinsurance can stabilize a primary insurer's loss experience. See the exhibit "Stabilization of Annual Loss Experience for a Primary Insurer With a $20 Million Retention."

Provide Surplus Relief

Insurers that are growing rapidly may have difficulty maintaining a desirable capacity ratio, because of how they must account for their expenses to acquire new policies. State insurance regulation mandates that, for accounting purposes, such expenses be recognized at the time a new policy is sold. However, premiums are recognized as revenue as they are earned over the policy's life. When an insurer immediately recognizes expenses while only gradually recognizing revenue, its policyholders' surplus will decrease as its capacity ratio increases.

Stabilization of Annual Loss Experience for a Primary Insurer With a $20 Million Retention

(1) Time Period (Year)	(2) Actual Losses ($000)	(3) Amount Reinsured ($000)	(4) Stabilized Loss Level ($000)
1	15,000	—	15,000
2	35,000	15,000	20,000
3	13,000	—	13,000
4	25,000	5,000	20,000
5	40,000	20,000	20,000
6	37,000	17,000	20,000
7	16,500	—	16,500
8	9,250	—	9,250
9	18,000	—	18,000
10	10,750	—	10,750
Total	$219,500	$57,000	$162,500

The total actual losses are $219.5 million, or an average of $21.95 million each time period. If a reinsurance agreement were in place to cap losses to $20 million, the primary insurer's loss experience would be limited to the amounts shown in the stabilized loss level column. The broken line that fluctuates dramatically in the graph below represents actual losses, the dotted line represents stabilized losses, and the horizontal line represents average losses.

Graph of Hypothetical Loss Data

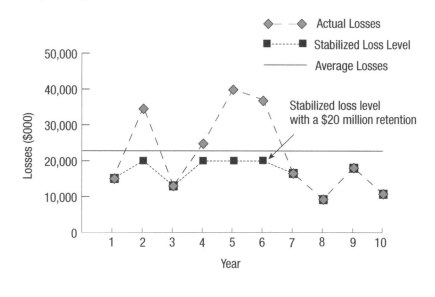

[DA03016]

Surplus relief

A replenishment of policyholders' surplus provided by the ceding commission paid to the primary insurer by the reinsurer.

Many insurers use reinsurance to provide **surplus relief**, which satisfies insurance regulatory constraints on excess growth. State insurance regulators monitor several financial ratios as part of their solvency surveillance efforts, but the relationship of written premiums to policyholders' surplus is generally a key financial ratio and one considered to be out of bounds if it exceeds 3 to 1 or 300 percent. Policyholders' surplus (also called "surplus to policyholders" or simply "surplus") is an insurer's net worth as reported on the financial statement prescribed by state insurance regulators. It represents the financial resource the primary insurer can draw on to pay unexpected losses.

Some reinsurance agreements facilitate premium growth by allowing the primary insurer to deduct a ceding commission on loss exposures ceded to the reinsurer. The ceding commission is an amount paid by the reinsurer to the primary insurer to cover part or all of a primary insurer's policy acquisition expenses. The ceding commission immediately offsets the primary insurer's policy acquisition expenses for the reinsured policies and often includes a profit provision, or an additional commission, if the reinsurance ceded is profitable.

Because the ceding commission replenishes the primary insurer's policyholders' surplus, the surplus relief facilitates the primary insurer's premium growth and the increase in policyholders' surplus lowers its capacity ratio.

Facilitate Withdrawal From a Market Segment

Reinsurance can also facilitate withdrawal from a market segment, which may be a particular class of business, geographic area, or type of insurance. A primary insurer may want to withdraw from a market segment that is unprofitable, undesirable, or incompatible with its strategic plan. When withdrawing from a market segment, the primary insurer has these options:

- Stop writing new insurance policies and continue in-force insurance until all policies expire (often referred to as "run-off")
- Cancel all policies (if insurance regulations permit) and refund the unearned premiums to insureds
- Withdraw from the market segment by purchasing portfolio reinsurance

To withdraw from a market segment, an insurer can stop writing new business or, to the extent permitted by applicable cancellation laws, cancel all policies in effect and return the unearned premiums to its insureds. However, these approaches can be unwieldy and expensive and could create ill will among insureds, producers, and state insurance regulators. They also create uncertainty about the insurer's outstanding claims, which must be settled, and about new claims, which might continue to be filed even after the insurer ceases operations.

Portfolio reinsurance

Reinsurance that transfers to the reinsurer liability for an entire type of insurance, territory, or book of business after the primary insurer has issued the policies.

Another approach available to the primary insurer is to transfer the liability for all outstanding policies to a reinsurer by purchasing **portfolio reinsurance**. Portfolio reinsurance can facilitate withdrawal from a market segment and prevent the formation of ill will due to policy cancellation. It is an exception to the general rule that reinsurers do not accept all of the liability for specified loss exposures of an insurer.

In portfolio reinsurance, the reinsurer accepts all of the liability for certain loss exposures covered under the primary insurer's policies, but the primary insurer must continue to fulfill its obligations to its insureds. For example, the primary insurer may decide to use portfolio reinsurance to withdraw from the errors and omissions insurance market. In this situation, the reinsurer typically agrees to indemnify the primary insurer for all losses incurred as of, and following, the date of the portfolio reinsurance agreement. However, the primary insurer continues to pay claims to (or on behalf of) its insureds who are covered by the underlying insurance.

Portfolio reinsurance can be expensive, particularly if the portfolio has been unprofitable and is expected to incur additional losses for the reinsurer. In many states, portfolio reinsurance must be approved by the state insurance department.

Sometimes a primary insurer wants to completely eliminate the liabilities it has assumed under the insurance policies it has issued. This can be accomplished through a **novation**. A novation is not considered portfolio reinsurance because the substitute insurer assumes the direct obligations to insureds covered by the underlying insurance. Usually, the approval of state insurance regulators or the insured is required to effect a novation.

Novation
An agreement under which one insurer or reinsurer is substituted for another.

Provide Underwriting Guidance

Reinsurance may also provide underwriting guidance. Reinsurers work with a wide variety of insurers in the domestic and global markets under many different circumstances. Consequently, reinsurers accumulate a great deal of underwriting expertise. A reinsurer's understanding of insurance operations and the insurance industry can assist other insurers, particularly inexperienced primary insurers entering new markets and offering new products. For example, one medium-size insurer reinsured 95 percent of its umbrella liability coverage over a period of years and relied heavily on the reinsurer for technical assistance in underwriting and pricing its policies. Without such technical assistance, certain primary insurers would find it difficult to generate underwriting profits from coverages with which they have limited expertise.

Reinsurers that provide underwriting assistance to primary insurers must respect the confidentiality of their clients' proprietary information. Reinsurers often learn about the primary insurer's marketing and underwriting strategies but should not reveal insurer-specific information to other parties.

REINSURANCE TRANSACTIONS

No single reinsurance agreement performs all the reinsurance functions. Instead, reinsurers have developed various types of reinsurance, each of which is effective in helping insurers meet one or more goals. A primary insurer often combines several reinsurance agreements to meet its particular needs. Each reinsurance agreement is tailored to the specific needs of the primary insurer and the reinsurer.

There are two types of reinsurance transactions: treaty and facultative.

Treaty reinsurance uses one agreement for an entire class or portfolio of loss exposures and is also referred to as obligatory reinsurance. The reinsurance agreement is typically called the treaty.

Facultative reinsurance uses a separate reinsurance agreement for each loss exposure it wants to reinsure and is also referred to as nonobligatory reinsurance.

Treaty Reinsurance

In treaty reinsurance, the reinsurer agrees in advance to reinsure all the loss exposures that fall within the treaty. Although some treaties allow the reinsurer limited discretion in reinsuring individual loss exposures, most treaties require that all loss exposures within the treaty's terms must be reinsured.

Primary insurers usually use treaty reinsurance as the foundation of their reinsurance programs. Treaty reinsurance provides primary insurers with the certainty needed to formulate underwriting policy and develop underwriting guidelines. Primary insurers work with reinsurance intermediaries (or with reinsurers directly) to develop comprehensive reinsurance programs that address the primary insurers' varied needs. The reinsurance programs that satisfy those needs often include several reinsurance agreements and the participation of several reinsurers.

Treaty reinsurance agreements are tailored to fit the primary insurer's individual requirements. The price and terms of each reinsurance treaty are individually negotiated.

Treaty reinsurance agreements are usually designed to address a primary insurer's need to reinsure many loss exposures over a period of time. Although the reinsurance agreement's term may be for only one year, the relationship between the primary insurer and the reinsurer often spans many years. A primary insurer's management usually finds that a long-term relationship with a reinsurer enables the primary insurer to be able to consistently fulfill its producers' requests to place insurance with them.

Most, but not all, treaty reinsurance agreements require the primary insurer to cede all eligible loss exposures to the reinsurer. Primary insurers usually make treaty reinsurance agreements so their underwriters do not have to exercise discretion in using reinsurance. If treaty reinsurance agreements permitted primary insurers to choose which loss exposures they ceded to the reinsurer, the reinsurer would be exposed to **adverse selection**.

Treaty reinsurance

A reinsurance agreement that covers an entire class or portfolio of loss exposures and provides that the primary insurer's individual loss exposures that fall within the treaty are automatically reinsured.

Facultative reinsurance

Reinsurance of individual loss exposures in which the primary insurer chooses which loss exposures to submit to the reinsurer, and the reinsurer can accept or reject any loss exposures submitted.

Adverse selection

The decision to reinsure those loss exposures that have an increased probability of loss because the retention of those loss exposures is undesirable.

Because treaty reinsurers are obligated to accept ceded loss exposures once the reinsurance agreement is in place, reinsurers usually want to know about the integrity and experience of the primary insurer's management and the degree to which the primary insurer's published underwriting guidelines represent its actual underwriting practices.

Facultative Reinsurance

In facultative reinsurance, the primary insurer negotiates a separate reinsurance agreement for each loss exposure that it wants to reinsure. The primary insurer is not obligated to purchase reinsurance, and the reinsurer is not obligated to reinsure loss exposures submitted to it. A facultative reinsurance agreement is written for a specified time period and cannot be canceled by either party unless contractual obligations, such as payment of premiums, are not met.

The reinsurer issues a **facultative certificate of reinsurance** (or facultative certificate) that is attached to the primary insurer's copy of the policy being reinsured.

Facultative certificate of reinsurance
An agreement that defines the terms of the facultative reinsurance coverage on a specific loss exposure.

Facultative reinsurance serves four functions:

- Facultative reinsurance can provide large-line capacity for loss exposures that exceed the limits of treaty reinsurance agreements.

- Facultative reinsurance can reduce the primary insurer's exposure in a given geographic area. For example, a marine underwriter may be considering underwriting numerous shiploads of cargo that are stored in the same warehouse and that belong to different insureds. The underwriter could use facultative reinsurance for some of those loss exposures, thereby reducing the primary insurer's overall exposure to loss.

- Facultative reinsurance can insure a loss exposure with atypical hazard characteristics and thereby maintain the favorable loss experience of the primary insurer's treaty reinsurance and any associated profit-sharing arrangements. Maintaining favorable treaty loss experience is important because the reinsurer has underwritten and priced the treaty with certain expectations. A loss exposure that is inconsistent with the primary insurer's typical portfolio of insurance policies may cause excessive losses and lead to the treaty's termination or a price increase. The treaty reinsurer is usually willing for the primary insurer to remove high-hazard loss exposures from the treaty by using facultative reinsurance. These facultative placements of atypical loss exposures also benefit the treaty reinsurer. For example, an insured under a commercial property policy may request coverage for an expensive fine arts collection that the primary insurer and its treaty reinsurer would not ordinarily want to cover. Facultative reinsurance of the fine arts collection would eliminate the underwriting concern by removing this loss exposure from the treaty. Often, the treaty reinsurer's own facultative reinsurance department provides this reinsurance. The facultative reinsurer knows that adverse selection occurs in facultative reinsurance. Consequently, the loss exposures submitted for reinsurance are likely to have an increased probability of loss. Therefore, facultative reinsurance is usually priced to reflect the likelihood of adverse selection.

- Facultative reinsurance can insure particular classes of loss exposures that are excluded under treaty reinsurance.

Primary insurers purchase facultative reinsurance mainly to reinsure loss exposures that they do not typically insure or on exposures with high levels of underwriting risk. Consequently, primary insurers use facultative reinsurance for fewer of their loss exposures than they use treaty insurance. Primary insurers that find they are increasingly using facultative reinsurance may want to review the adequacy of their treaty reinsurance.

The expense of placing facultative reinsurance can be high for both the primary insurer and the reinsurer. In negotiating facultative reinsurance, the primary insurer must provide extensive information about each loss exposure. Consequently, administrative costs are relatively high because the primary insurer must devote a significant amount of time to complete each cession and to notify the reinsurer of any endorsement, loss notice, or policy cancellation. Likewise, the reinsurer must underwrite and price each facultative submission. See the exhibit "Hybrids of Treaty and Facultative Reinsurance."

Hybrids of Treaty and Facultative Reinsurance

Reinsurers sometimes use hybrid agreements that have elements of both treaty and facultative reinsurance. The hybrid agreements usually describe how individual facultative reinsurance placements will be handled. For example, the agreement may specify the basic underwriting parameters of the loss exposures that will be ceded to the reinsurer as well as premium and loss allocation formulas. Although hybrid agreements may be used infrequently, they demonstrate the flexibility of the reinsurance market to satisfy the mutual needs of primary insurers and reinsurers. The two hybrid agreements briefly described next illustrate common reinsurance agreement variations.

- In a *facultative treaty*, the primary insurer and the reinsurer agree on how subsequent individual facultative submissions will be handled. A facultative treaty could be used when a class of business has insufficient loss exposures to justify treaty reinsurance but has a sufficient number of loss exposures to determine the details of future individual placements.

- In a *facultative obligatory treaty*, although the primary insurer has the option of ceding loss exposures, the reinsurer is obligated to accept all loss exposures submitted to it. Facultative obligatory treaties are also called *semi-obligatory treaties*.

[DA05757]

TYPES OF REINSURANCE

Each reinsurance agreement negotiated between a primary insurer and reinsurer is unique because its terms reflect the primary insurer's needs and the willingness of reinsurers in the marketplace to meet those needs. Several forms of reinsurance have been developed to serve the functions of reinsurance and to help insurers meet their goals.

The two types of reinsurance transactions are treaty reinsurance and facultative reinsurance. These types can be further categorized based on the manner in which the primary insurer and the reinsurer divide the obligations under the reinsurance agreements. The principal approaches that reinsurers use to allocate losses are broadly defined as pro rata reinsurance and excess of loss reinsurance. These types of reinsurance reflect how the primary insurer and reinsurer will share premiums, amounts of insurance, and losses.

The exhibit shows the types of reinsurance and their relationships, and augments the description of the subcategories of pro rata and excess of loss reinsurance. In practice, a reinsurance agreement might contain several of the various types of reinsurance agreements to meet the specific needs of a primary insurer. Unlike primary insurance contracts, reinsurance agreements are not standardized. See the exhibit "Types of Reinsurance."

Pro Rata Reinsurance

Under **pro rata reinsurance**, or proportional reinsurance, the primary insurer cedes a portion of the original insurance premiums to the reinsurer as a reinsurance premium. The reinsurer usually pays the primary insurer a ceding commission for the loss exposures ceded. The ceding commission reimburses the primary insurer for policy acquisition expenses incurred when the underlying policies were sold. In addition to policy acquisition expenses, insurers incur loss adjustment expenses. Loss adjustment expenses that can be related to a specific loss are usually shared proportionately by the primary insurer and the reinsurer.

The amount of insurance, the premium, and the losses (including loss adjustment expenses) are divided between the primary insurer and the reinsurer in the same proportions as the risk. For example, if the reinsurer covers 60 percent of the liability for each loss exposure the primary insurer insures, then the reinsurer would be entitled to 60 percent of the policy premiums and would be responsible for 60 percent of each loss. The amount of the ceding commission paid to the primary insurer is usually negotiated and is taken from the reinsurance premium remitted to the reinsurer. When the ceding commission is a fixed percentage of the ceded premium with no adjustment for the primary insurer's loss experience, it is referred to as a **flat commission**.

The reinsurance agreement may also include a **profit-sharing commission**, or profit commission, which is negotiated and paid to the primary insurer after the end of the treaty year if the reinsurer earns greater-than-expected profits

Pro rata reinsurance
A type of reinsurance in which the primary insurer and reinsurer proportionately share the amounts of insurance, policy premiums, and losses (including loss adjustment expenses).

Flat commission
A ceding commission that is a fixed percentage of the ceded premiums.

Profit-sharing commission
A ceding commission that is contingent on the reinsurer realizing a predetermined percentage of excess profit on ceded loss exposures.

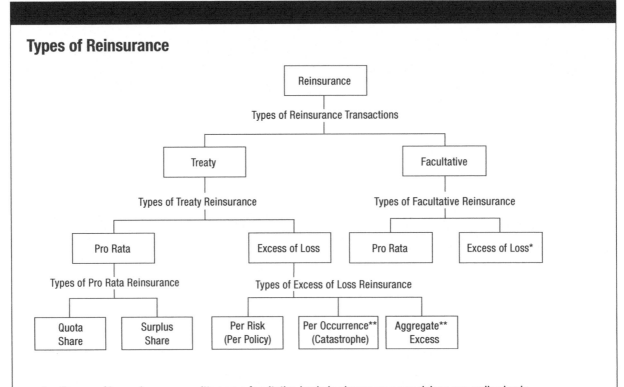

Types of Reinsurance

*   Excess of loss reinsurance written on a facultative basis is always on a per-risk or per-policy basis.

**   Per occurrence and aggregate excess of loss reinsurance relate to a type of insurance, a territory, or the primary insurer's entire portfolio of in-force loss exposures rather than to a specific policy or a specific loss exposure.

[DA05080]

on the reinsurance agreement. The profit-sharing commission percentage is predetermined and applied to the reinsurer's excess profits; that is, the profits remaining after losses, expenses, and the reinsurer's minimum margin for profit are deducted. Profit commission is also called "contingent commission" because its payment is contingent on the reinsurance agreement's profitability.

Sometimes, as an alternative to the flat commission and profit-sharing commission, the ceding commission initially paid to the primary insurer may be adjusted to reflect the actual profitability of the reinsurance agreement. This type of commission is called a **sliding scale commission** and could result in the commission being lower than the commission initially paid.

Pro rata reinsurance is generally chosen by newly incorporated insurers or insurers with limited capital because it is effective in providing surplus relief. Its effectiveness results from the practice of paying ceding commissions under pro rata treaties, a practice not common under excess of loss treaties.

Pro rata reinsurance can be identified as either quota share or surplus share. The principal difference between them is how each one indicates the primary insurer's retention.

Sliding scale commission

A ceding commission based on a formula that adjusts the commission according to the profitability of the reinsurance agreement.

Quota Share Reinsurance

The distinguishing characteristic of **quota share reinsurance** is that the primary insurer and the reinsurer use a fixed percentage in sharing the amounts of insurance, policy premiums, and losses (including loss adjustment expenses). Quota share reinsurance can be used with both property insurance and liability insurance but is more frequently used in property insurance.

For example, an insurer may arrange a reinsurance treaty in which it retains 45 percent of policy premiums, coverage limits, and losses while reinsuring the remainder. Such a treaty would be called a "55 percent quota share treaty" because the reinsurer accepts 55 percent of the liability for each loss exposure subject to the treaty.

Most reinsurance agreements specify a maximum dollar limit above which responsibility for additional coverage limits or losses reverts to the primary insurer (or is taken by another reinsurer). With a pro rata reinsurance agreement, that maximum dollar amount is stated in terms of the coverage limits of each policy subject to the treaty. For example, a primary insurer and a reinsurer may share amounts of insurance, policy premiums, and losses on a 45 percent and 55 percent basis, respectively, subject to a $1 million maximum coverage amount for each policy.

In addition to a maximum coverage amount limitation, some pro rata reinsurance agreements include a per occurrence limit, which restricts the primary insurer's reinsurance recovery for losses originating from a single occurrence. This per occurrence limit may be stated as an aggregate dollar amount or as a **loss ratio** cap. The per occurrence limit diminishes the usefulness of pro rata reinsurance in protecting the primary insurer from the effects of catastrophic events. Primary insurers exposed to catastrophic losses usually include **catastrophe excess of loss reinsurance** in their reinsurance programs.

The exhibit shows how the amounts of insurance, policy premiums, and losses would be shared between a primary insurer and a reinsurer for three policies subject to a quota share treaty. See the exhibit "Quota Share Reinsurance Example."

These observations can be made about quota share reinsurance:

- Because the retention and cession amounts are each a fixed percentage, the dollar amount of the retention and the dollar amount of the cession change as the amount of insurance changes. On policies with higher amounts of insurance, the primary insurer will have a higher dollar retention.

- Because the primary insurer cedes a fixed percentage under a quota share treaty, even policies with low amounts of insurance that the primary insurer could safely retain are reinsured.

- Quota share treaties are straightforward because of the fixed percentage used in sharing premiums and losses. The primary insurer can combine

Quota share reinsurance

A type of pro rata reinsurance in which the primary insurer and the reinsurer share the amounts of insurance, policy premiums, and losses (including loss adjustment expenses) using a fixed percentage.

Loss ratio

A ratio that measures losses and loss adjustment expenses against earned premiums and that reflects the percentage of premiums being consumed by losses.

Catastrophe excess of loss reinsurance

A type of excess of loss reinsurance that protects the primary insurer from an accumulation of retained losses that arise from a single catastrophic event.

Quota Share Reinsurance Example

Brookgreen Insurance Company has a quota share treaty with Cypress Reinsurer. The treaty has a $250,000 limit, a retention of 25 percent, and a cession of 75 percent. The following three policies are issued by Brookgreen Insurance Company and are subject to the pro rata treaty with Cypress Reinsurer.

- Policy A insures Building A for $25,000 for a premium of $400, with one loss of $8,000.
- Policy B insures Building B for $100,000 for a premium of $1,000, with one loss of $10,000.
- Policy C insures Building C for $150,000 for a premium of $1,500, with one loss of $60,000.

Division of Insurance, Premiums, and Losses Under Quota Share Treaty

	Brookgreen Insurance Retention (25%)	Cypress Reinsurance Cession (75%)	Total
Policy A			
Amounts of insurance	$6,250	$18,750	$25,000
Premiums	100	300	400
Losses	2,000	6,000	8,000
Policy B			
Amounts of insurance	$25,000	$75,000	$100,000
Premiums	250	750	1,000
Losses	2,500	7,500	10,000
Policy C			
Amounts of insurance	$37,500	$112,500	$150,000
Premiums	375	1,125	1,500
Losses	15,000	45,000	60,000

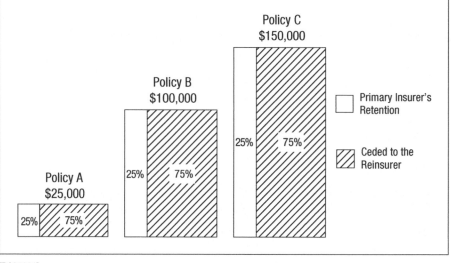

[DA05081]

premium and loss amounts and determine the amounts owed to the reinsurer in premiums and owed by the reinsurer in losses.

- Because the primary insurer and the reinsurer share liability for every loss exposure subject to the quota share treaty, the reinsurer is usually not subject to adverse selection. The loss ratio for the reinsurer is the same as that of the primary insurer for the ceded loss exposures.

One type of quota share treaty, a **variable quota share treaty**, has the advantage of enabling a primary insurer to retain a larger proportion of the small loss exposures that are within its financial capability to absorb, while maintaining a safer and smaller retention on larger loss exposures.

Surplus Share Reinsurance

The distinguishing characteristic of **surplus share reinsurance** is that when an underlying policy's total amount of insurance exceeds a stipulated dollar amount, or line, the reinsurer assumes the surplus share of the amount of insurance (the difference between the primary insurer's line and the total amount of insurance). Surplus share reinsurance is typically used only with property insurance.

The primary insurer and the reinsurer share the policy premiums and losses proportionately. The primary insurer's share of the policy premiums and losses is the proportion that the line bears to the total amount of insurance. The reinsurer's share of the premiums and losses is the proportion that the amount ceded bears to the total. For example, if the line is $50,000 and the amount ceded is $200,000, the primary insurer would receive 20 percent ($50,000 ÷ $250,000) of the policy premium and pay 20 percent of all losses, while the reinsurer would receive 80 percent ($200,000 ÷ $250,000) of the policy premium and pay 80 percent of all losses.

The exhibit shows how a primary insurer and a reinsurer would share amounts of insurance, policy premiums, and losses under a surplus share treaty using the same three policies shown in the quota share treaty exhibit. See the exhibit "Surplus Share Reinsurance Example."

The reinsurance limit—the total limit or capacity—of a surplus share treaty is expressed in multiples of the primary insurer's line. A primary insurer with a nine-line surplus share treaty has the capacity under the treaty to insure loss exposures with amounts of insurance that exceed its retention by a multiple of nine. For example, if the line is $300,000 for a nine-line surplus share treaty, the primary insurer has a total underwriting capacity of $3 million, calculated as the $300,000 line, plus nine multiples of that $300,000 line. In addition to being expressed as a number of lines, the reinsurance limit of a surplus share treaty can also be expressed as an amount of insurance the reinsurer is willing to provide, such as $2.7 million ($300,000 multiplied by nine lines).

Variable quota share treaty
A quota share reinsurance treaty in which the cession percentage retention varies based on specified predetermined criteria such as the amount of insurance needed.

Surplus share reinsurance
A type of pro rata reinsurance in which the policies covered are those whose amount of insurance exceeds a stipulated dollar amount, or line.

Surplus Share Reinsurance Example

Brookgreen Insurance Company has a surplus share treaty with Cypress Reinsurer and retains a line of $25,000. The treaty contains nine lines and provides for a maximum cession of $225,000. Therefore, the retention and reinsurance provide Brookgreen with the ability to issue policies with amounts of insurance as high as $250,000. The following three policies are issued by Brookgreen Insurance Company and are subject to the surplus share treaty with Cypress Reinsurer.

- Policy A insures Building A for $25,000 for a premium of $400, with one loss of $8,000.
- Policy B insures Building B for $100,000 for a premium of $1,000, with one loss of $10,000.
- Policy C insures Building C for $150,000 for a premium of $1,500, with one loss of $60,000.

Division of Insurance, Premiums, and Losses Under Surplus Share Treaty

	Brookgreen Insurance Retention	Cypress Reinsurance Cession	Total
Policy A			
Amounts of insurance	$25,000 (100%)	$0 (0%)	$25,000
Premiums	400	0	400
Losses	8,000	0	8,000
Policy B			
Amounts of insurance	$25,000 (25%)	$75,000 (75%)	$100,000
Premiums	250	750	1,000
Losses	2,500	7,500	10,000
Policy C			
Amounts of insurance	$25,000 (16.67%)	$125,000 (83.33%)	$150,000
Premiums	250	1,250	1,500
Losses	10,000	50,000	60,000

Policy A
No participation
by the reinsurer

Policy B
$100,000
25% / 75%

Policy C
$150,000
16.67% / 83.33%

Primary Insurer's Retention

Ceded to the Reinsurer

These observations can be made about surplus share reinsurance:

- The surplus share treaty does not cover policies with amounts of insurance that are less than the primary insurer's line. Many primary insurers use surplus share reinsurance instead of quota share reinsurance so that they do not have to cede any part of the liability for loss exposures that can be safely retained.

- The amount of insurance for a large number of loss exposures may be too small to be ceded to the treaty but, in the aggregate, may cause the primary insurer to incur significant losses that are not reinsured. For example, many homeowners policies in the same region that do not exceed the primary insurer's line could incur extensive losses from a single occurrence, such as a hurricane.

- Because the percentage of policy premiums and losses varies for each loss exposure ceded, surplus share treaties are more costly to administer than quota share treaties. Primary insurers must keep records and, in many cases, periodically provide the reinsurer with a report called a **bordereau**.

- Surplus share treaties may provide surplus relief to the primary insurer because the reinsurer usually pays a ceding commission for those policies ceded. Loss exposures with amounts of insurance that are less than the primary insurer's line are not reinsured, so a surplus share treaty typically provides less surplus relief than does a quota share treaty.

Bordereau

A report the primary insurer provides periodically to the reinsurer that contains a history of all loss exposures reinsured under the treaty.

Unlike the simplified example shown in the "Surplus Share Reinsurance Example" exhibit, many surplus share treaties allow the primary insurer to increase its line from a minimum amount to a maximum amount, depending on the potential loss severity of the exposed limit. For example, Brookgreen Insurance Company's surplus share treaty may allow the company to increase its line on a "superior" loss exposure from $25,000 to $50,000. In this case, the nine-line surplus share treaty would give Brookgreen Insurance Company the large line capacity to insure loss exposures with amounts of insurance as large as $500,000, which is calculated as the $50,000 line plus nine multiplied by the $50,000 line. The primary insurer's ability to vary its line also allows it to retain some loss exposures it may otherwise be required to cede. The flexibility provided by the reinsurer in the surplus share treaty is usually communicated to the primary insurer's underwriters through a **line guide**, or line authorization guide.

Line guide

A document that provides the minimum and maximum line a primary insurer can retain on a loss exposure.

When the total underwriting capacity of the primary insurer's surplus share treaty is insufficient to meet its large-line capacity needs, the primary insurer can arrange for additional surplus share reinsurance from another reinsurer. When a primary insurer arranges more than one surplus share treaty, the surplus share treaty that applies immediately above the primary insurer's line is referred to as the first surplus. Other surplus share treaties are referred to in the order that they provide additional large-line capacity, such as second or third surplus treaties.

Excess of loss reinsurance (nonproportional reinsurance)

A type of reinsurance in which the primary insurer is indemnified for losses that exceed a specified dollar amount.

Attachment point

The dollar amount above which the reinsurer responds to losses.

Excess of Loss Reinsurance

In an **excess of loss reinsurance** agreement, also called "non-proportional reinsurance," the reinsurer responds to a loss only when the loss exceeds the primary insurer's retention, often referred to as the **attachment point**. The primary insurer fully retains losses that are less than the attachment point, and will sometimes be required by the reinsurer to also retain responsibility for a percentage of the losses that exceed the attachment point.

Excess of loss reinsurance can be visualized as a layer, or a series of layers, of reinsurance on top of the primary insurer's retention. See the exhibit "How Excess of Loss Reinsurance Is Layered."

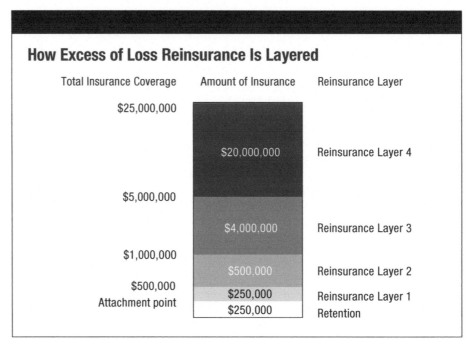

[DA05084]

An excess of loss reinsurer's obligation to indemnify the primary insurer for losses depends on the amount of the loss and the layer of coverage the reinsurer provides. The reinsurer providing the first layer of excess of loss reinsurance shown in the exhibit would indemnify the primary insurer for losses that exceed $250,000 (the attachment point) up to total incurred losses of $500,000. This reinsurer describes its position in the primary insurer's excess of loss reinsurance program as being "$250,000 in excess of (denoted as 'xs') $250,000." The reinsurer in the second layer of the excess of loss reinsurance program would indemnify the primary insurer for losses that exceed $500,000 up to total incurred losses of $1 million, or "$500,000 xs $500,000." Losses that exceed the capacity of the primary insurer's excess of loss reinsurance remain the primary insurer's responsibility unless otherwise reinsured. In the exhibit, loss amounts in excess of $25 million are the primary insurer's responsibility.

Excess of loss reinsurance premiums are negotiated based on the likelihood that losses will exceed the attachment point. The reinsurance premium for excess of loss reinsurance is usually stated as a percentage (often called a rate) of the policy premium charged by the primary insurer (often called the **subject premium** or underlying premium). Therefore, unlike quota share and surplus share reinsurance, the excess of loss reinsurer receives a nonproportional share of the premium.

Generally, reinsurers do not pay ceding commissions under excess of loss reinsurance agreements. However, the reinsurer may reward the primary insurer for favorable loss experience by paying a profit commission or reducing the rate used in calculating the reinsurance premium.

The primary insurer's attachment point is usually set at a level where claims that are expected are retained. However, if the primary insurer's volume of losses is expected to be significant, an excess of loss reinsurance agreement may have a low attachment point. This type of reinsurance agreement is sometimes referred to as a **working cover**. A working cover enables the primary insurer to spread its losses over several years. The primary insurer and the reinsurer anticipate that profitable years will offset unprofitable ones. Primary insurers selling a type of insurance with which they have little expertise may choose to purchase a working cover until they better understand the frequency and severity of losses that the portfolio for that particular type of insurance produces. Reinsurers typically require a working cover to contain an occurrence limitation of two or three times the reinsurance limit. This requirement prevents the working cover from being exposed to catastrophic events, such as an earthquake.

Sometimes a co-participation provision is contained within an excess of loss reinsurance agreement. The purpose of this provision is to provide the primary insurer with a financial incentive to efficiently manage losses that exceed the attachment point. A co-participation provision is usually denoted by specifying a percentage before the position of its layer. For example, if the fourth layer in the "How Excess of Loss Reinsurance Is Layered" exhibit had a 5 percent co-participation provision, that layer would be specified as "95% of $20,000,000 xs $5,000,000."

In addition to indemnifying losses in a layer of coverage, the reinsurer's obligation may also extend to payment of loss adjustment expenses. Loss adjustment expenses are often a substantial insurer expense, especially for insurance for liability loss exposures. Therefore, excess of loss reinsurance agreements are usually very specific regarding how loss adjustment expenses attributable to specific losses are handled. In rare circumstances, they may be excluded from

Subject premium
The premium the primary insurer charges on its underlying policies and to which a rate is applied to determine the reinsurance premium.

Working cover
An excess of loss reinsurance agreement with a low attachment point.

the reinsurance agreement, but these are the two most common approaches to handling loss adjustment expenses:

- Prorate the loss adjustment expenses between the primary insurer and the reinsurer based on the same percentage share that each is responsible for the loss. This approach is commonly referred to as "*pro rata* in addition."
- Add the loss adjustment expenses to the amount of the loss when applying the attachment point of the excess of loss reinsurance agreement. This approach is commonly referred to as "loss adjustment expense included in the limit."

If loss adjustment expenses are prorated, the primary insurer pays all of the loss adjustment expenses when the loss amount does not exceed the attachment point. If loss adjustment expenses are added to the loss amount, the reinsurer may have to pay a claim in which the loss amount alone does not exceed the attachment point. Primary insurers and reinsurers usually assess the potential for loss adjustment expenses independent of the actual loss potential when negotiating the excess of loss reinsurance agreement. Commonly, reinsurance agreements provide that loss adjustment expenses are prorated for property insurance and most types of liability insurance. However, excess of loss reinsurance covering liability insurance that usually involves substantial litigation often specifies that loss adjustment expenses are added to the amount of the loss when applying the attachment point. For instance, medical malpractice insurance often involves substantial loss adjustment expenses in the form of legal fees even if the claim can be settled with a nominal loss payment or no payment at all.

There are five types of excess of loss reinsurance, each of which usually has a specific use. See the exhibit "Five Types of Excess of Loss Reinsurance."

Per Risk Excess of Loss

Per risk excess of loss reinsurance

A type of excess of loss reinsurance that covers property insurance and that applies separately to each loss occurring to each risk.

The first type of excess of loss reinsurance is **per risk excess of loss reinsurance**, which is often referred to as property per risk excess of loss and is generally used with property insurance. It applies separately to each loss occurring to each risk, with the primary insurer usually determining what constitutes one risk (loss exposure).

The exhibit indicates how a reinsurer would respond if the primary insurer defined three separate buildings under a per risk excess of loss reinsurance agreement as three separate risks. In this example, a tornado damaged all three buildings in one occurrence. Because each building is a risk, the attachment point and reinsurance limit apply separately to each. The attachment point and reinsurance limit are stated as a dollar amount of loss. See the exhibit "Example of Per Risk Excess of Loss Reinsurance Applying $950,000 xs $50,000."

Per occurrence limits are commonly included with per risk excess of loss reinsurance agreements. A per occurrence limit restricts the amount that

---

Five Types of Excess of Loss Reinsurance

1. Per risk excess of loss
2. Catastrophe excess of loss
3. Per policy excess of loss
4. Per occurrence excess of loss
5. Aggregate excess of loss

[DA05083]

Example of Per Risk Excess of Loss Reinsurance Applying $950,000 xs $50,000

Building Number	Loss Amount	Primary Insurer's Retention	Reinsurer's Payment
1	$ 500,000	$ 50,000	$ 450,000
2	350,000	50,000	300,000
3	700,000	50,000	650,000
Total	$1,550,000	$150,000	$1,400,000

[DA05086]

the reinsurer pays as the result of a single occurrence affecting multiple risks. Had a per occurrence limit of $1 million been imposed in the example in the exhibit, the reinsurer would have been responsible for only $1 million of losses (instead of $1.4 million) because the three losses arose out of the same occurrence (the tornado). Catastrophe excess of loss reinsurance is usually purchased in conjunction with per risk excess of loss reinsurance to protect the primary insurer from one occurrence affecting multiple risks.

Catastrophe Excess of Loss

The second type of excess of loss reinsurance is catastrophe excess of loss reinsurance, which protects the primary insurer from an accumulation of retained losses that arise from a single catastrophic event. It may be purchased to protect the primary insurer and its reinsurers on a combined basis but is more frequently purchased to protect the primary insurer on a net basis after all other reinsurance recoveries are made. Examples of catastrophic events include tornadoes, hurricanes, and earthquakes. Such events, especially major hurricanes, can result in losses totaling billions of dollars.

As with per risk excess of loss reinsurance, the attachment point and reinsurance limit for catastrophe excess of loss reinsurance are stated as dollar amounts of loss. The attachment point is subject to negotiation, but it is usually set high enough so that it would be exceeded only if the aggregation of losses from a catastrophe would impair the policyholders' surplus of a primary insurer. Additionally, losses exceeding the attachment point are usually subject to a co-participation provision.

Loss occurrence clause

A reinsurance agreement clause that defines the scope of a catastrophic occurrence for the purposes of the agreement.

Because the attachment point and reinsurance limit apply separately to each catastrophe occurring during a policy period, the catastrophe excess of loss reinsurance agreement defines the scope of a catastrophic occurrence through a **loss occurrence clause** (sometimes called an hours clause). The loss occurrence clause specifies a time period, in hours, during which the primary insurer's losses from the same catastrophic occurrence can be aggregated and applied to the attachment point and reinsurance limits of the catastrophe excess of loss reinsurance agreement. Such clauses usually specify a time period of 72 consecutive hours (three days) for hurricane losses and 168 consecutive hours (seven days) for earthquake losses. When making a claim against the catastrophe excess of loss reinsurance agreement, the primary insurer can usually choose the date and time when the period of consecutive hours commences to maximize the amount of recovery under the agreement. The exhibit provides an example of the operation of a loss occurrence clause in a catastrophe excess of loss reinsurance agreement and shows how a primary insurer can select the period of coverage to its advantage. See the exhibit "Example of the Operation of a Loss Occurrence Clause in a Catastrophe Excess of Loss Reinsurance Agreement."

Example of the Operation of a Loss Occurrence Clause in a Catastrophe Excess of Loss Reinsurance Agreement

Day	Losses	Period of Coverage Providing Maximum Recovery
1	$1,000,000	
2	1,000,000	
3	2,000,000	$7,000,000
4	4,000,000	
Total	$8,000,000	

The total losses that could potentially be applied to the reinsurance agreement are $7 million if the seventy-two-hour period starts on the second day, as opposed to $4 million if the period had started on the first day.

[DA05087]

In this example, the primary insurer sustains $8 million in losses from a hurricane over a four-day period. The primary insurer has a $6 million xs $1 million catastrophe excess of loss reinsurance treaty with a loss occurrence clause that stipulates a period of seventy-two consecutive hours for a hurricane. In this simplified example, selecting the specific hour of the day that coverage begins is not an issue, and no co-participation provision applies. Given the distribution of losses over the four days, the primary insurer should elect to start the seventy-two-hour period on the second day to maximize its reinsurance recovery.

Payments from the reinsurer to the primary insurer for catastrophe losses reduce the reinsurance coverage limits available for future losses, but catastrophe excess of loss reinsurance agreements often include a provision requiring the primary insurer to pay an additional premium to reinstate the limits of the agreement after a loss. This provision allows the reinsurer to obtain additional premiums and gives the primary insurer confidence that sufficient limits are available should another catastrophe occur during the reinsurance agreement's term.

Primary insurers and their reinsurers usually do not anticipate that the catastrophe excess of loss reinsurance will be triggered every year. Catastrophe protection is purchased for the unlikely, but possible, event that may cause unstable operating results or that cannot be absorbed by the primary insurer's policyholders' surplus. A primary insurer's need for catastrophe reinsurance and the amount purchased depends on its catastrophe loss exposures. The exhibit provides an example of how the amount of loss retained by the primary insurer and the amount of loss owed by the reinsurer are determined under catastrophe excess of loss reinsurance. See the exhibit "Catastrophe Excess of Loss Reinsurance Example."

Per Policy Excess of Loss

The third type of excess of loss reinsurance, **per policy excess of loss reinsurance**, is used primarily with liability insurance. The exhibit provides an example of how a reinsurer would respond under a $900,000 xs $100,000 per policy excess of loss treaty. In this example, three separate general liability policies issued by the same primary insurer incur losses from *separate events*. See the exhibit "Example of Per Policy Excess of Loss Reinsurance Applying $900,000 xs $100,000."

Per Occurrence Excess of Loss

Per occurrence excess of loss reinsurance, the fourth type of excess of loss reinsurance, is usually used for liability insurance. It applies the attachment point and the reinsurance limit to the total losses arising from a single event affecting one or more of the primary insurer's policies. See the exhibit "Example of Per Occurrence Excess of Loss Reinsurance Applying $4,900,000 xs $100,000."

Per policy excess of loss reinsurance
A type of excess of loss reinsurance that applies the attachment point and the reinsurance limit separately to each insurance policy issued by the primary insurer regardless of the number of losses occurring under each policy.

Per occurrence excess of loss reinsurance
A type of excess of loss reinsurance that applies the attachment point and reinsurance limit to the total losses arising from a single event affecting one or more of the primary insurer's policies.

Catastrophe Excess of Loss Reinsurance Example

Brookgreen Insurance Company (Brookgreen) decides to sell earthquake coverage in southern California but wants to limit its losses to approximately $1 million from any one earthquake. Brookgreen conducted a study and estimated that its maximum loss from any one earthquake, given its spread of earthquake loss exposures in southern California, would be $10 million. Brookgreen purchases catastrophe excess of loss reinsurance of 95 percent of $9,250,000 xs $750,000. If Brookgreen were to sustain a $10 million loss from an earthquake, it would retain $1,212,500 and the reinsurer would pay $8,787,500. These figures are calculated as follows:

Step 1—Determination of the loss amount exceeding the attachment point

Amount exceeding the attachment point	=	Amount of loss (subject to the reinsurance limit)	−	Retention
	=	$10,000,000	−	$750,000
	=	$9,250,000		

Step 2—Determination of the co-participation

Amount of co-participation	=	Amount exceeding the attachment point	×	Co-participation percentage
	=	$9,250,000	×	0.05
	=	$462,500		

Step 3—Determination of the amount of loss owed by the reinsurer

Amount owed by the reinsurer	=	Amount exceeding the attachment point	−	Amount of co-participation
	=	$9,250,000	−	$462,500
	=	$8,787,500		

Step 4—Determination of the amount retained by Brookgreen

Amount retained by Brookgreen	=	Retention	+	Amount of co-participation
	=	$750,000	+	$462,500
	=	$1,212,500		

[DA05088]

The exhibit provides an example of how a per occurrence excess of loss treaty applies to the three policies used in the "Example of Per Policy Excess of Loss Reinsurance Applying $900,000 xs $100,000" exhibit. In the exhibit, a $100,000 attachment point applies to the total losses of the policies covering the same event, and there is a $4.9 million reinsurance limit. A per occurrence excess of loss treaty covering liability insurance usually has an attachment point that is less than the highest liability policy limit offered by the primary insurer.

Example of Per Policy Excess of Loss Reinsurance Applying $900,000 xs $100,000

Primary Insurer has a $900,000 xs $100,000 per policy excess of loss treaty. The table below shows three policies for which Primary Insurer is indemnified by Reinsurer because the amount of loss arising out of each of the policies exceeds Primary Insurer's attachment point.

Policy	Loss Amount	Primary Insurer's Retention	Reinsurer's Payment
1	$ 300,000	$ 100,000	$ 200,000
2	500,000	100,000	400,000
3	600,000	100,000	500,000
Total	$1,400,000	$300,000	$1,100,000

[DA05094]

Example of Per Occurrence Excess of Loss Reinsurance Applying $4,900,000 xs $100,000

Primary Insurer has a $4,900,000 xs $100,000 per occurrence excess of loss treaty. The table below shows how losses are accumulated to determine whether the attachment point has been exceeded. Primary Insurer is indemnified by Reinsurer because the total amount of the loss arising out of all three policies exceeds Primary Insurer's attachment point.

Policy	Loss Amount		Primary Insurer's Retention		Reinsurer's Payment
1	$ 300,000				
2	500,000				
3	600,000				
Total	$1,400,000	=	$100,000	+	$1,300,000

[DA05095]

Clash cover, a type of per occurrence excess of loss reinsurance for liability loss exposures, can be provided for a combination of different types of liability insurance, including auto liability, general liability, professional liability, and workers compensation. Clash cover has an attachment point higher than any of the limits of the applicable underlying policies.

For example, a primary insurer could issue a workers compensation policy and a general liability policy with an each occurrence limit of $1 million. To obtain higher limits of coverage for an occurrence that may involve injury to

Clash cover

A type of per occurrence excess of loss reinsurance for liability loss exposures that protects the primary insurer against aggregations of losses from one occurrence that affects several insureds or several types of insurance.

both employees and nonemployees, a clash cover could be purchased in layers. If an explosion results in both workers compensation and general liability claims, the primary insurer would be covered by the clash cover because the claims arise from a single occurrence (the explosion). The clash cover retention is not in addition to the retention of any other applicable per occurrence excess of loss reinsurance; it is net of those retentions.

As another example, Brookgreen Insurance Company (Brookgreen) insures the general liability loss exposure of six contractors working on a single job site. Each of the six contractors' policies has a limit of $1 million. Brookgreen has per occurrence excess of loss reinsurance of $3 million xs $250,000. Brookgreen also has a clash cover of $3 million xs $1 million. An explosion injures employees and nonemployees. The injured parties are awarded damages that total $6 million from the six contractors' policies. The losses from this single occurrence are paid as indicated in the exhibit. See the exhibit "Application of a Clash Cover to One Occurrence Involving Multiple Claims."

Application of a Clash Cover to One Occurrence Involving Multiple Claims

Policy	Damages	Brookgreen Insurance Co. Retention	Per Occurrence Reinsurer	Clash Cover Reinsurer
1	$1,000,000	$ 250,000	$ 750,000	$ 0
2	1,000,000	—	1,000,000	0
3	1,000,000	—	1,000,000	0
4	1,000,000	750,000	250,000	0
5	1,000,000	—	Limit exhausted	1,000,000
6	1,000,000	—	—	1,000,000
Total	$6,000,000	$1,000,000	$3,000,000	$2,000,000

[DA05096]

Brookgreen exhausted its per occurrence excess of loss reinsurance retention ($250,000) with payment of the $1 million loss from Policy 1. The per occurrence excess of loss reinsurer paid the remaining losses until the per occurrence limit of $3 million was exhausted. Brookgreen paid the remaining $750,000 under Policy 4 to fulfill its $1 million retention under the clash cover. The clash cover reinsurer then paid the remaining losses.

Both catastrophe excess of loss reinsurance (for property insurance) and clash cover (for liability insurance) are also referred to as pure risk covers because they are expected to cover only rare events, not common claims covered by other excess of loss treaties.

Clash cover may be useful for types of liability insurance in which loss adjustment expenses are likely to be very high and the underlying per occurrence reinsurance limits include these expenses rather than pro rate them. Examples include professional liability (such as medical malpractice, directors and officers liability, and accountants professional liability) and expenses associated with environmental claims (for example, asbestos and pollution liability). Primary insurers also use clash cover when they want protection from extra-contractual damages and excess of policy limits losses.

Extracontractual damages are damages awarded to an insured as a result of an insurer improperly handling a claim. This improper behavior is known as bad faith, and it implies that the insurer has failed to deal fairly with the insured. Damages awarded to an insured for an insurer's bad faith in claim handling are usually not considered to be a loss covered by the underlying policy and therefore are usually not subject to indemnification by a reinsurer unless the reinsurance agreement specifically provides coverage.

Extracontractual damages
Damages awarded to the insured as a result of the insurer's improperly handling a claim.

Excess of policy limits losses result when an insured sues an insurer for failing to settle a claim within the insured's policy limits when the insurer had the opportunity to do so. Excess of policy limits losses are also extracontractual obligations of the insurer but are usually distinguished from extracontractual damages by reinsurers because they are covered losses that, as a result of a mistake of the primary insurer, exceed policy limits. As with other extracontractual obligations, the reinsurance agreement specifies whether excess of policy limits losses are subject to indemnification by the reinsurer.

Excess of policy limits loss
A loss that results when an insured sues an insurer for failing to settle a claim within the insured's policy limits when the insurer had the opportunity to do so.

Aggregate Excess of Loss

The fifth type of excess of loss reinsurance is **aggregate excess of loss reinsurance**. This type of excess of loss reinsurance can be used for property or liability insurance and covers aggregated losses that exceed the attachment point and occur over a stated period, usually one year. The attachment point in an aggregate excess of loss treaty can be stated as a dollar amount of loss or as a loss ratio. When the attachment point is stated as a loss ratio, the treaty is called "stop loss reinsurance." With stop loss reinsurance, the primary insurer's retention may be a loss ratio of 90 percent, and the reinsurer would indemnify losses up to a loss ratio of 120 percent. The reinsurance agreement in this instance would specify the attachment point and reinsurance limit as "30% xs 90% loss ratio." The primary insurer retains responsibility for losses above a loss ratio of 120 percent.

Aggregate excess of loss reinsurance
A type of excess of loss reinsurance that covers aggregated losses that exceed the attachment point, stated as a dollar amount of loss or as a loss ratio, and that occur over a specified period, usually one year.

Aggregate excess of loss treaties are less common and can be more expensive than the other types of excess of loss reinsurance. The treaty usually specifies an attachment point and reinsurance limit that does not result in the primary insurer earning a profit on the reinsured policies when the policies were unprofitable overall. Most aggregate excess of loss treaties also contain a co-participation provision of 5 to 10 percent to provide the primary insurer with an incentive to efficiently handle claims that exceed the attachment point. See the exhibit "Aggregate Excess of Loss Reinsurance Example."

Aggregate Excess of Loss Reinsurance Example

Brookgreen Insurance Company (Brookgreen) offers liability insurance to a tavern. This general liability policy has an each occurrence limit of $1 million and a general aggregate limit (capping the number of per occurrence dollars the insurer will pay during the policy period) of $2 million.

Brookgreen purchases facultative per occurrence excess of loss reinsurance for this policy in excess of $500,000. This insurance protects Brookgreen against any loss above $500,000 but would not respond to any loss below $500,000. If the tavern suffered three separate losses of $450,000 each, Brookgreen would not recover from the reinsurer even though the total of all losses under the policy during the policy period exceeded $500,000.

Because of concern about aggregation of losses from this and similar loss exposures, Brookgreen decides to purchase a $7 million xs $3 million aggregate excess of loss treaty that is applicable to all of its liability insurance. This treaty further stabilizes losses by indemnifying Brookgreen for accumulations of losses exceeding $3 million. For example, Brookgreen insures a cosmetics manufacturer whose wrinkle cream causes an increase in susceptibility to skin cancer. Brookgreen settles a class action suit brought by customers who used the product for $15 million. Brookgreen's net loss is $8 million (the $3 million retention plus $5 million loss amount that exceeds the $7 million limit).

[DA05097]

Because of the stabilizing effect of aggregate excess of loss reinsurance on a primary insurer's loss ratio, it may be argued that it is the only type of reinsurance needed. However, aggregate excess of loss reinsurance has limited availability. When used, the aggregate excess of loss reinsurer usually expects to pay losses only after the primary insurer has been reimbursed under its other reinsurance agreements.

While a catastrophe excess of loss reinsurance agreement only protects against catastrophe losses (loss severity), an aggregate excess of loss reinsurance agreement provides the reinsured with broader protection. This is because the aggregate excess of loss reinsurance agreement includes catastrophes and unforeseen accumulations of non-catastrophic losses during a specified period (addressing both loss severity and loss frequency).

REINSURANCE ACCOUNTING BASICS

Different accounting frameworks have established rules and procedures for the accounting and reporting of different types of reinsurance.

Reinsurance introduces accounting considerations that are unique to the reinsurance transaction and to reinsurers. Lags associated with the reporting of many reinsurance transactions and the use of bordereau reports both influence values in insurers' financial statements. Users of financial statements should understand the accounting practices and rules for these types of reinsurance transactions:

- Assumed reinsurance
- Ceded reinsurance
- Commutations
- Prospective versus retrospective reinsurance[3]

Assumed Reinsurance

In general, the accounting rules applicable to insurers writing direct insurance contracts also apply to those writing assumed reinsurance contracts. Differences may occur, however, due to different risk transfer rules and different definitions of loss versus loss adjustment expense (LAE).

Risk Transfer Rules

For both generally accepted accounting principles (GAAP) and statutory financial reporting in the United States, accounting rules exist regarding the amount of risk transfer required for a contract to be categorized as reinsurance (as opposed to being accounted for as a deposit). The risk transfer rules may apply to accounting for all reinsurance contracts, or only to the ceded reinsurance portion and not the assumed reinsurance portion of the same contract. The same risk transfer rules may apply to insurance contracts. Complications can also exist in cases where one contract provides insurance risk transfer for a portfolio of contracts that includes both insurance and noninsurance contracts.

Loss Adjustment Expense (LAE)

Reinsurance contracts covering tort liability insurance risks commonly include coverage for both losses and legal defense costs. The covered legal defense costs are frequently coded as LAE and reported by the ceding company separately from losses. The assuming company may, however, record such costs as assumed losses. Therefore, the categorization of defense costs (and other such expenses) may change from LAE to losses when transferred from the ceding company to the assuming company. This will distort analyses of losses versus LAE on a combined industry basis (that is, combined experience of insurers and reinsurers) or in comparisons of primary insurer experience and reinsurer experience.

Ceded Reinsurance

Two alternative approaches for an accounting framework's treatment of ceded reinsurance exist:

- Ceded reinsurance entries are recorded in the same place as, and as offsets to, the corresponding direct or assumed reinsurance entries.
- The purchase of reinsurance is recorded as the purchase of an asset.

These two approaches may sometimes be combined in a single accounting framework. For example, U.S. GAAP treats ceded reinsurance premiums and losses as negative premiums and negative losses for income statement purposes, but treats ceded loss reserves as an asset rather than as an offset to a liability for balance sheet purposes. See the exhibit "Example— Ceded Reinsurance Impact on Income Statement, Assuming Treatment as Negative."

If the accounting instead requires segregated reporting of the effect of ceded reinsurance, it may require that the ceded reinsurance be treated as a net expense in the calculation of underwriting income. In the example, the net cost of ceded reinsurance would be $1 (equal to an earned premium cost of $20 less recoveries of both $13 for losses and $6 for expenses). See the exhibit "Example—Treatment of Ceded Reinsurance as Purchase of an Asset for Balance Sheet Purposes (Such as Under U.S. GAAP)."

Commutations

The commutation of a reinsurance agreement finalizes the remaining obligations under the agreement of either party to the other. It can occur due to a commutation clause written into the original contract or through negotiation between the parties in executing and/or resolving disputes under the contract. The accounting for commutations is not dependent on how the commutation arose.

A commutation does not negate the original contract. Instead, it finalizes obligations under the contract, generally through a fixed payment or series of fixed payments from the reinsurer to the reinsured.

The final payment or series of payments is typically accounted for as a paid loss. Consistent with the finalization of all remaining obligations, all other balance sheet entries are removed. As the final payment is typically based on the economic value remaining in the contract, it generally reflects the time value of money; therefore, it would normally be less than a full undiscounted loss reserve. However, this may not always be the case. Where the commutation reflects the economic value of the future payments otherwise due under the reinsurance contract, the economic value would also include an

Example—Ceded Reinsurance Impact on Income Statement, Assuming Treatment as Negative

Assume the company has (and has historically maintained) a 20 percent quota share ceded reinsurance contract for all direct insurance, with a ceding commission of 30 percent.

Assume the loss ratio on direct business is 65 percent, and the only direct expense is a 30 percent commission.

Assume the direct earned premium for the year is $100 and the direct loss reserve at year-end is $200.

Income Statement

Direct Earned Premium	$100
Ceded Earned Premium	-20
Net Earned Premium	80
Direct Incurred Losses	$65
Ceded Incurred Losses Net	-13
Incurred Losses	$52
Direct Commissions	$30
Ceded Commissions	-6
Net Commissions	24
Net underwriting income	$4

Balance Sheet

Direct Loss Reserve	$200
Ceded Loss Reserve	-40
Net Loss Reserve	160

This example assumes that the relative entries in an account are added together to derive a total. For example, if the company writes $100 in direct premium and then cedes $20 in premium, it assumes that the premium entries are +$100 and -$20. These values are then added to get the net of $80. Some accounting systems record direct and ceded entries as positive values and then subtract the ceded value from direct to calculate the net values for an account. In such a system, the premium entries would be +$100 and +$20, and the preparer and/or user of the information would have to know to subtract ceded amounts from direct and assumed amounts.

[DA06371]

adjustment for risk. This risk adjustment would increase the economic value, offsetting the reduction for the time value of money, in some cases resulting in a value greater than the expected undiscounted recoveries. See the exhibit "Written Illustration of the Income Statement Impact of the Commutation of Two Companies."

Example—Treatment of Ceded Reinsurance as Purchase of an Asset for Balance Sheet Purposes (Such as Under U.S. GAAP)

Assume the same facts as in the "Example—Ceded Reinsurance Impact on Income Statement, Assuming Treatment as Negative," but with different balance sheet treatment.

Balance Sheet

Assets		Liabilities	
Ceded Loss Reserve	$40	Direct Loss Reserve	$200

[DA06372]

Written Illustration of the Income Statement Impact of the Commutation of Two Companies

As an example, assume that Ceding Company A and Assuming Company B enter into a commutation that finalizes their obligations and rights under a contract, in return for a final payment from B to A of $100. Assume that before the commutation, Ceding Company A recorded a ceded loss reserve under the contract (accounted for as a negative loss reserve) of -$150, and that Company B recorded an assumed loss reserve of +$110. The final value of $100 reflects both the time value of money and a compromise as to expected future payments. The income statement effect of the commutation for the two companies would look like this:

Ceding Company (A)

Paid losses	-100
Change in loss reserves	+150
Incurred losses	50

Assuming Company (B)

Paid losses	+100
Change in loss reserves	-110
Incurred losses	-10

[DA06374]

Prospective Versus Retrospective Reinsurance

Some reinsurance frameworks distinguish between **prospective reinsurance** and retrospective reinsurance. The accounting considerations presented thus far (that is, assumed reinsurance, ceded reinsurance, and commutations) represent typical accounting rules for prospective reinsurance.

Prospective reinsurance
Reinsurance purchased to cede future losses.

An example of a retrospective reinsurance contract is a **loss portfolio transfer**. The reinsurer may participate in such a transfer either over a predetermined time or subject to an aggregate limit. Another example is an aggregate loss cover purchased for an existing portfolio of liabilities. This type of aggregate loss cover reinsurance contract is used by an insurer as protection against adverse development beyond a specified point for an existing portfolio of claim liabilities. Aggregate loss cover can be both prospective and retrospective, depending on the date that the contract is effective and the period of claims for which protection is provided. Retrospective aggregate loss covers have been used in numerous acquisitions of insurers, whereby the buyer of the insurer will want some protection against the acquired book of loss reserves developing adversely.

Loss portfolio transfer
A type of retroactive plan that applies to an entire portfolio of losses.

Historically, special retrospective reinsurance accounting rules were established by insurance accounting frameworks that did not allow discounting. Prior to these special retrospective reinsurance rules, some insurers were reportedly using retrospective reinsurance to generate earnings, as they would cede existing loss reserves held at undiscounted values for a ceded premium that reflected the time value of money. Consequently, special rules were implemented for retrospective reinsurance to prevent or limit such potential abuse.

Retrospective reinsurance accounting generally requires that the recoveries under the contract be held on a present value basis, with some exceptions. It may also require separate disclosure of the benefits or effects of such contracts, so that any distortion of these contracts on the ceding company's financial statements can be isolated.

Where such rules exist, exceptions are sometimes incorporated into the rule whereby certain contracts are excluded from the present value or special disclosure requirements. When this occurs, it is typically said that "prospective accounting applies" to the retrospective reinsurance contract.

Reinsurance Reporting Lags

Reinsurance contracts specify the reporting requirements of the ceding company to the assuming company. These reports serve multiple purposes. One purpose is to effect the necessary payment transactions under the contract, including ceded premiums and losses according to the policy terms. Another purpose is to provide the assuming company sufficient data to perform its own reserve analysis (either for the particular contract or contract claims or for the assuming company's portfolio of contracts or claims). A third purpose is to enable the assuming company to meet its own accounting and financial reporting requirements.

Significant lags can occur in the filing and receiving of these reinsurance reports. The lags can result from the time necessary for the ceding company to accumulate the data required. Lags may also result from the need to coordinate input from multiple parties. For example, a ceding entity may be in a pool, and the pool administrator may need to first collect the relevant data from all the pool members before submitting reports to the pool reinsurers. Delays can also be caused by multiple handoffs and consolidations. This can occur for some retrocession contracts where first the ceding companies must report to their reinsurers, who then must process the data before submitting their report to retrocessionaires. To further delay the reporting, there may be multiple layers of retrocessionaires. Delays of several years have been observed for higher-level retrocession contracts that involve parties from multiple countries and/or continents.

Some accounting frameworks require the assuming company to record estimated transactions when the lags and the dollars involved are material. This may involve recording estimated values for premiums, losses, and LAE (including estimated "paid" values) based on historical or anticipated experience. These estimates would typically be adjusted once the actual values are known or when improved estimates are available.

Bordereau Reporting

For certain reinsurance contracts, such as many facultative or individual claim excess of loss contracts, the ceding company's report includes individual claim (and possibly premium) transaction detail. In contrast, the reporting for certain other reinsurance contracts is only in a summarized, aggregated form. Such summarized reports are called bordereau.

Bordereau reports may include product line detail or type of loss detail. Some bordereau reports include only high-level summary data of subject losses and premiums. Additional detail would be available only through special requests or inspections, with the ability or inability to do so depending on the contract terms. The level of detail in the bordereau reports can directly influence the level of detail in the assumed company's accounting records. For example, if no line-of-business splits are available in the bordereau, the assuming company cannot report its assumed share except on a highly summarized line of business basis. An assuming company receiving a bordereau report may also be limited in its ability to split the subject losses into various categories unless the detail in the bordereau supports such reporting.

PROPERTY-CASUALTY INSURER TAXATION

Although insurers enjoy certain federal income tax advantages that are not available to noninsurers, they are required to pay state taxes that are unique to the business of insurance.

If they meet the requirements for insurer tax treatment, property-casualty insurers are subject to special tax rules in addition to general corporate tax rules levied on businesses by the United States tax system. These special rules include those regarding reserving for future liabilities and discounting future liabilities.

The federal income tax system is governed by the **Internal Revenue Code (IRC)** enacted by Congress and enforced by the Internal Revenue Service (IRS), which is part of the executive branch of government. In addition to being subject to federal taxes, insurers are subject to state and local corporate income taxes as well as some special tax levies that are unique to the business of insurance.

Internal Revenue Code (IRC)
Title 26 of the United States Code, enacted in 1986, comprising the laws governing federal taxation in the U.S., including those applicable to property-casualty insurers.

Requirements for a Company to Be Taxed as an Insurer

The rules governing the taxation of insurers apply only to those that satisfy the definition of an "insurance company" according to the IRC. If more than half of a company's business during the tax year is the issuance of insurance or annuity contracts or the reinsuring of risks underwritten by insurance companies, then the IRC considers the company an insurance company for tax purposes.

The IRC further divides insurance companies into life insurers and nonlife insurers based on the type of reserves held. If in any tax year an insurer's average loss reserves for life insurance exceed 50 percent of its total loss reserves, it is taxed as a life insurer.

If average life reserves are less than 50 percent of total loss reserves, the company is taxed as a nonlife insurer. Property-casualty insurers are included in the nonlife category.

The determination of a company's status as an insurer and as a life or nonlife insurer is based on facts and circumstances. A company's status as either a life or nonlife insurer under state law does not automatically determine the company's status as an insurer for federal tax purposes.

Even if a state recognizes a company as an insurer, if the "more than 50 percent insurance business" rule is not met during a specific tax year, the company will not be considered an insurer for federal tax purposes. Consequently, none of the company's business activities, even its insurance activities, will be eligible for the special tax rules applicable to insurers.

Although the IRC defines an insurer, it does not define "insurance activities." The definition of insurance activities has evolved from case law and various IRS rulings. Activities generally acknowledged as insurance activities are those that shift a risk of loss from an insured to an insurer, distribute risk among many insureds, and involve an insurance contract.

Like the determination of a company's status as an insurer, the determination of activities as insurance activities depends on the facts in each situation. The transfer, sharing, and distribution of the insurance risk to all parties insured by a bona fide insurance contract are essential to the concept of true insurance activities.

The IRC provides that, for federal income tax purposes, the annual statement prepared by insurers following statutory accounting practices (SAP) as prescribed by the National Association of Insurance Commissioners (NAIC) is to be used as a guide for calculating the underwriting and investment components of gross income. However, the NAIC Annual Statement does not override the IRC guidelines for federal income tax purposes, and the IRS can require adjustments to the values reported in the Annual Statement that are used in the preparation of the income tax returns for insurers.

Federal Tax Treatment of Underwriting Income

The general corporate tax rules that apply to both insurers and noninsurers alike include those related to tax rates, depreciation, tax credits and carryovers, and employee benefits. However, there are special provisions applicable to the calculation of underwriting income for property-casualty insurers.

These are three special provisions that apply to the computation of taxable underwriting income for property-casualty insurers:

- Earned premium is increased by 20 percent of the change in the unearned premium reserve, leading to higher reported taxable income.
- Insurers are allowed to deduct estimates for future liabilities in the form of loss reserves.
- Loss reserves are discounted using methods dictated by the IRS.

Determination of Taxable Underwriting Revenue

Underwriting income
Income an insurer earns from premiums paid by policyholders minus incurred losses and underwriting expenses.

Underwriting income is calculated as premiums earned minus incurred losses, incurred loss adjustment expense, and underwriting expenses. These amounts are net of return premiums, reinsurance, and salvage. The computation of taxable underwriting income follows that same general formula, but certain adjustments cause the underwriting income reported in the NAIC Annual Statement to differ from the underwriting income reported on the income tax statement.

In the statutory annual statement, calendar-year earned premiums are computed by adding written premiums to the unearned premium reserve at the beginning of the year and then subtracting the unearned premium reserve at the end of the year.

In the tax computation of earned premium, written premiums are added to 80 percent of the unearned premium reserve at the beginning of the year, and then only 80 percent of the end-of-year unearned premium reserve is subtracted from the total. The result of this adjustment is that earned premiums are increased (or decreased) by 20 percent of the change in the unearned premium reserve over the course of the tax year.

If an insurer's unearned premium reserve is growing, taxable earned premiums are higher than statutory earned premiums. If an insurer's unearned premium reserve is shrinking, then taxable earned premiums are lower than statutory earned premiums.

Determination of Deductible Underwriting Expenses

The general formula for computing calendar-year incurred losses for statutory purposes is to add the end-of-year loss reserves to paid losses for the year and then to subtract the beginning-of-year loss reserves. Underwriting expenses are calculated in a similar manner. Both the incurred losses and the incurred expenses include estimated amounts as well as known amounts.

The general tax rule for deducting any expense or operating cost is that the expense is deductible when all events have occurred that are necessary to establish a true liability and determine a reasonably accurate amount for that expense or operating cost. Paid losses are easily established, but it is not always feasible to establish the full liability for losses during a tax year because of delays in the loss settlement process. However, the strict use of paid losses alone as the deductible loss expense violates the matching principle that expenses should be matched to the revenue associated with those expenses. Therefore, the IRC allows property-casualty insurers to deduct estimates for unpaid losses for both reported losses and **incurred but not reported (IBNR) losses**, even though this violates the general tax rules for expense recognition applicable to noninsurers.

The triggering event for the deduction is the occurrence of a loss. Although property-casualty insurers can deduct reserves for losses that have occurred but have not yet been reported, the insurers are not permitted to deduct reserves for events or losses that have not yet occurred.

For example, an insurer may forecast that it will incur average windstorm losses of $10 million over the next ten years, averaging $1 million per year. However, it will not be able to recognize any deductions for losses or reserves set aside to pay for those losses until a windstorm actually occurs. After the occurrence of a windstorm, the insurer will be able to deduct reasonable reserves set aside to pay claims associated with that windstorm even if they have not yet been reported to the insurer. Similarly, insurers know there are delays between the occurrence of auto accidents and the filing of insurance claims. Based on historical data using appropriate actuarial methods, they

Incurred but not reported (IBNR) losses
Losses that have occurred but have not yet been reported to the insurer.

can use reasonable estimates of the dollar amounts of those IBNR claims that have occurred but that have not been reported.

Loss reserves are reported in the NAIC Annual Statements filed with the NAIC, and the IRS uses the statutory statement as the basis for determining taxable income. However, the amounts reported on the NAIC Annual Statement are subject to challenge by the IRS for tax purposes. The amounts most often challenged for reasonableness are the reserves for losses and loss adjustment expenses. The burden of proving that the reported reserves are reasonable rests with the insurer. If the IRS has determined the reserves to be unreasonable, the insurer must prove both the reasonableness of its reported reserves and the unreasonableness of the IRS's proposed adjustment. See the exhibit "Example of the Calculation of Taxable Underwriting Income for a Property-Casualty Insurer."

Discounting Loss Reserves

Another significant difference between the statutory loss and loss adjustment reserves reported in a property-casualty insurer's NAIC Annual Statement and in its federal income tax return is that the reserves deducted for income tax purposes are discounted to their **present value**. Eventually, the insurer will receive the full dollar amount of tax deduction for its losses incurred because paid losses are fully deductible.

Present value

The value today of money that will be received in the future.

The practical effect of reserve discounting is to spread the deduction for incurred losses and loss adjustment expenses over multiple years to better match investment earnings on reserves for losses and loss adjustment expenses that have been incurred but not yet paid.

The industry discount rate, which is calculated and published annually by the IRS, is based on these two factors:

- The interest rate that is determined annually by the IRS—This interest rate is an average of the federal midterm rates earned on U.S. Treasury obligations with maturities between three and nine years.
- Loss and loss adjustment expense payment patterns—The IRS recalculates these patterns every five years using the most recent industry data published by A.M. Best.

Insurers can elect to calculate and use their own discount factors rather than using the IRS industry factors, but must elect to do so by a specific date. Once an insurer makes that election, it cannot change again until the next election window opens.

The election window is spaced at five-year intervals (for example, 2007, 2012, 2017, and so forth). If an insurer elects to use its own loss payment experience to compute the discount factors, it must still follow IRS guidelines to calculate the discount factors and use the interest rate published by the IRS.

Example of the Calculation of Taxable Underwriting Income for a Property-Casualty Insurer

The computation of taxable income for property–casualty insurers is described in Title 26 U.S. Code Section 832. Underwriting income is computed as adjusted earned premiums minus adjusted incurred losses minus incurred expenses.

Annual Statement	Adjusted Premium Earned	Tax Return
1,000,000	Beginning unearned premium reserve*	800,000
5,500,000	Gross premiums written	5,500,000
−25,000	Return premiums	−25,000
−275,000	Reinsurance premiums	−275,000
−1,200,000	Ending unearned premium reserve*	−960,000
5,000,000	Total	5,040,000

Annual Statement	Adjusted Losses Incurred	Tax Return
3,000,000	Losses paid during year	3,000,000
−400,000	Salvage recovered during year	−400,000
−300,000	Reinsurance recovered during year	−300,000
8,000,000	Unpaid losses at end of year**	7,600,000
−7,000,000	Unpaid losses at beginning of year**	−6,650,000
500,000	Anticipated salvage at beginning of year***	495,000
−600,000	Anticipated salvage at end of year***	−594,000
3,200,000	Total	3,151,000

Annual Statement	Expenses Incurred****	Tax Return
125,000	Expenses unpaid at beginning of year	125,000
1,500,000	Expenses paid during year	1,500,000
−150,000	Expenses unpaid at end of year	−150,000
1,475,000	Total	1,475,000
325,000	Underwriting Income	414,000

*   For tax purposes, only 80% of the unearned premium reserve is included in the calculation.

**   Each of the major lines of business has a separate discount factor; in this example, the average loss discount factor used is 0.950.

***   IRS promulgates discount rates and procedures for estimated salvage; this example uses 0.99 as the discount factor.

****   Excludes all loss adjustment expenses, which should be included in incurred losses.

The procedures for computing taxable underwriting income are laid out in Title 26 U.S. Code Section 832–Insurance Company Taxable Income. The numbers in the example have been fabricated. [DA11296]

Salvage value

An amount an insurer can recover by disposing of insured property for which the insurer paid a total loss.

A separate set of discount factors is published to discount the estimated future **salvage value** associated with the incurred losses. Salvage values are estimates of future recoveries from disposing of property that the insurer has taken title to following a total loss. Those discount factors are applied to the estimated values of future salvage recoveries associated with each set of accident-year incurred losses for each line of business used in the reserve discounting procedure. See the exhibit "Example of Loss Reserve Discount Factors for Accident Year 2013."

Apply Your Knowledge

Taxable revenue and loss expenses are adjusted relative to the amounts reported in the statutory annual statement. When evaluating a property-casualty insurance company that is increasing its premium volume, it would be expected that:

a. Taxable revenue and deductible loss expenses are both lower than the statutory revenue and loss expenses reported in the NAIC Annual Statement.

b. Taxable revenue is lower and the deductible loss expenses are higher than the statutory revenue and loss expenses reported in the NAIC Annual Statement.

c. Taxable revenue is higher and the deductible loss expenses are lower than the statutory revenue and loss expenses reported in the NAIC Annual Statement.

d. Taxable revenue and deductible loss expenses are both higher than the statutory revenue and loss expenses reported in the NAIC Annual Statement.

Feedback: c. Taxable revenue will be higher, and deductible loss expenses will be lower. The earned premium is adjusted to include 20 percent of the change in the unearned premium reserve, which would be increasing for an insurer that is growing. Deductible loss expenses would be lower because the unpaid reserves are discounted for tax purposes.

Types of State Taxes

Admitted insurer

An insurer to which a state insurance department has granted a license to do business within that state.

In addition to state income taxes, insurers are subject to other taxes levied by state taxing authorities. All states levy a gross premium tax that applies only to insurers. This tax is imposed on the gross premiums written by an **admitted insurer** during a calendar year on insurance policies for insureds within the state.

Example of Loss Reserve Discount Factors for Accident Year 2013

For losses incurred in calendar year 2013, these are the loss reserve discount factors that are applied to the unpaid losses in each subsequent tax year. Discount factors are published for each of the major lines of business, based on industry payout patterns and the average mid-term interest rate U.S. Treasury securities.

	Private Passenger Auto Liability	Commercial Auto Liability	General Liability– Occurrence	General Liability– Claims Made	Workers Compensation
2013	0.9680	0.9548	0.9120	0.9303	0.9034
2014	0.9663	0.9600	0.9167	0.9360	0.8894
2015	0.9673	0.9624	0.9211	0.9377	0.8795
2016	0.9660	0.9615	0.9189	0.9431	0.8753
2017	0.9618	0.9574	0.9147	0.9438	0.8738
2018	0.9585	0.9524	0.9070	0.9467	0.8701
2019	0.9580	0.9428	0.9016	0.9529	0.8782
2020	0.9596	0.9306	0.8968	0.9577	0.8891
2021	0.9687	0.9311	0.9056	0.9551	0.8956
2022	0.9790	0.9408	0.9171	0.9766	0.9086
2023	0.9894	0.9507	0.9292	0.9865	0.9224
2024	0.9894	0.9606	0.9421	0.9894	0.9372
2025	0.9894	0.9706	0.9561	0.9894	0.9530
2026	0.9894	0.9805	0.9716	0.9894	0.9703
Beyond	0.9894	0.9894	0.9894	0.9894	0.9894

This is an example of the computation of the discounted loss reserves for $5,000,000 of workers compensation incurred losses in tax years 2013 through 2017. As the losses are paid and the reserves are reduced over time, the discount factors for accident year 2013 continue to be applied to the remaining unpaid losses. This method allocates the investment income available to insurers over time, based on the prevailing interest rates in 2013.

Remaining Unpaid Loss as of:	Remaining Unpaid Portion of Incurred Losses	Discount Factor Applied to Unpaid Reserves	Discounted Reserve for Federal Income Tax Purposes
12/31/2013	3,905,135	0.9034	3,527,900
12/31/2014	2,825,190	0.8894	2,512,600
12/31/2015	2,199,695	0.8795	1,934,700
12/31/2016	1,822,280	0.8753	1,595,000
12/31/2017	1,550,600	0.8738	1,354,800

The discount factors are taken from Internal Revenue Bulletin 2013-49, available at www.irs.gov/irb/2013-49_IRB/ar09.html and accessed July 8, 2014.
[DA11297]

The premium tax rate varies from 1 percent to 4 percent, although it is typically in the 2 percent range. Surplus lines premiums are also subject to premium taxes, but those taxes are typically collected and remitted by surplus lines brokers rather than by the insurer.

The **Nonadmitted and Reinsurance Reform Act (NRRA)** limits regulatory authority of surplus lines transactions to the home state of the insured and establishes federal standards for collecting surplus lines premium taxes. The NRRA states that only an insured's home state may require a surplus lines broker to be licensed and to collect premium taxes, with the exception of workers compensation insurance. [4]

Almost all states use retaliatory and reciprocal taxes to equalize taxation of insurers among states with varying levels of premium taxes. **Retaliatory premium taxes** are levied by a taxing state on premiums written in that state by admitted insurers not domiciled (incorporated) in the state, but only if the premium taxes in the insurer's state of domicile are greater.

Reciprocal provisions in the taxing state allow nondomestic insurers to pay the taxing state lower premium taxes if the premium taxes in the insurer's state of domicile are lower. These taxes are intended to encourage equal treatment of insurers by other states, thereby allowing insurers equal access to all markets.

In addition to the gross premium tax, many states levy various taxes or assessments solely on insurers. The purpose of these taxes is usually evident from the name of the tax. Examples include these:

- Fire marshal tax—This tax helps fund the state fire marshal's office in carrying out duties such as enforcing local laws and ordinances relative to the prevention of fires; inspecting buildings and public service facilities for the means and adequacy of exit in case of fire; and investigating the cause, origin, and circumstances of fires.

- Fire department tax—This tax helps fund local fire departments within the state.

- Guaranty fund assessments—The guaranty fund protects policyholders against insolvent insurers. The fund does not prevent an insurer's insolvency, but it mitigates its effects. All states have property-casualty insurance guaranty funds that pay, up to a specific limit, the eligible unpaid claims of insolvent insurers licensed in the particular state.

- Workers compensation funds—These funds are used to administer state workers compensation laws, to provide claim payments to employees, and to cover claims when employers are uninsured.

SUMMARY

Reinsurance is the transfer of insurance risk from one insurer to another through a contractual agreement under which the reinsurer agrees, in return

Nonadmitted and Reinsurance Reform Act (NRRA)

Legislation passed on July 21, 2011, as part of the Dodd-Frank Wall Street Reform and Consumer Protection Act to create a more effective surplus lines tax payment and regulatory system.

Retaliatory premium taxes

Premium taxes imposed on insurers licensed, but not domiciled, in a state.

for a reinsurance premium, to indemnify the primary insurer for some or all the financial consequences of the loss exposures covered by the reinsurance contract. Reinsurance performs these principal functions for primary insurers: increase large-line capacity, provide catastrophe protection, stabilize loss experience, provide surplus relief, facilitate withdrawal from a market segment, and provide underwriting guidance.

The two types of reinsurance transactions are treaty reinsurance and facultative reinsurance. Treaty reinsurance agreements provide coverage for an entire class or portfolio of loss exposures and involve an ongoing relationship between the primary insurer and the reinsurer. Treaty reinsurance agreements are usually obligatory; loss exposures must be ceded to and accepted by the reinsurer. Facultative reinsurance agreements insure individual loss exposures. Under a facultative agreement, the reinsurer is usually not obligated to accept the loss exposure submitted by the primary insurer.

Reinsurance agreements can be categorized as either pro rata (proportional) or excess of loss (nonproportional) reinsurance. Pro rata reinsurance involves the proportional sharing of amounts of insurance, policy premiums, and losses (including loss adjustment expenses) between the primary insurer and the reinsurer. Pro rata reinsurance can be either on a quota share basis or on a surplus share basis. With excess of loss reinsurance, the reinsurer responds to a loss only when the loss exceeds the primary insurer's retention (often referred to as the attachment point).

The different accounting frameworks have established rules and procedures for the reporting of different types of reinsurance. Lags in the reporting of claims and premium detail underlying reinsurance contracts as well as bordereau reporting influence the values that appear in insurers' accounting systems and financial reports. Users should understand how the rules and procedures affect the financial reporting of reinsurance transactions.

The Internal Revenue Code applies special tax rules to insurers, which are segregated into two categories: life insurers and nonlife insurers. Property-casualty insurers follow most of the same income tax rules that noninsurers follow, but with a few major exceptions with respect to calculating taxable underwriting income. In addition, insurers are subject to state corporate income taxes as well as other special tax levies that are unique to the insurance business.

ASSIGNMENT NOTES

1. Many of the definitions of terms in this section were adapted from the Reinsurance Association of America's (RAA) *Glossary of Terms*. The RAA's website is www.reinsurance.org (accessed March 31, 2010).

2. Insurers that are publicly traded are usually referred to as "stock insurers" to differentiate them from "mutual insurers," which are owned by their policyholders.

3. Material is adapted with permission from the Casualty Actuarial Society Study Note, "Basic Insurance Accounting—Selected Topics" by Ralph Blanchard.

4. Edwards Wildman, "States' Implementation of NRRA in 2013," Excess and Surplus Lines Laws in the United States, http://surplusmanual.edwardswildman.com/espreface/ (accessed July 23, 2014).

Index

Page numbers in boldface refer to pages where the word or phrase is defined.

E

F

G

H

I

J

L

M